# OTHER MEN'S LIVES

D1483827

Captain William J. Reddan
Commander Company B. 114th Infantry,
29th Division (Blue & Gray), A.E.F.

# OTHER MEN'S LIVES

Experiences of a Doughboy,
1917–1919

William J. Reddan

WESTHOLME
Yardley

Westholme Publishing, LLC
904 Edgewood Road
Yardley, Pennsylvania 19067
Visit our Web site at www.westholmepublishing.com

ISBN: 978-1-59416-283-1
Also available as an eBook.

Printed in the United States of America

# CONTENTS

# INTRODUCTION

*Only the dead have seen the end of war.* —Plato

I AND MY TWO SISTERS AND TWO BROTHERS are only here because our grandfather, William J. Reddan, was an unlikely survivor of the October 12, 1918, battle of Bois de Ormont, as captain of Company B, 114th Infantry, 29th Division of the American Expeditionary Forces (A.E.F) in Europe. Our father, his youngest of seven children, was born almost a decade after he came home from the "Great War."

World War I had been raging in Europe for over three years before American soldiers physically entered the conflict, landing in France in early 1918. Congress had declared war in April 1917, only a few months after President Woodrow Wilson was sworn in for his second term, despite campaigning—and winning the election by a small margin—on the platform of keeping the U.S. out of the war.

On the Western Front, which was the main theater (the war was being fought by the Germans on both their western and eastern borders), each side was locked down in trenches dug sometimes 40 feet below ground, reinforced by concrete, plank, mud and guarded by barbed wire, dug in a zig-zag pattern, and stretching for hundreds of miles. Each side fought to gain or lose a few feet or maybe—at most—a mile of ground. The area between enemy trenches was called "No Man's Land" and was anywhere between 50 to 250 yards apart. The use of artillery and mortar rounds, rifles, mines, machine guns, poison gas (chlorine and mustard), airplanes, and tanks left towns and forests transformed into ghostly macabre dead zones.

The war's statistics were grim. After the signing of the Armistice on the 11th hour of the 11th day of the 11th month of 1918, more than 35 percent of all German men between the ages of 19 and 22 had been killed; one-half of all Frenchmen ages 20 to 32 died. British casualties, in battles like the Somme (1916) numbered in the tens of thousands—and that was just on the first day of battle. Though total numbers are difficult to confirm, it was commonly agreed by historians that at the war's end there were over 38 million casualties, including more than 21 million wounded, many left to live a life of suffering from amputations, disfigurement, diseases, shell shock (after the war, tens of thousands of American veterans languished in psychiatric facilities suffering from shell shock, what we call post traumatic stress disorder today), and survivor's guilt.

*Other Men's Lives*, privately published in 1936, recounts my grandfather's experiences as a participant in the Meuse Argonne Offensive (America's big push to help the major Allies, France and England). It also recites, document by document (including German intelligence), how "incompetent superiors" ordered him into battle, to try and capture German gun positions on reports that "only a few troops [enemy] up there, the position is held lightly." Had it not been such a false narrative, and contributed to the almost complete annihilation of his company, it would otherwise have been laughable.

"A reckless exposure of infantry" was written in the field book of a German soldier found in the carnage after the battle (referring to the American assault).

Only my grandfather and thirteen of his battle-weary men returned after twelve hours of fighting in Ormont Woods (France). He writes, "I finally and reluctantly gave orders to the THIRTEEN survivors of the company to 'get out of here.'"

My grandfather died twelve years before my birth, but our house was filled with memories of his legacy, tenaciously securing justice and recognition for the men in his company who never made it home. He called them: "my buddies."

*Other Men's Lives* articulates his diary of war, bearing witness to the slaughters, diseases, and incomprehensible suffering (among them, "trench foot", rats, lice, frostbite). His experiences became a raging internal fire he wouldn't let die. In fact, he took it to his grave.

WILLIAM JOSEPH REDDAN was born April 10, 1883, in Manchester, England to Irish parents Michael and Julia (the family fled Ireland to England years before his birth during times of an economic crisis, known as the Irish Potato Famine). In 1894, he immigrated to the United States with his mother, Julia, and older sister, Mary, on the ship *Aurania*, becoming a U.S. naturalized citizen in 1906. The family settled in Orange, New Jersey.

It was during my high school years in the early 1970s when I became interested in reading his book. I saw the country had been torn apart for years by The Vietnam War. As a teenager—with two younger brothers who could be called to fight—I was overwhelmed with emotion, fear, and questions about war . . . especially one fought in lands as far away and long ago like World War I.

From inside my 1970s community at the Jersey Shore, the effects of Vietnam were painstakingly evident through interactions with not only the soldiers—many former classmates—but also their wives, girlfriends, parents, siblings, children, and neighbors. I witnessed a range of emotion in families, whose initial joy at welcoming their soldier home, often turned to rage, despair, or hopelessness as the veteran's inability to integrate back into family and post-war life took control. To me, it seemed: No matter how distant the fight, when soldiers returned home, their presence infected communities in distressing, disabling, and disconcerting ways. How can one recover from the sudden embodiment of horrific wartime experiences, to seamlessly assimilate into everyday Americana?

With the Vietnam War making headlines, I thirsted for a first personal perspective on war and opened my father's copy of *Other Men's Lives*. I read and re-read the following inscription, hand-written in the front of the book:

Oct. 23rd 1936
To the 'boss' of the house—my son—
Joseph Leslie Reddan
May you be spared from ever participating in the horrors of war, is the prayer of your loving, soldier, 'Dad'.
May God bless you and give you a long and happy life.
Wm J. Reddan
Captain, Commanding,
Company B.
114th U.S. Infantry
29th Division
A.E.F

I devoured his book in short order, absorbing specific anecdotes brimming with grim reality. My grandfather writes on page 224 of his book:

One of the fortunes of war was rather ironically demonstrated on this same road; a small detachment of German prisoners was being escorted to the rear by one of our men. The solder was hustling the prisoners down the open road at a fast walk, when without warning the enemy artillery opened up and killed the prisoners. The guard escaped without a scratch. On another occasion while standing on a small knoll, watching a few carrying parties coming up the road, I saw one of our men carrying a box on his shoulder. All at once that soldier seemed to be enveloped in a blue flame. When the flame and smoke had cleared away a few seconds later the soldier had disappeared. There was no trace of him, merely a hole in the road where he had been . . . Who that soldier was, where he came from, what company he belonged to, I do not know. On the casualty list he would be carried as "Missing in Action." Somewhere in this great country of ours, a father, a mother or perhaps a wife bid that soldier good-bye and anxiously looked forward to his return; but it was not to be.

And this from the same page:

Another task falling to the lot of my battalion was burying our dead comrades; this was the most disagreeable work from several angles. It was a rough job having to bury men that we had soldiered alongside of, shared our "grub" with, and slept with one a few days before. Now they were gone. More than one husky soldier broke down when he came across the dead body of his "buddy."

After reading *Other Men's Lives*, I was numbed at the realization of the unthinkable ordeal he and his men faced, perishing violently or surviving to (always) question the days. As my family can certainly attest, I became obsessed to learn all that I could about the Great War (as it was then called, although by the 1970s, less than half a century later, America had already become involved in three more declared wars—World War II, Korea, and Vietnam). So I delved into reading as much as I could about wars in general, preferring first-person narratives, in lieu of generally accepted historical perspectives (which could be infested with re-writing, bias, nationalistic jingo, and/or hero worshipping).

I've been a certified public accountant for twenty years with a client base of senior citizens. I've prepared tax returns for many veterans of America's wars (and covert wars). Often I would engage my clients in conversation about their service, hoping to learn from their experiences, and also giving them a venue—if they chose—for an awake and attentive audience. Over the years, I've learned that most clients who served combat duty in Vietnam were ready, willing, and able to disclose their experiences, down to details which were for them, pure horror. However, those from World War II and Korea were more likely to change the subject when I casually brought up their service. I'm always hoping to learn from their shared experiences and cobble new knowledge into a better understanding of my grandfather's combat experiences and the conclusions he reached and defiantly held.

I searched out information on wars' toll on returning military personnel, and reached out to peace groups for articles, references, recommendations. One organization run by David Swanson, World Beyond War, organizes communities to educate about past wars, not only from an historical perspective, but also from economic, social, and moral considerations. In his most recent publication, speaking about the 100th anniversary of World War I, Mr. Swanson wrote:

> As well recounted in Michael Kazin's *War Against War: The American Fight for Peace 1914-1918*, a major peace movement had the support of a great deal of the United States. When the war finally ended (after the US had actually been in it for about 5% of the length of the war on Afghanistan thus far), just about everybody regretted it. The losses in life, limb, sanity, property, civil liberties, democracy, and health were incredible. Death, devastation, a flu epidemic, prohibition, a permanent military and the taxes to go with it, plus predictions of World War II: these were the results, and a lot of people remembered that they had been warned, as well as that the ending of all war had been promised.

I knew that my grandfather had given copies of his book to his wife, Catherine (who also passed away before my birth) and his seven children, each with a personal inscription. Researching the internet revealed he had also presented an inscribed copy to each of the thirteen survivors of his company, as well as to other soldiers he met during his journey.

I corresponded with or spoke to antique book sellers, historians, authors, reporters, and used online searches, social media and World War I blogs to find more information and also copies of *Other Men's Lives*. One book purchased was offered at an estate sale in upstate New York at $500, and contained a beautiful hand-written inscription to a soldier in his command.

Thanks to my grandfather, my library of used, battered, and well-read war books—all wars, including Gulf War, Iraq, Afghanistan, and others—exceeds my collection of fiction, fun, reference, and tax books combined.

It was through these online blogs that I connected with the grandson of one of the survivors of Company B who fought in the battle in Ormont Woods: Sergeant Thomas J. Hynes. A few years ago, Sergeant Hynes' grandson and I met at my home and related stories of what we knew about the war, comparing military memorabilia, including the combat helmet worn by his grandfather, which contained a bullet hole! Sergeant Thomas J. Hynes was wounded in battle (shot in the head); yet despite his grave injury, continued pushing on helping others, and going over the top, fighting the enemy.

My father, Joseph, grandpa's youngest child, passed away in 2012 after a four-year contentious battle with Alzheimer's disease. In the years before dad died, around 2010, my sister and I tried to find competent long-term care for dad, whose health was declining rapidly. On one visit to a nursing facility, which was located just ten minutes from my home, and during the interview process with the home's administrator, I asked her the ages of the youngest and oldest patients in the home. She replied the youngest was 40 (we were able to meet her) and the oldest, a man who was 109. Curious, I inquired if the man was a World War I veteran. Why, yes, he was.

The nursing home's administrator said the story she had been told was that this 109-year-old man was from north Jersey, lied about his age to join the military (he was only 17), served in the Meuse-Argonne Offensive in France in 1918, and had been taken as a prisoner of war by the Germans.

Though we were unable to meet him that day, I could hardly contain my excitement about the prospect. I asked his name and was told it was Everett Littlefield. When I got home, I immediately pulled out my grandfather's book. There on page 335 of the appendix in *Other Men's Lives*, in an alphabetical listing of men who served in 1917–1918 ("not a complete list"), is the name: Everett A. Littlefield. My hands were shaking. Here was a man who had known and served with my grandfather in 1918 (92 years earlier) who lived not ten minutes from my home! I couldn't wait to talk to him. Unfortunately, I never got the chance as he passed away before I could do so (he was in very ill health, with limited access to visitors).

A few years ago, while cleaning out my father's closet, I found a copy of my grandfather's scrapbook, "The Answer to Other Men's Lives, History repeating itself," where he clipped out newspaper articles, not only questioning the competency of officers in the military, but also following the trail (if any) of military postulating on "what went wrong in France." The scrapbook, now eighty years old and as delicate as a dried leaf, contains newspaper clippings taped to pages, passages underlined, and comments noted on their content by grandpa.

For twenty years after the war, in addition to writing *Other Men's Lives*, my grandfather (he was mustered out of service in 1919 as a major) told his story throughout New Jersey in public platforms, newspaper articles, interviews, and letters to the editor. In his letter to the editor published in the *Newark Sunday Call* on October 20, 1941, Major Reddan recalled the bitter experiences of the 29th Division during the war "thrown into battle under inefficient and timid officers":

> It was political intrusion that created such havoc in the 29th Division. Officers with little or no military experience, but with political affiliations, were appointed to command and later sent units into battle to be annihilated.

Once completed, the manuscript for *Other Men's Lives* was sent to several publishers, who refused to publish it. So, after self-publishing the book, he pursued his investigation into what happened at Bois de Ormont: Why was there no legislative investigation? No military investigation? Why were the people of NJ unimpressed and uninterested in finding out what happened to their sons? Why was weeding out incompetent officers such a challenge?

Halfway through the scrapbook (pieces dating from August 28, 1939) is an article "Watching the Crowds, Weeding Misfit Officers, Good News to Veterans" published in the *Newark Sunday Call* on July 13, 1941. The article, in which the author, Edward Sothern Hipp, admits reading *Other Men's Lives* "several times despite the fact that it . . . abounds in split infinitives and offers French words which are correct only phonetically . . . but is written from the heart," also notes that, "it would be a blessing to Uncle Sam's new Army if every officer and every non-com who aspires to be an officer were required to read *Other Men's Lives*. They would profit from the confession of an officer, who led his men to slaughter in the Bois d'Ormont, back in October 1918, because incompetent superiors willed it." Of the Meuse Argonne offensive, Mr. Hipp wrote "There may have been similar tragic incidents during that fierce campaign; but Captain Reddan alone had the courage to write a book about it."

Next to this article, my grandfather hand wrote the following inscription:

> At last the men of Company B—114th U.S. Inf., who were sacrificed to political greed and inefficiency are remembered. I have kept my promise to these men and their sacrifices have helped to straighten out a rotten mess. My men have not died in vain.
>
> WM J Reddan

My grandfather's story was never challenged, nor was he ever sued for libel.

After the bombing of Pearl Harbor in December 1941, the US entered World War II. My grandfather continued keeping current with war news, cutting out articles, in particular about the 29th Division's (the "Blue and Grey") activities in the war.

Two of his four sons were in service during the war; his oldest, William, was stationed in England. His second oldest, Douglas, was stationed in South America. By the spring of 1944, with a desperate need for more soldiers, my grandfather's third son, Corr, was scheduled to be deployed into action in the Pacific Theater (due to a congenital birth defect affecting his hearing, Corr was not earlier cleared for military duty. Corr was born in February 1920, just nine months after my grandfather's return to the States). My father was then a senior in high school.

The last article in his scrapbook, entitled "U.S. Invasion Losses 15,883," published in the *Newark News* on June 17, 1944, reported on the Normandy landings (known as D-Day). The article noted that the 29th Division's casualties, suffered on the beachheads east of Douve, France, were somewhat "heavier than anticipated." He may have recalled his regimental chaplain's description of his appearance after a particularly desperate battle in the same country a quarter century earlier:

> I was the most disreputable, filthy-looking, wild-eyed man he ever laid eyes upon, spotted with blood as I was from helping the wounded during the fight. My uniform was ripped and torn from trying to get through the barbed wire; I was plastered with mud from dropping into shell-holes, and had not shaved in more than three days. The only part of my equipment in place was my gas-mask and the service pistol at my side where it could be reached in a hurry if necessary. I have often thought of those days and wondered what our friends at home would have thought

of us if they could have seen that dirty, filthy, even half-crazy outfit that had so often been complimented on its smart, soldierly appearance.

Fourteen days later, on July 1, 1944, while standing on the beach of Manasquan, New Jersey, Major William Joseph Reddan suffered a massive, fatal heart attack. He was sixty-one years old. I believe his heart couldn't take any more news of people participating in the "horrors of war."

Lynn (Reddan) Petrovich
Oakhurst, New Jersey
April 2017

# FOREWORD

THE story of OTHER MEN'S LIVES has been written at the urgen requests of numerous civilian and military friends, in an effor to set forth the part played in the World War by Company I 114th U. S. Infantry, the organization it was my privilege t command during its service—then to see it annihilated an the lives of our "Buddies" wasted as a result of inefficiency.

Being a soldier, and not a professional writer or historia apologies are offered for whatever may be lacking in tecl nique, but no apologies are made for our part in the fightin; The story is not intended to be a literary masterpiece or even treatise on military matters. It is simply a recital of experienc and observations made during the war.

In recounting personal experiences the pronoun "I" is neces sarily prominent. Personal anecdotes and incidents relating t promotions, decorations or even of men failing in the perform ance of duty are mentioned as concrete examples of the exist ing conditions—not with any intention of extolling one man' bravery or efficiency and with no desire to besmirch another' war record. These were the prevailing conditions in our o ganization and doubtless existed, more or less, in other unit of the army.

In November, 1918, a telegram was sent to a United State Senator requesting an investigation to be made, as, "somethin went wrong in the 114th Infantry, at *Ormont Farm.*" It i hoped that this book will serve to answer that telegram as we as to demonstrate the adverse conditions under which w served, terminating in a "reckless exposure of Infantry," a recorded in the German field reports of our attack on *Bois d Ormont.*

WM. J. REDDAN

To the Memory of our Comrades who made the Supreme Sacrifice
this book is reverently dedicated.

W. J. R.

# HONOR ROLL

## COMPANY B, 114TH U. S. INFANTRY, 29TH DIVISION, A.E.F.

Members of Company B who lost their lives while in the service of
their country

| | | | |
|---|---|---|---|
| 2nd Lieut. | Mitchell, Robert L. | K.I.A. | 12 Oct. 1918 |
| Sergeant | Wittenweiler, Frank G. | K.I.A. | 12 Oct. 1918 |
| Corporal | Bauer, William H. | K.I.A. | 12 Oct. 1918 |
| " | Kunz, Francis W. | D.O.C. | 27 Oct. 1918 |
| " | LeGlise, Thomas M. | K.I.A. | 12 Oct. 1918 |
| " | Meath, Frank A. | K.I.A. | 12 Oct. 1918 |
| Private 1st Cl. | Allen, Frank F. | K.I.A. | 12 Oct. 1918 |
| " " " | Carey, William J. | D.O.C. | 19 May 1919 |
| " " " | Corrigan, John P. | K.I.A. | 12 Oct. 1918 |
| " " " | Del Favero, Peter | K.I.A. | 12 Oct. 1918 |
| " " " | Doody, William J. | K.I.A. | 12 Oct. 1918 |
| " " " | Ellison, James J. | K.I.A. | 12 Oct. 1918 |
| " " " | Glennon, John T. | K.I.A. | 12 Oct. 1918 |
| " " " | Heusser, Edward F. | K.I.A. | 12 Oct. 1918 |
| " " " | Hintzen, Walter | K.I.A. | 12 Oct. 1918 |
| " " " | Jaggers, James F. | D.O.C. | 8 Oct. 1918 |
| " " " | Kurowski, John | K.I.A. | 12 Oct. 1918 |
| " " " | Naccaralla, Antonio | K.I.A. | 12 Oct. 1918 |
| Private | Ball, William H. | K.I.A. | 12 Oct. 1918 |
| " | Beccaccine, Frank | D.O.W. | 12 Oct. 1918 |
| " | Betak, Joseph | D.O.C. | 10 Oct. 1918 |
| " | Brown, William H. | D.O.C. | 6 Oct. 1918 |
| " | Chance, Clyde | K.I.A. | 12 Oct. 1918 |
| " | Climie, John S. | K.I.A. | 12 Oct. 1918 |
| " | Dean, Albert J. | K.I.A. | 12 Oct. 1918 |
| " | DeBella, Vincent | K.I.A. | 12 Oct. 1918 |
| " | Delaney, John J. | K.I.A. | 12 Oct. 1918 |
| " | Downard, Hugh G. | K.I.A. | 12 Oct. 1918 |
| " | Doyle, James L. | K.I.A. | 12 Oct. 1918 |
| " | Goldstein, Hyman | K.I.A. | 12 Oct. 1918 |
| " | Higgins, William H. | D.O.W. | 19 Oct. 1918 |

| Private  | Klien, Otto W. ............... K.I.A. | 12 Oct. 1918 |
|----------|---------------------------------------|--------------|
| "        | McChesney, Edward D. ...... K.I.A. | 12 Oct. 1918 |
| "        | Morabito, Alfred ........... K.I.A. | 12 Oct. 1918 |
| "        | O'Grady, John J. ........... D.O.W. | 17 Oct. 1918 |
| "        | Rosen, Israel ............... K.I.A. | 12 Oct. 1918 |
| "        | Steinberg, Joseph ........... D.O.W. | 26 Oct. 1918 |
| "        | Strauss, Raymond ........... K.I.A. | 12 Oct. 1918 |
| "        | Sylve, Herman .............. K.I.A. | 12 Oct. 1918 |
| "        | Thompson, Dave T. .......... K.I.A. | 27 Oct. 1918 |
| "        | Wilcox, Charley F. .......... D.O.W. | 14 Oct. 1918 |
| "        | Wylie, William ............. D.O.W. | 27 Oct. 1918 |
| "        | Zilka, Otto ................. K.I.A. | 12 Oct. 1918 |
| "        | Zukowski, Peter ............. D.O.W. | 16 Oct. 1918 |
| Mechanic | Umbreit, Lawrence P. ........ K.I.A. | 27 Oct. 1918 |

K.I.A. —Killed in action.
D.O.W.—Died of wounds.
D.O.C.—Died of other cause (sickness, etc.).

# DEFINITIONS OF ARMY EXPRESSIONS

| | |
|---|---|
| A.E.F. | American Expeditionary Forces in Europe |
| A.W.O.L. | Absent without official leave |
| "Pass the Buck" | To transfer responsibility |
| Buck Private | The lowest grade in the army |
| "Buddy" | A pal. A comrade |
| "Bumped off" | Killed |
| "Carry on" | Continue |
| Casual | A wounded or disabled soldier |
| Chow | Army slang for food |
| Citation | An official order, reward for bravery or leadership |
| "Cooties" | Army slang for lice |
| Croix de Guerre | Cross of War. French military decoration |
| "Doughboy" | An infantryman |
| D. S. C. | Distinguished Service Cross. U. S. decoration |
| "Dud" | A shell that fails to explode |
| Dump | In the forward zones, storage of ammunition |
| G. C. | Combat Group—front lines usually held by them |
| G. H. Q. | General Headquarters of the A.E.F. |
| "Gone West" | Killed or died |
| "Frog" | American slang for the French soldier |
| Leave | Authorized absence from duty |
| Liaison | Contact between units |
| M. P. | Military Police |
| "Mud Sloggers" | The Infantry |
| N. C. O. | Non-Commissioned Officer |
| No Man's Land | The ground in between opposing forces |
| O. P. | Observation post for noting enemy activities |
| "Over the Top" | Going into an attack |
| P. C. | Post of Command |
| Pillbox | Concrete emplacement for machine guns |
| "Poilu" | French soldier |
| "Rookie" | Recruit—as when a man first joins the army |
| "Shavetail" | A Second Lieutenant |
| "The Skipper" | The Captain of a Company |
| Shock Troops | Specially selected troops for hard fighting |
| "Tin hat" | Army slang for the steel helmet |

A few of the pet names applied by the A.E.F. to designate the enemy: "The Boche," Fritz, Heinie, "The Huns," Krauts, etc.

In several instances French words have been spelled as pronounced by the 'doughboy.'

# ILLUSTRATIONS

## ACKNOWLEDGMENTS

To the authors and publishers of the several books, pamphlets, etc., from which quotations are used; also to those gentlemen who read the original manuscript, the author's sincere appreciation is extended.

\*      \*      \*      \*      \*      \*      \*

Extracts from OUR GREATEST BATTLE, by Frederick Palmer. Copyright, 1919, by Dodd, Mead & Co., Inc.

Extracts from the HISTORY OF THE TWENTY-NINTH DIVISION, "Blue and Gray," 1917-1919. Published by Colonel J. A. Cutchins and Colonel George Scott Stewart, Jr.

Extracts from Source Book OPERATIONS OF THE 29TH DIVISION, East of the *Meuse River,* October 8th to 30th, 1918. As prepared by Major W. S. Bowen, Coast Artillery Corps, U.S.A., at the C. A. School, Ft. Monroe, Va., 1922.

Extracts from GERMAN DOCUMENTS TO ACCOMPANY OPERATIONS OF THE 29TH DIVISION, as prepared by Colonel George Ruhlen, Coast Artillery Corps, U.S.A., at the C. A. School, Ft. Monroe, Va., 1923.

# OTHER MEN'S LIVES

## CHAPTER I

## CALL TO THE COLORS

### MOBILIZATION

SUNDAY, March 25th, 1917. A day well remembered by the members of the First Brigade, National Guard of New Jersey and their families. The last day for many of them to ever again appear in civilian clothing.

The War that had been raging in Europe, from August, 1914, to this date, had in no way affected the military organization of the United States. Whatever the diplomatic relations with the belligerent nations might have been, the National Guard had no intimation that a sudden call for active service was to be expected at any time. No preparations being made for a possible National Emergency.

From June to November, 1916, the First Brigade had been in the Federal Service at Douglas, Arizona. During that period any serious discussion of the possibility of the United States entering the European War was frowned upon. As our regiment travelled across country, returning from this tour of duty, placards were noticed on display advocating the re-election of President Wilson as "He has kept the United States out of the War."

In compliance with orders, previously issued, Company H, Fifth Regiment, Infantry, N.J.N.G., had been preparing for the annual Federal Inspection, which was to be held on Tuesday, March 27th. All day Sunday the officers of the company and some of the non-commissioned officers, with a detail, had been checking records and laying out property to be inspected by the Regular Army Officers. About six o'clock the detachment went home with orders to report to the armory the following evening at seven o'clock to complete the work.

Imagine my surprise about 7.30 Sunday evening, when the following order was received by telephone at my home, from the Commanding Officer, First Battalion, Fifth N. J. Infantry: "Captain Reddan, you will assemble your company at the armory and prepare for active service. Our regiment has again been ordered into the field."

Orders were immediately sent to the members of the company to report at the armory. Before midnight more than two-thirds of the company had reported. During the night the remainder of the organization was contacted, and on Tuesday the last man, a sergeant, who was in Ohio on business, saw the mobilization order in the paper and reported for duty.

The tour of duty on the Mexican Border had not been a sinecure. There had been many gruelling "hikes" under a scorching sun, when the soldier's pack seemed to weigh five hundred pounds, with blistered feet and still several miles to go before reaching camp, the men growling and grouching among themselves: "If I ever get out of this man's army, they will have to lasso me to get me back in again. I quit a good job to be a hero—now look at me." It was the usual growl of the soldier, never satisfied; when he is at one place he wants to be somewhere else. These same men were the first to report for duty when the order for assembly was issued. They came in all smiles, ready to go the limit. Where they were going or what the duty might be, they did not know or care. It was a "gathering of the clan." Back with the gang. "Good luck to all of us and may the devil take the enemy," whoever he might be.

Monday morning Companies H and I, 5th Infantry, were assembled at the Orange armory. Later in the day Company K, of Montclair and Company A, of Passaic, joined us, completing the battalion formation.

Recruiting was started immediately to bring the organizations up near to war strength, 150 men and 3 officers per company. Our first instructions were to recruit the companies up to one hundred men. At this time, officially, we were not at war with any nation.

While at the Orange armory little was done in preparation for the real work that was to come later. There were several assemblies each day, company and battalion drills were held, the recruits being trained by the corporals and sergeants. Equipment was issued as far as possible with existing shortage. The men had a great deal of freedom, being allowed to return to their homes at night. Arrangements had been made with the local restaurants to provide meals. From the tales that came out later, evidently many deals and schemes were worked to swap a meal ticket for smokes. If I know anything about soldiers, I'll wager that the storekeeper was on the losing end of the game.

Many social affairs were held, dances almost every evening. I was detailed, with several non-commissioned officers, to take up the instruction of the Civilian Units, then being formed to aid the police, as well as to replace the National Guard that was about to leave for other duty. This work was interesting. The members of the organizations, composed of all classes—bankers, lawyers, clerks and mechanics—were very anxious to learn and seemed much in earnest. I have often thought of the first night that they were able to march, in formation, from the Orange High School, down Main Street, then to the armory, and there perform a simple drill before my Battalion Commander. These men were very proud of themselves and I was quite proud of them.

While recruiting was in progress many men tried to enlist, only to discover they had some physical defect that was a bar to their entering the Service. A number of applicants were rejected for this reason. An old Spanish-American war veteran, whom I had known for many years, came into my orderly room one day, highly indignant that the medical officers had rejected him, due to age and general physical condition. He insisted that he was as good as any man in the company and that "he could stand as much hardship as any of them 'kids' in the outfit." The only way his wrath could be appeased was by telling him that it was necessary to have some men with military experience at home, to train the recruits for possible replacements. The old story over again: "Once a soldier, always a soldier."

Remaining at Orange about ten days, the battalion was then ordered to the central part of New Jersey, establishing a line of guards on railroads and other public utilities from Perth Amboy on the east to Phillipsburg on the west. Company K was stationed at Neshanic and Company H with headquarters at Metuchen, guarding industrial plants which were turning out war materials, in addition to covering bridges, railroads, etc. In bitter cold weather, with considerable snow, this was a severe tour of duty, especially on those men who were unaccustomed to outside work. Many of the men of my company having worked in offices and factories were not hardened for the conditions. They stood the hardship quite well and only a few cases of minor illness developed.

The details on guard were being continually inspected by the company officers and occasionally by the higher commanders. Some of these Inspectors were lenient, merely looking over company quarters and a few of the nearby posts. At times an officer would appear, who insisted on making a thorough inspection of each and every post. On one occasion an inspecting officer visited each post, questioned the guards about their duties and their special orders, etc. All went well until we reached the double post at the Anaconda Copper Co. plant, in Perth Amboy. This detail also covered the Pennsylvania R.R. bridge crossing the Raritan River; the Inspector and I arrived at the factory shortly before two o'clock in the afternoon and inspected the men at the plant. It was a cold, blustery day, and, having no desire to cross the railroad bridge on the ties and in the wind I had crossed over at other times, I suggested that we remain at the plant until the guard was changed—in about ten minutes. The Inspector insisted on making the trip over the trestle. After going about fifty yards beyond the end of the bridge the wind caught us and it certainly did blow. We tried to watch our footing on the railroad ties, with overcoats tangling around our legs, our campaign hats down over the eyes one minute and blowing off the next. That wind was just howling around us. A little more of this and the Inspector decided that he could do just as well at the plant. We turned back and completed the inspection when the old guard came in. That inspector never made any more trips to that plant.

Although diplomatic relations had been severed several weeks previously, the United States, officially, was at peace with the Central Powers. On April 6th, 1917 the Congress of the United States declared "That a State of War existed between the United States and Germany." At last we were in it. Guard duty continued just the same with the additional task of watching for enemy sympathizers and spies. We had several false alarms, but generally conditions remained quiet.

While stationed at Metuchen we made many friends and the members of Company H, officers and men, appreciated the many kindnesses of the ladies of the town, who provided a reading room for us in addition to other conveniences. The services of Mayor Washington Wilson and the Borough Council, the Recorder and Chief of Police Hutchinson were especially helpful to me.

On May 7th, the First Battalion commenced to change station to Pompton Lakes, N. J., a detail being sent ahead to prepare the new camp. Company H left Metuchen at 7 A.M., marching to North Plainfield, joining the other three companies of the battalion about half-past eight. The battalion marched to Orange, arriving shortly after five o'clock that evening. It was planned to continue the march the next day, but all of use were so completely exhausted after the day's "hike," that permission was granted to lay over, at our home station, until the 9th. The battalion left Orange at 8.30 A.M., marching through Montclair, Singac, Riverdale, Pompton Plains and so on to the new camp at Pompton Lakes.

In my military service I have participated in many long and forced marches, but this was the most severe "hike" it has ever been my privilege to take part in. Oftentimes, in France, I saw these same men, after serving in the fighting zones for weeks, come out of the lines and then make a night march of ten or fifteen kilometers, and at the end of the march appear in better physical condition than they were at the finish of the march to Pompton. There had been no preparation for such a strenuous effort. Guard duty for more than a month had in no way tended to harden the men for any such long march.

Company H made the "stroll" in fairly good shape, probably due to the fact that the Infantry packs had been sent by motor truck, thereby saving the men considerably. We thought the march from Metuchen to Orange was hard. The "hike" from Orange to Pompton will never be forgotten by any man who had the "privilege" of taking part in it. At every rest period, men and officers would drop alongside of the road and not move until the command was again given to "fall in." Towards the end of the march it became necessary to increase the rest periods from ten minutes in each hour, as prescribed in regulations, to twenty minutes per hour. When we eventually reached the camp the squad tents were up, which was a blessing. When the companies were dismissed each man found a place in a tent, removed his shoes and lay down. If it had been necessary to travel an extra five miles I believe that more than half of us would have had to be carried in. There was no trouble keeping the men in camp that night, their feet just naturally refused to move them or to do any more duty, for the time being.

May 10th was spent in arranging camp and in preparation for more guard duty. Company K was assigned to railroads and munitions plants. Company H was ordered to protect the Newark Water Line from Lake Canistear to Smith Mills, also furnishing details for railroad guard, north and west of Paterson.

The stay at Pompton Lakes was much more pleasant than the time spent in Metuchen. Shortly after arriving there the weather became warm, and living in a tent is always preferred by a soldier. Leaves of absence were granted quite frequently, the men being excused from camp in the afternoon until reveille the next morning, if not required for duty. The usual procedure in getting from camp to home was to go over to the Pompton Turnpike and try hitch-hiking to Montclair and then a trolley to Newark or the Oranges. The Erie Railroad was the mode of return. A train from Montclair arrived at Pompton about 2.30 A.M. and was usually filled with soldiers. Looked more like a regular troop train than a passenger train. The conductors must have had a delightful time trying to collect tickets from that "gang."

Many men were deprived of passes for minor infractions of regulations, or perhaps not having their equipment in the required condition. I recall one soldier, found delinquent at inspection, ordered to stay in camp over the week-end as punishment. Shortly before noon, leaving camp in an automobile driven by one of the orderlies, I saw a soldier about a mile out on the Turnpike, soliciting a ride. As we came along he signalled to us to take him along. I directed the orderly to let him ride with us. To my surprise it was the soldier whom I had ordered to stay in camp, at the inspection. It was too bad he took a chance, but on this occasion he did not "get away with it." Of all the traffic on that road he had the misfortune to select the car his Captain was riding in. To be sure, that soldier did not visit in Orange that week-end. I took him back to camp and left him in the Guard House, where he would be safe until my return Monday morning. Hard on the soldier, but wars are won by soldiers obeying orders and this was the place to learn to be a soldier.

During the stay at this station it was a hard task to enforce real discipline. Being so close to home, there was a constant temptation for the men to go A.W.O.L. (absent without official leave). If a man was gone for a few days and then returned, usually he would be tried by the summary court officer and fined one dollar for each day's absence, in addition to losing his regular pay for the time he was absent. In a few cases, of continued unauthorized absence, the culprit, instead of being fined, would be sent to the Passaic County Jail, for periods up to fifteen days. I did not like this method. After all, these men were not criminals; they did not know how to play the game. This had some effect but the conditions did not improve until the regiment was transferred to the larger southern camp.

Conditions on the outposts were even worse than in the main camp. In the case of Company H, strung out along the Water Line, with only a small railroad running but a few trains out there, it was impossible for me to keep proper supervision over the posts. As a result the non-commissioned officers had a bad time trying to maintain discipline. Many a corporal or sergeant lost his stripes, through no real fault of his own, except being too easy on the men under his command. At that time the N.C.O.'s had not learned to be as "hard-boiled" as they were a few months later.

The only men receiving any progressive instruction were the recruits, who had come to us from the recruiting depots at Paterson and Orange. These men were kept in the battalion camp and given instruction by the sergeants, under the supervision of the lieutenants. The recruits also provided the necessary details for the usual camp routine. In other words they were introduced to a stack of pots and pans that had to be washed, scoured and polished; also the delightful pastime of peeling potatoes, half a barrel for a meal.

Details on the outposts were relieved every week or two and new men sent out to replace them. This was necessary in the posts at isolated spots. It became very lonesome out there after a week or so. Also the matter of food supplies became a problem due to lack of rapid transportation. Automobiles and trucks were not as plentiful as they became later. For one of our company wagons to make the trip to Lake Canistear would have required a day to get out there and another day for the return trip.

Numerous athletic contests were held at the camp and, as usual, Company H took an active part and brought home many of the prizes. Band concerts were a popular form of entertainment, under the able leadership of Chief Musician

George McNeice. We even had a few dances on the grass in front of battalion headquarters. Naturally, being so close to our homes, we had many visitors. On Sunday the camp had the appearance more of a circus than of a military post in time of war. Altogether these diversions helped to pass the time pleasantly, and combined with routine duties kept us fairly well occupied. All was not pleasure, however. Preparations were being made for whatever might be in front of us. A great deal of attention was given to equipment, of which we were already feeling a shortage.

Early in August the 2nd and 3rd Battalions of the 5th Infantry joined us at the camp and the entire regiment was, at last, relieved from the monotonous guard duty and in a position to make a beginning on the intensive training, with each company and battalion under command of the proper officers. Late in August Company C was ordered to Camp McClellan.

During the months in service, from March to September 1st, we had received no official information as to the possible duty for which the National Guard would be used. Naturally our thoughts often wandered into the future, trying to guess what was in store for us. Many evenings, after mess, the officers would gather around the major's tent and then speculation would run wild as to our chance of ever getting to France. Some of the officers were positive that the Guard organizations would be used for domestic service only. Since then I have often wondered if the wish was not father to the thought, in those cases. Others were just as sure that we would be sent to the battle front in a very short time. Only a few seemed to realize that we would require months of intensive training before we would be of any use, except as "cannon fodder." It was not until modern war was seen, in all its horror, and what it all really means, that I understood the necessity for thoroughly trained men and the elimination of the weaklings. Our battalion commander was very anxious to join the division that former President Theodore Roosevelt had offered to raise for immediate service in France. During these discussions it became very clear that a few of our brother officers could not appreciate the "Honor of Dying for their Country." The arguments waged back and forth until about September 1st when orders were received to prepare for another move.

On September 5th the regiment started to break camp and load baggage on the trains. At nightfall the regiment was homeless, sleeping, as best they could on the ground. It was a pretty sight, with the camp fires burning. Little did we realize that it would be almost two years later before the few of us who were survivors of Company H would again sleep in New Jersey. Or that many of those now sleeping on this field, in less than one year would be sleeping their last, long sleep, on the blood-soaked fields, northwest of VERDUN.

September 6th, no need for reveille. Everybody was awake bright and early, breakfast was hurried through, kitchens taken down, packed, and all equipment, except that carried by the troops, loaded on the freight cars. During the morning many of the friends and families of the troops came up to see us off. By noon the loading was completed, lunch eaten, and then the final policing of the camp grounds.

In the afternoon the battalion was formed and marched to the railroad station. Waiting around the depot until 5 o'clock, we boarded the troop train, and at 6 P.M. pulled out amid the good wishes of our friends and families. To my mind the hardest part of war is in the leave-taking of those left behind, then the long wait for news and the uncertainty of what is happening. It is much harder on the families than on the troops; we, at least, have the change of station and the excitement of travelling.

Passing through Paterson, the train moving slowly, we were serenaded by a large crowd and then moved on to Jersey City. At this point the train remained all night, due to a defect in the train equipment. At daylight we again started on our way, reaching Washington, D. C. that afternoon. Laying over for an hour, the journey was continued to Anniston, Alabama.

While the 5th New Jersey Infantry had been stationed in the vicinity of Pompton Lakes other units of the New Jersey National Guard, 1st, 2nd and 4th Infantry Regiments, had been doing guard duty the same as we. The remaining organizations had been assembled at the State Encampment, Sea Girt, N. J. the latter part of July 1917. They were the 3rd Infantry, 1st Field Artillery, 1st Squadron Cavalry and Brigade Commander and Staff. The troops at Sea Girt came to be looked upon as the 29th Division. There was a sign on one of the buildings designating it as 29th Division Headquarters. This was the beginning of much of our later troubles in that division. Creating the impression of some influence working to have the division built around the 'Jersey' troops, without regard for troops from other States who were to concentrate at Camp McClellan under the command of Major-General Charles G. Morton, who had established headquarters at that station in August.

In order to properly realize just what was taking place during the concentration of the troops at Sea Girt—to comprehend the reasons for many of our difficulties at Camp McClellan and later in France—also to understand why so many officers were relieved of command or retained when they should have been relieved, at the reorganization that took place later on, it will be necessary to consider some conditions that had existed in the New Jersey National Guard for many years prior to the World War, as well as events that had transpired during 1916 and 1917.

For years the Guard in New Jersey had been a convenient means, to some officers, to either public employment or elective office, and these gentlemen were not a bit slow to use their military rank as a stepping-stone when seeking elective office. A bit of a war record would be a wonderful help. Our entry into the war found this group in a strong political position, smart enough to take advantage of it and plan for possibilities after the war was over. It was a peculiar thing but the organizations not affiliated with the group referred to were the troops ordered for the Mexican Border Service, and after that duty were the same troops to receive the first order for duty in the war.

In June, 1916 the First Brigade, N.J.N.G., composed of the 1st, 4th and 5th Infantry Regiments, with the 1st Squadron of Cavalry and Batteries A and B, Field Artillery, Signal Company, Field Hospital and Ambulance Company, under the command of Brigadier General Edwin W. Hine, were ordered to the Mexican Border. In order that the military units might make a rapid mobilization and departure for service, the Adjutant General, Brigadier General Wilbur F. Sadler, Jr. worked night and day to get the 'Jersey' regiments off to a 'flying start'. General Sadler was complimented later for having us among the first to report ready for duty. Unfortunately for us General Sadler became ill due to overwork, and died November 10th, 1916. The death of the Adjutant General was a severe loss to the State, but more of a loss to the National Guard. He had been the Adjutant General since 1909 and during that time had worked unceasingly to improve the militia organizations. In that period more progress was made than at any time in its history, the Guard passing from the old militia days to that of an organization capable of being whipped into soldiers, in a short time, that could be used in any part of the world.

December 5th, 1916 Charles W. Barber was appointed to fill the vacancy of Adjutant General, relieving Major Nelson B. Gaskell who was filling the position temporarily. General Barber had been retired from the regular service a short time before, having entered the army at the close of the Spanish-American War, in which he had served as an officer in the same regiment with the Honorable Walter E. Edge, Governor of New Jersey in 1917.

The general opinion among the officers with whom I talked at the time was that the appointment of General Barber would be for the best interests of the Service, in view of the fact that he had had some service in the Guard and years of service in the Regulars. We felt that he would understand the problems of the National Guard and his experience would help to build up the organizations ready to enter the Service and take our part in the war that we all felt was "just around the corner." If we had only been able to see into the future and note all the trouble, bitterness and suffering this appointment was to bring to us later, I believe the appointment would not have been so easily obtained.

In March, 1917 we lost another good friend of the National Guard. Brigadier General Edwin W. Hine, having reached the age limit, was relieved of command and placed on the retired list. General Hine had been connected with the New Jersey Guard since the early '80s. He had served as Colonel of the 2nd N. J. Volunteers in the Spanish-American War and after that as Colonel of the 5th N. J. Infantry, then promoted to command the First Brigade. He was a gentleman and a really good officer at all times, who thoroughly understood the civilian soldiers.

The retirement of General Hine left a vacancy for a Brigadier General, which, under the Constitution of New Jersey, would have to be filled by election. The Field Officers of the First Brigade voting at an election in the spring of 1917 were prepared to follow the usual procedure and elect one of the colonels, or such other officer as they saw fit, to fill the vacancy. When these officers were assembled they were permitted to understand that the Adjutant General of New Jersey would be acceptable. To whom? Any other man being elected might discover the physical or mental examinations rather hard to pass. As we were now at war with The Central Powers the regimental commanders withdrew from the race, figuring that with his greater experience General Barber would be the most valuable man for the position. The irony of the whole thing was, that within one year most of the officers who had taken part in the election were relieved by the man they had elected, or by his orders were transferred and later relieved.

## CHAPTER II

# CAMP McCLELLAN

### THE REORGANIZATION

ARRIVING at Anniston, Alabama, early in the morning of September 9th we had finally reached our Southern Home, Camp McClellan. Named in honor of a northern officer from New Jersey, the camp was built in a southern state with the men of the division, then in the making, coming from both northern and southern States, signifying the complete unity of purpose in the task that lay before us.

As the regiment was marching the short distance to the camp grounds we saw, in a pathway on our left, an officer on horseback, looking us over very critically. By the two stars on his shoulder we knew that he was a Major General. Having seen Generals before, and their meaning nothing in our young and inexperienced lives, we merely spruced up a little, gave him a side glance and continued on our way. If we had only known who he was, and his reputation for discipline, we would have passed out right then and there. He was none other than the celebrated Major General Charles G. Morton, Commanding General of the 29th Division, without a doubt one of the strictest disciplinarians in the entire United States Army. We learned all about him in short order. He made life a misery for us for a long time to come, but I believe every man of the division realizes now that in spite of all obstacles, and they were many, he made soldiers of us and fitted the organizations for the real fighting later on.

A casual glance at Major General Morton did not leave a very imposing impression, but looks are apt to be deceiving, as we soon discovered. The general was about 55 years old, probably five feet ten inches tall, stockily built, gray hair and moustache, with a cold, hard look in his gray eyes that seemed to see every button on the uniform, every shoe lace, even every hair in a soldier's head. We soon discovered that he saw all these things and many more that we never intended him to see. Nothing escaped 'Eagle Eye Charlie'.

We spent the next few days making camp and getting settled. The ground assigned to us for a camp site being on a hill, the mess shack on top, the company street dropping down hill from the kitchen and the officers' quarters on the other side of the rise, I was unable to see into the company street from my tent. The area had evidently been a cotton field, although a number of tree stumps had to be dynamited after the tents had been erected. Many of the tents were damaged by the flying pieces, providing another job for a soldier, patching torn canvas.

There was no time lost. The day after our arrival drills were started, the daily schedule being: Reveille 5.45 A.M., Breakfast 6.20, Sick Call and Fatigue 7 o'clock, Drill 7.30 to 11.30, Mess 12 noon, Drill 12.50 to 4.30 P.M., Guard Mount 5 o'clock, Retreat 5.45, Mess 6 P.M., Officers and Non-commissioned Officers' Schools 7 o'clock, Taps 10 P.M. This schedule was in effect each day, excepting Wednesday afternoon when we were allowed liberty if not on special duty. Saturday morning was given over to inspection, which meant a thorough check of personnel, equipment, quarters and everything connected in any way with the army. These inspections were not severe in the early days, but as training progressed and our military education improved the slightest slip was sure to bring down swift punishment. Sunday morning another inspection was held though not as thorough as the one the previous day—just a check on quarters and the company area.

Within a few days after our arrival we received an introduction to "Morton" discipline. Orders were issued that men were not to leave the company street unless completely dressed, also the sentries would not allow soldiers out of camp unless dressed strictly according to regulations. We soon discovered there was to be no more of the freedom of Pompton Lakes. This required a pass, properly authenticated, to get out, then inspected. The smallest thing out of place, even a missing button, would mean 'Stay in Camp.' Such things as a hatcord missing or wearing other than the canvas leggings of the infantry, even though they had not been issued, meant being placed under arrest and return to the company. Several of the mounted organizations, who had a reputation for being smartly uniformed while in the National Guard, brought leather puttees with them to the camp and on their first trip into town wore them. All went well until the 'Old Man' either saw or heard about the leather 'Putts' and that was the last of them. We were an infantry division and the common 'Doughboy' uniform, in the smallest detail, was the only one permitted.

It was plain to be seen the State troops were about to receive a brand of discipline such as they had never known. It was going to be tough on officers and men who had been playing soldier for years, without a thought of what the real service was, or what it meant to be a soldier. Now it was a case of make good or get out and let other men take your place. At least that appeared to be General Morton's plan, but we had better wait and see other plans working.

The 5th Infantry had been at this station only a short time when the usual army rumors were flying around thick and fast. Definite information as to the future of the National Guard was kept a dark secret, except that some kind of a reorganization was about to take place, with a switching around of officers. In conversation with others all kinds of stories were heard. Some claimed the companies were to be increased from 150 to 250 enlisted men with two captains and 5 or 6 lieutenants, the additional men to come from the new National Army. Others thought the Regular Army officers would take command of the National Guard organizations, all captains and higher ranking officers in the Guard being transferred to command the new army.

The first definite knowledge of a change came at a conference of the 5th regiment officers, when the regimental commander announced that in view of a consolidation there would be a surplus of officers, especially captains. He suggested that any captain who desired to stay with the new regiment apply for a discharge, as of his rank. This would be granted and then the officer would be immediately reappointed as a first lieutenant in the reorganized regiment. None of our officers accepted this generous offer. Whoever thought up such a scheme did not use much brain power. It would have been the cause of endless jealousy. The scheme was entirely opposite to the plans and later orders of the division commander, who ordered that when a non-commissioned officer was reduced, or an officer promoted, they were to be transferred to another unit in order to prevent friction or favoritism.

Some of the officer personnel in the old regiment would have to be eliminated, either by transfer or discharge. The majority of our officers had attended every kind of a service school possible and had spent years of their lives in an honest effort to be ready for just such an emergency as now confronted us. This type of officer made good later on in the fighting. Also remember the Reserve Officers' Training Camps were turning out officers, after three months at school and without previous military training, with ranks as high as major.

In the five weeks since arriving at this camp, up to October 11th, there was little accomplished in the matter of real training. No one appeared to know just what was to happen. As a result most of the time was devoted to trying to find out who was to be retained and who was slated to go. Training received but scant consideration and this condition was reflected in the enlisted men, who realized something was about to happen. Numerous transfers out of the companies had already been made, particularly to the new Machine Gun Battalions and Engineer Regiment being formed. A few of the junior lieutenants had been transferred to other branches of the service, and Company F had been sent to the engineers.

This was the beginning of the end of the New Jersey National Guard as we had known it—the breaking of all local ties. The authorities responsible succeeded to such an extent that when we left Camp McClellan in June, we had in this same company 3 officers from New Jersey, 3 officers from Maryland, about 125 enlisted men from 'Jersey' and more than one hundred men from a dozen other states. This before we saw any fighting. Returning to this country in 1919 we had two officers from New Jersey, two from Massachusetts, one from North Carolina, one from Virginia, one from Maryland. Forty-eight enlisted men were all that remained of the original three hundred from the State of New Jersey, the remainder of the returning company being from the other 47 states.

The last conference of officers, 5th Infantry, was held October 10th, 1917, and the make-up of the new regiment explained to us. The program was very simple, merely uniting two companies of the old regiment into one company of 250 men and six officers, in the new regiment, which had been designated as the 114th U. S. Infantry. Considering all the deep secrecy that had surrounded this contemplated reorganization, I had expected some profound military strategy was in the making that would cause the Central Powers to surrender if they should discover the New Jersey National Guard was in the war.

Company K of Montclair, N. J. and Company H of Orange, were to be consolidated and form a new company, designated as Company B, under the command of Captain Roscoe R. Johnson, formerly of K Company. Under the same date, October 11th, General Order No. 8, headquarters 57th Brigade, Infantry, was issued specifying the officers named therein were transferred, as surplus, to the 54th Depot Brigade, and for them to report to the Commanding General of that organization at ten o'clock the next morning. The writer was among the undesirables.

After mess, that night, Company H was assembled, the order for the consolidation read to them and they were advised to obey the order without grumbling. Wishing them luck wherever the fortunes of war should take them, I left. At times it had been necessary for me to be strict with these men, for their own good as I saw it. Whenever it became necessary to punish a man, no matter how serious the offense, personal feelings were not allowed to enter. In leaving them now it appeared as though my service with these men was finished. No man can read the future.

Reading this General Order No. 8, years after its first appearance, noting the names of the officers who were transferred, according to newspaper articles published at the time, because they were considered as not measuring up to the professional qualifications of the men who were retained, I recall at least five of these same officers, discarded from the old regiment, who commanded organizations in battle later. A number of us were recalled to the 114th Infantry and even commanded battalions of the same regiment in the worst battle of the whole war, at Verdun. If it were not for the seriousness of the thing and the useless waste of human lives resulting from this condition it would have been a comedy.

Many times, then and since the war, I have talked with men who knew something of the workings at this reorganization and have been unable to discover what system was applied in making the selection of the company commanders who were to be retained in the new regiment. It has been impossible to get any satisfactory explanation. Officers in a position to know, or who were responsible for the selections, have either evaded the question or given some lame excuse a child could see through. It was quite evident that consideration was not given to seniority, age, physical fitness or even to ability. In some cases, later, officers who had been retained, had to be relieved due to inability to function on the front lines or were unable to stand the strain. In France, one of these officers asked to be relieved of his command, admitting he could not stand the terrific strain up there. Another had to be relieved for what looked very much like ordinary cowardice. Many were relieved, for various reasons, even before the regiment left the States. A rotten story, isn't it? Imagine yourself serving under such conditions.

The division commander left these selections entirely in the hands of the brigade commanders; they in turn gave the regimental commanders some leeway in making their choice. In the case of the 57th Brigade, made up principally of New Jersey Troops, and the Commanding Officer, also from the same State, indebted to the political faction in New Jersey for his appointment as the Adjutant General in 1916, it is not impossible to see signs of favoritism in the selections. As I discovered later, who you were and who you knew politically played a bigger part in being retained with the new organizations and in promotions than did ability.

These same conditions continued right up to the battle zone and reached such a wretched state that Major General Morton found it necessary to relieve several of the higher ranking officers. On two occasions during active operations, in France, a General Officer remarked:

"The 57th Brigade is seething with politics and I'll break it up if it is necessary to relieve half of the officers in the brigade to do it."

A fine condition to exist in the face of a real war. The people at home bending every effort, making all kinds of sacrifices to bring the war to a successful and speedy end, yet, here were officers of the United States Army, with the lives of other men in their keeping, juggling these lives for their own preferment or personal advantage. Making this statement is distasteful, but the truth is usually unpleasant. These are facts, vouched for by many officers of the former New Jersey National Guard. This is one reason why so few of the wartime company commanders were willing to go back into the new regiments organized after the war in New Jersey. "A burnt child dreads the fire." We received a good burning.

On the morning of the 11th, in company with the other officers who had been relegated to the 'dump,' I left the regiment. Even here our feelings were not spared. As we walked down the road we could see the sly, superior, sarcastic grins on the faces of those who had been retained. What is the old saying about "He who laughs last, laughs best?"

So my thirteen years of service with the New Jersey National Guard came to a sudden and confusing halt. Sacrificed to political expediency. I was not of the 'Elite.' When I again came into a command with this regiment it was as a mere captain of the United States Army, with all sentiment crushed out of me and a determination to either succeed, or, "Enemy bullets have no respect for rank." After all is said and done, this being left out at the reorganization was of more value to me than all the severe training put together. It taught me how to fight.

## CHAPTER III

## 54TH DEPOT BRIGADE

### THE MADHOUSE

WITH the other undesirables, or misfits as you may choose to call them, I arrived at the camp of the 54th Depot Brigade about eleven o'clock Saturday morning. Even being magnanimous, truth compels me to say that this camp was a madhouse. Surplus officers and enlisted men from all regiments of the division were arriving at the same time, all trying to report, looking for orders, assignments, etc. I eventually located quarters, set up a cot, stowed my equipment and then did the one thing all good soldiers do at every opportunity— went A.W.O.L. (absent without official leave). It was plain to be seen, with all the confusion existing in this camp, one soldier, more or less, would not be missed. As my family was staying at a little town about six miles outside of camp it appeared to be a wonderful opportunity for a short vacation. Returning to camp early Monday morning I discovered I had not been missed.

During the existence of the Depot Brigade it was not uncommon for officers to leave for periods varying from a few days to several weeks. One man was jokingly accused of making trips to New York, Washington and other points of interest to him. It was not difficult to account for any absence; there was no check up. In the daytime it was often necessary for the former company commanders, who had been responsible for property, to go to the new regiments and assist in the transfer of accounts from the old to the new commanders. The higher authorities, if they even missed us, probably

22

thought we were attending business in our old companies. Altogether, the Depot Brigade was a calamity.

In the next few days there were many meetings with friends of the former New Jersey Guard, who, like myself, had been left out in the cold at the reorganization. These men had been known to me for a number of years and, generally, had been considered as above the average. In many cases I had the opportunity, later, to observe their value while in action. Many of them were commended for their ability, also decorated for bravery in action. It was peculiar, but when the division completed its training and entered the fighting only a few of the individuals who had been responsible for these conditions in the National Guard were with the 57th Brigade.

It is not to be expected that you can classify a man as inefficient one day, then a month later order him back to his former position and have him enter upon his duties as though he relished the job. Among the 'Jersey crowd' none of us had any desire to be assigned to the new regiments. All seemed to feel we could accomplish more if assigned to duty with troops outside of the 29th Division.

One favorite pastime in this hour of gloom was to look out toward the end of the war and wonder what price we would pay for this duty. So far the service had been nothing but heartache with but little chance of improvement in the near future. We sat around at night, jokingly telling what we would do when we returned from the war, probably as broken-down, wounded old soldiers. One of our officers, since politically prominent in Essex County, N. J., decided he would peddle shoe-laces on the corner of Market and Broad Streets—he had it all figured out—his old comrades would patronize him. Another officer, who was too bashful to ask for any favors, we assigned to the corner of Main and Day Streets, in Orange, to sell newspapers and lead pencils. So passed the time, nothing to do but bemoan our luck and hope for a brighter future. In much the same manner I have seen the men in the companies, waiting for the command to go

"Over the Top," joking about their chances of being wounded and hoping if hit, that it would be only a small wound so they could sport a wound stripe.

Towards the end of October, with several others, I was assigned, for temporary duty, with the Personnel Section of 29th Division Headquarters. Our duty was to visit each regiment and question the men about their occupations in civil life; to inquire into their experience such as working on motors, driving automobiles, railroading, the building trades or anything that might be of value to the army. The information was then filed for future reference. Later, when requisitions were made for specialists in any line, these cards were gone over and men selected for assignment in accordance with the information given by the men themselves. Many a soldier was transferred to a railroad yard, possibly to a bakery company or to an Aviation Depot, when the soldier wanted to be an infantryman; they would wonder what offense they had committed to cause them to be transferred, never realizing they had talked too much when telling how much they knew.

Upon completion of duty with the Personnel Section I was assigned to one of the Division General Courts Martial Boards. Most of the cases coming before us were of men who had been absent without leave. The sentences were usually a fine and in some cases confinement in the Division Stockade for a short period. At this time the courts were more lenient than they were later; most of the offenders were new to army rules and regulations, and sentences were imposed more as a deterrent than as a punishment. Where necessary some rather stiff sentences were meted out. I recall one trial, in which three soldiers were tried for a prolonged absence, about three months. The punishment in these cases was that two soldiers received six years each and the third man seven years' confinement, all to be served at the Military Prison, Fort Leavenworth, Kansas.

Early in November the 54th Depot Brigade was disbanded and all members of it transferred and attached to the active organizations, as surplus. In this new shuffle, the men who came from northern States were attached to regiments that had originated in the southern States, and vice versa, the idea apparently being to make the division a part of the United States Army, to eliminate all local or sectional ties and sentiment. Such a plan might have worked in some divisions, but in the 29th, with politicians from Virginia, Maryland and New Jersey, all striving to make the most of a golden opportunity, it was asking too much of embryo soldiers.

When the attached officers reported to the units designated, another difficulty appeared. No one in authority seemed to know what to do with us. The thought undoubtedly in the minds of those officers who had survived the reorganization, was that an officer of equal rank, attached to his unit was a menace. The surplus officer could easily be used to replace him. All that was needed was a division order and the position of the attached officer and the assigned was reversed. As a result of this condition it became the general rule to give no information or instruction that might be useful in any way to assist the attached officers to keep up with the new system of training then being introduced. All we did was to 'hang around' camp and watch the training from a distance. Yet we were expected to be ready to take command of an outfit on a moment's notice. If an officer was not right up to the minute in ability to instruct or for any reason showed the slightest let-up, he was ordered before a reclassification board, and he was finished. Altogether it was a fine mess. Many times I was ready to apply for a discharge, but something kept urging me to "stick it out" and beat the game. I knew that if given the opportunity making good would not be too hard for me.

Oh! Yes! I had opportunities to study the conditions, and the rotten political situation in the 29th Division. The enlisted men and the majority of officers in the division were real soldiers, asking no odds or favors, and are deserving of all the credit possible, but to those officers, so-called gentlemen, who were responsible for these conditions and for the stigma cast on numerous good men, especially in the New Jersey regiments, I have nothing but the utmost contempt.

Changes among the officers who had been retained at the reorganization were continually taking place. The 58th Brigade had several commanders within the first few months. The National Guard generals in command were being relieved and other, supernumerary generals placed in command, and they in turn would be relieved, until all General Officers of the National Guard had been ousted, except in the 57th (New Jersey) Brigade. The same procedure was applied to the colonels and so on down through the various grades, including the captains. It appeared as if all Field Officers were to be forced out, and any officer, no matter what his rank, would have to be so careful or so proficient that he was never caught in any mistakes or slip-ups.

This everlasting changing and transferring was raising the devil with morale. It was not conducive to the rapid progress necessary in training for the work for which we had entered the service,—fighting. The spirit seemed to have left everyone. Pride in one's organization, esprit de corps, so necessary to military efficiency,—there was no such thing in the 29th Division, at that period. The prospects for an early departure for foreign service appeared very dim at the time.

One instance is recalled demonstrating the point referred to—lack of spirit. A board had been appointed for the purpose of examining officers to determine their efficiency and ability to command troops. Officially it was named the Efficiency Board, unofficially it was called the "Gasoline Board." The general opinion being that an officer, when ordered before the board, was finished, even before his trial commenced. One story going the rounds was about a lieutenant ordered before the board for some slip-up or infraction. After the trial several of the higher officers were discussing the trial and its effect on other officers. A Regular Army colonel remarked to one of his majors: "This ought to teach some of our officers a lesson." To which the major replied: "I am afraid, sir, more men than we realize would welcome a trial as one way to get out of this madhouse." However, all the officers who went before this board were not discharged. Some were transferred to other divisions and gave excellent service. Perhaps life was more bearable in other outfits.

There is no intention of belittling the conscientious effort made by the major portion of the division personnel, but rather of emphasizing the complete lack of preparation for the task our country was facing. This very lack of preparation provided a wonderful opportunity for a powerful, political minority, by favoritism and intrigue to maneuvre the selection of officers to their own advantage. As a result of these conditions the New Jersey organizations for more than a year were made to realize they were not in the good graces of certain very high officers of the 29th Division. These facts have never appeared in the public press. It is easily understood that the war correspondents attached to the Division dared not publish anything but the rosiest picture of what was transpiring. On several occasions I talked with one of these correspondents, from New Jersey, and he expressed himself very forcibly about the conditions in the Division.

In the fall of 1917, a new system of training was inaugurated, under the general supervision of French and British officers, men who were experts in their special subjects. They had seen considerable service on the Western Front, and from their service were able to give us the latest methods of 'kultur.' Our old system of fighting was discarded to a great extent. Bayonet fighting was completely changed. It now became real work to go through the exercises; every ounce of energy and strength was put into a lunge into a sack of straw. No more high or low parries and thrust; now it was long point, short point, jab, butt stroke, etc. We also heard of grenades, bombs, machine guns, automatic rifles, gas, flame throwers— all the paraphernalia of modern war, things we had never heard about or, if we had, only as a fad or experiment. We became thoroughly familiar with them before long, we were apt pupils when we had a chance to learn.

In my opinion a mistake was made in the schedule of training, no consideration being given to the surplus officers. If permitted to attend the schools of instruction in the division they would have been ready to take active command the moment they were assigned to a unit. Another thing, the un-assigned officers certainly had plenty of time to study; they had nothing else to do. The only way we were able to gain any instruction in the new ideas was to stand on the sidelines and watch the men at work on the bayonet runs or drill fields, or perhaps to overhear smatterings of lectures. It almost appeared as though instruction was deliberately being kept from us. Perhaps we might tell the enemy that the United States was considering sending the 29th Division across to look the war over.

Shortly before Thanksgiving, in a conversation with the Commanding Officer, 112th Machine Gun Battalion, the unit to which I had been attached, request was made by me for permission to attend the course of instruction in machine gunnery about to start in a few days. The major was interested and promised to see what could be done. Some time later he informed me he had taken the matter up with division head-quarters and learned there was no authority for surplus officers to attend the service schools, but, if the instructor, Captain John Lean of the British Army, had no objection, the major would see that the necessary time was allowed. What time would have to be allowed is beyond me as I had nothing else to do. Talking with Captain Lean, explaining the circum-stances, he expressed a willingness to have me take the course as the knowledge would be valuable even though later as-signed to an infantry company.

Looking back over my war service I am convinced that every infantry officer should know something of machine gun fire, its possibilities and limitations. Many times during active service the power of machine guns was wasted by infantry officers who failed to appreciate what could or could not be done by these weapons. On one occasion, in France, I saw a machine gun section, uselessly sacrificed by the simple com-mand of an officer ordering them, in broad daylight, to join an infantry company, that was under severe artillery fire dur-ing an advance. If this section had been given a position on high ground in rear of the attacking troops, it would have been able to materially assist the infantry, by overhead fire.

This school was my first experience with soldiers of the foreign armies. The N.C.Os, especially impressed me. For snap and smartness there is nothing to equal the British sergeant-major. To hear one of them talking to their officer or giving a command is the acme of brevity and precision; their commands sound like the crack of a rifle. These instructors were very thorough and painstaking, always willing to make a point clear. The lectures were made interesting by accounts of actual front line conditions. One noticeable point was the willingness to give the enemy credit for being a good fighter with a wonderful machine behind him. However, they were insistent the Allies would eventually win the war.

Shortly before the school finished my battalion commander asked if an assignment to command a machine gun company of colored troops at Camp Dodge, Iowa, interested me. As this seemed to offer an opportunity for active service and above all a chance to get away from this Division in which there appeared to be no progress, I agreed to take the command. When the New Year came two other officers and myself, who had been scheduled to go out there, were notified the order had been rescinded and we would remain at Camp McClellan.

Early in December we were informed that twenty per cent of the command would be granted leave for the Christmas holidays. In many outfits orders were published showing who were the lucky men. Plans were made for getting away and in numerous cases money was sent to allow a soldier to get home once more before going overseas. Those who were to go counted on leaving camp on the 22nd or 23rd. About the 19th orders were changed so that only five per cent would be allowed on leave. This was a severe disappointment in the case of the enlisted men. It was the cause of considerable A.W.O.L. Who can blame a soldier for leaving camp without permission, when he had been on his good behavior for months, trying to obtain a pass, and after being told he was to go home, found, as he is about to leave for the train, that orders have been changed and that he could not go. No explanation made, he was simply directed to remain in camp. People will say a soldier's duty is to obey orders, no matter how distasteful or disappointing. I agree with them, but the greatest punishment I know of is to promise a man a leave of absence and then to take it away from him. There were two occasions where it was necessary for me to use this punishment. In one case I have always regretted the necessity.

For some reason, probably due to the fact that an attached officer was not charged against the quota of any organization, I was granted leave for seven days from December 23rd; also was able to obtain an additional 24-hour pass, allowing me an extra day.

On the evening of the 21st I went up to Jacksonville to complete arrangements with my family, who were also going home. While in town two artillerymen accosted me and in a pitiful way explained they had received leave orders, but by a friend in their battery had been told that new orders had been issued and that they were not on the new list. Explaining that they had seen me in Jacksonville on several previous occasions, they asked me to tell them how to get out of town and on the train due to leave early the next morning, without being caught by the military police. To me it has always remained as a laughable incident of the war, to have these men, strangers to me, ask that I become a party to their going A.W.O.L. According to men who served in my command I was never considered as the type of officer who would 'wink' at regulations or as exceptionally lenient with men who were violating the rules. Perhaps it was the Christmas spirit. Whatever it was, I did not call the M.Ps. and have these men returned to camp. After asking a few questions, I directed them to follow the small railroad out of Jacksonville a few miles, where they would strike the main line going north; by keeping out of sight they ought to be able to get safely on board the train for Washington. I have often thought of those boys and wondered what was their fortune in the war.

The next morning Jacksonville was the scene of considerable activity as we were about to leave. Our Military Police were very much on the job to see that only those with the proper credentials boarded the train. Everyone on the train was in high glee at the prospects of getting home again. The trip was uneventful except for one thing. Between dinner Saturday night and breakfast Sunday morning the dining car had been taken from the train. This made the 'rustling' of food a real problem. The only opportunity to procure food was from the stands and restaurants at water tank stops and small towns. As these stops were for only short periods, usually not more than fifteen minutes, you can imagine the chaos when that mob of hungry soldiers descended on those food stands, all wanting to be waited on immediately. As my family was traveling with me my food problem was considerably increased. I found the simplest way was to get around to the back of these food stalls, wave a small piece of the International Flag (dollar bill), thereby keeping from starving to death.

Washington, D. C., was reached about ten o'clock, Sunday night, more than ten hours late. Then a mad rush for the dining room, afterwards trying to arrange reservations for the balance of the trip to Newark. In memory it appears as though the entire trip was just one rush and dash after another. Rather reminds me of the Argonne Forest, just dashing from one place to another.

While waiting for the train which was scheduled to leave at 2.30 A.M., a soldier of the 114th Infantry, now a respected citizen and business man of the Oranges, approached and explained that he and another soldier were on their way home, and having expended all their money were unable to continue the journey. "Would the Captain loan them enough to get home on," the loan to be repaid as soon as they reached Orange. I knew this soldier's father and realized the Holidays would be rather lonesome for the parents if the boy did not get home. To my query as to whether they were traveling on leave he replied that they were. Officially, I should have asked to see his travel orders, but as such a request would undoubtedly have caused embarrassment and complications for this young man I gave him enough money to take both of them to their destination. Several weeks after my return to Camp McClellan this soldier came to my quarters to repay the loan. He explained that he had missed me at home and since his return to camp had been unavoidably detained. The reason he had not been to see me earlier was a thirty-day stay in the division stockade as a 'reward' for going A.W.O.L. He probably figured the trip home was worth the punishment. So do I. Twice on this trip I had been asked to aid soldiers go absent without leave. Something must have gone wrong; perhaps I was getting soft-hearted.

The trip from Washington to Newark was uneventful. The train was very crowded and it was almost impossible to make any reservations. Had it not been for an enlisted man, who heard me trying to coax sleeping accommodations from the ticket agent, it would have been necessary to make the trip in a day coach. This soldier offered his reservation for the use of my family, while he made the trip curled up in a chair. This was the real spirit of the service—Unselfishness. Everybody was glad to reach home about eight o'clock the next morning, Christmas Eve.

While at home I was impressed by the way the civilians spoke and acted. There seemed very little understanding of the problems the country was facing, even among those people who had men in the service. It appeared to me as though they believed the war could be won without our men getting into it. Apparently they thought someone else might do a little fighting, but any idea of their own men getting to France never entered their minds. Work was plentiful and everyone seemed to have plenty of money. The drives, of various sorts, appeared to be successful, with a great show of patriotic 'ballyhoo,' but very little appreciation of the realities of the situation we were facing. They certainly never thought of the price the young men of the Oranges were to pay before another year had passed, and how materially these boys were to help, with their lives and bodies, in bringing to an end more than four years of war. It was a good thing the folks at home, and we in the field, could not see what the future had in store for us.

The stay at home was very enjoyable, but all too short— only seven days, three of which were used for travelling. I reported back to Camp McClellan, at noon December 31st, 1917. Due to the holiday next day there was no duty for me until January 2nd when I was directed to conduct a class in machine gun firing. Before the class even started, orders were again changed and I was assigned to attend the division Gas school for one week. Orders were issued and changed so fast we never knew what to expect next or where we were at.

On returning to camp I discovered that all National Guard Colonels had been changed, some of them relieved and discharged, others sent to service schools. The general rumor was that the officers sent to these schools would have to be super-men in order to get through, the real reason being to get them out of the Service. All of these colonels were replaced by officers of the regular army. Apparently the rumors were unfounded as most of these officers did come back to the division. I served under one of these colonels for several months, later on.

Mention is made of the rumors, circulating thick and fast throughout the division, as it seemed to be the favorite pastime. There was some justification for the rumors, changes were being made so rapidly that none of us could even imagine just where we stood. Some officers were being relieved for physical disability, more for lack of administrative ability, others were resigning, completely disgusted with conditions and unwilling to make any attempt to comply with regulations. Many that I talked with considered the whole affair a mess, and the possibility of the 29th Division ever getting to France appeared mighty small. After these experiences if the Division did get overseas it would be more of a mob than a fighting unit.

We had a long, hard road to travel, "The Devil's Own

Highway," before we did reach a state of efficiency which enabled us, as a combat unit, to stand up under the gruelling test, called Modern War. It is only fair to state that from the latter part of September to the middle of December 1917, the division had not been under the command of Major General Morton, our respected General having been in France as an observer. During his absence the division, under a temporary commander, provided an ideal breeding spot for any and all sorts of scheming and intrigue.

At the time of reorganization the 1st Regiment Infantry, Delaware National Guard, had been included in the new 114th Infantry and designated the Third Battalion, the surplus men of the regiment being distributed throughout the Division. About the beginning of the New Year an order was received directing the Delaware regiment, including all men of the National Army from that state, who had been assigned to the division, to be reassembled and transferred from the 29th Division to duty as a Pioneer regiment.

Upon completion of the course at the Gas school I was detailed, as instructor, for pistol firing in the 112th Machine Gun Battalion. This continued until January 22nd when I received an order to report to the Commanding General 57th Infantry Brigade, as Major Markey informed me, to take command of the Machine Gun Company, 113th Infantry. Upon reporting to Brigadier General Barber I was questioned as to my ability to command a company of 250 men. The General was referred to my former battalion commanders. He then directed that I report to the commanding officer of the 114th Infantry, Colonel Fred. Stritzinger, who in turn ordered me to report to Major John C. Taylor, commander of the First Battalion, from him I gained the information that a new captain was to be assigned to Company B, 114th Infantry. After talking with the major for a short time, he directed me to report back to Colonel Stritzinger, who then sent me to General Barber and again the question came up as to my ability. The answers were the same as at the previous interview. There was no thought of whether I wanted to be assigned to the command or not. Possibly they thought I would consider that an honor was conferred on me by merely being considered for the position.

The thought has occurred to me that I was like a horse being offered for sale, with each prospective purchaser giving the horse a thorough inspection, for fear of being 'Chiseled.' Every one of these officers 'looked me over' as if I was the horse. The peculiar part of the entire matter was that of these gentlemen, who so thoroughly inspected this horse, not one of them completed his service with the 29th Division.

The treatment received from the higher officers was very crude and primitive. I was certainly given a 'merry run-a-round.' Of course, as a mere line captain, those above me in rank were not required to be even civil. Unfortunately the Irish in me objected very strenuously to being treated as a menial without any rights. The treatment had to be 'swallowed' without complaint. During the interview I made no attempt to impress these gentlemen. There was no desire on my part to go back to the 'Jersey' brigade. The unfair manner in which the first selection of officers had been made was still fresh in mind. Also, the reports heard of conditions in the 114th were not encouraging, and the commanding officer of the regiment had the reputation of being anything but loving.

Since the war the remark has been heard that influence was used to have me back with the regiment. If any pressure was used it was without any of my knowledge. When orders did come for me to report I remarked to an officer friend: "I hope I do not get Company B, I don't want it and shall make no effort to hold the position." This officer advised me to go in and win, so that there would be at least one commanding officer with the men from home.

The men of the old company will be surprised at the above statement, but it will explain to them why I appeared so hard and cold when I did go back to command Company B. Experience with the 29th Division had taught me many things, especially to expect no consideration from any one in the division. It was apparent that the first appointments of officers had been made by influence and favoritism, and now three months later, when changes were necessary due to unfitness, the powers who had made the original selections were compelled to fall back on the old discarded officers to take command and help to pull the brigade out of a hole. Most of us who were recalled stayed with the regiment until its muster out in 1919; some were promoted to higher rank and many were decorated for ability and bravery in action. We even had the pleasure of seeing those officers who had been instrumental in having us relieved in turn being thrown out of the division.

Even at that early date it was plain to be seen the New Jersey infantry was not standing in the good graces of Division Headquarters. Also, Brigade was driving the regiments hard with little co-operation or help, the attitude being "Orders are issued, obey them," regardless of conditions or facilities for carrying out orders. A complete lack of understanding existed all down the line. It appeared to me as a case of 'bluff,' with some of our officers trying to impress their superiors with their own ability at the expense of the juniors, who could not successfully fight back. I most certainly believe that the regular army officers, who relieved our colonels, were sent in with one idea in mind and that to break the spirit of the National Guard officers—to use a rather strong expression "To put the fear of God in their hearts." This condition broke many a good officer's spirit so that when ordered before the 'Efficiency' boards they made no attempt to defend themselves, glad that it was all over and of the opportunity to get out of the madhouse.

About this time the following rumor was being circulated through the camp, most likely without any foundation, but certainly showing what every officer was looking forward to. One morning the division commander met the division inspector before breakfast, and the following conversation took place:

Major: "Good morning, sir."

General: "Good morning, Major, how are things this morning?"

Major: "Very good, Sir, I have relieved two colonels, one lieutenant colonel, one major and three captains so far this morning."

General: "Very fine Major, you are doing well and the day is young yet."

You can imagine what the end of the day would produce.

A fine condition to build up an organization spirit on. A volume on this subject alone would not suffice to tell the complete story. Yet, we were supposed to be in training for war.

## CHAPTER IV

## COMPANY B. 114TH U. S. INFANTRY

### TRAINING FOR 'OVER THERE'

FRIDAY morning, January 23rd, 1918, in compliance with orders issued by the Commanding General of the 29th Division, I again went through the routine of reporting to Brigadier General Barber, Colonel Stritzinger and Major Taylor, who directed me to relieve Captain Roscoe R. Johnson, commander of Company B. The usual procedure on an occasion of this kind would be for the major to accompany me to the orderly room of Company B where he would officially notify Captain Johnson that a new commander was about to take command of the company. For some reason I was not shown this courtesy. The order was obeyed, but I felt that my stay with the regiment would be short, when I, in turn, would be relieved. There was no other course for me to take except to resign from the army. This I had no intention of doing. If any one wanted to get rid of me there was only one way to do it—throw me out.

In the course of taking over the command of Company B, while talking with the regimental adjutant, Captain William M. Mead, he remarked that he was glad I was to be with the regiment; that the request for me, had been made by the commander of the 114th Infantry at the suggestion of Major Taylor. In reply I, undoubtedly, failed to show any appreciation of the 'Honor' by explaining to the Adjutant that there was no desire on my part to serve with the regiment, and if left to me to say, service in another division would be more agreeable.

When assuming command of the company the battalion

commander gave me no assistance or information about the condition of the organization. It was left to my own initiative to gather the information desired. It did not take long to size up the company. Decidedly it did not conform to my idea of a potential fighting unit. For some reason, possibly a little 'Irish' combativeness, I decided the outfit could be whipped into shape. The going would be hard and endless for some, many would fall by the wayside unable to stand the strain, but when the task was completed the survivors would have a record to be proud of for the rest of their lives.

Assuming command I found these officers assigned with the company: 1st Lieutenant L. D. Walker, on special duty as regimental exchange officer, 1st Lieutenant R. C. McNally, on special duty for the Brigade Commander, both of these officers being excused from ordinary company duty. 2nd Lieutenant A. T. Derrom was the only assigned officer actually performing duty with the company and, therefore, the only one having any interest in the organization. Attached were Captain R. A. Kennedy, a cavalry officer, also Captain Joseph J. Brooks, an infantryman, both good men, but as attached officers they had no interest in the success of the company. It was of no advantage to them to build up the organization. While these gentlemen remained with the outfit they gave me every co-operation and were of considerable value in the absence of the prescribed number of lieutenants.

During the afternoon of the first day I learned some things about conditions in the company that were far from encouraging. Many of the men had gone home, absent without official leave; also the men were confined to the company area by direction of the regimental surgeon. On the field, drill was very unsatisfactory, executed in a manner more to pass the time and comply with orders, rather than any desire to learn. Discipline was very lax and the appearance of the company was far from what might reasonably be expected of an organization that had spent six months on the Mexican Border, in 1916, and ten months in the Federal Service in preparation for this war. This condition was due, without a doubt, to the so-called reorganization with all its attendant transfers and general changing around. Taken as a whole the situation facing me was very discouraging.

It was plain to be seen that some changes would have to be made. They would come in good time. Material was available for good non-commissioned officers, who, with the proper support, would develop into real combat leaders. It would take a tremendous amount of hard work to develop them. General Pershing had said "The standard of efficiency will be that of West Point." Another General had remarked, "To win this war, the American Army will need discipline such as it has never known." I decided this would be the standard of Company B, as long as we remained together. If I failed, the men and officers would know that I had been around.

Mention has been made of the 'buck passing' by higher grades to the next lower rank. The following incident will serve as an example of the method, also the unreasonableness and inability of certain commanders to protect their junior officers.

The morning after assuming command the usual Saturday inspection was to be held. This would give me an opportunity to make a physical check of the personnel and equipment. It should also give me some idea of the general condition of the company as well as a point from which I could hope to make a start. In the few hours with the outfit I had made no effort to correct the faults, merely directing the usual inspection to be held at the hour designated in orders. As any soldier will tell you, these Saturday inspections are the real thing. In an organization that is up to standard they give an inspector some idea of its efficiency. This inspection showed me that Company B was in anything but good condition, either physically or in military efficiency.

These Saturday general inspections were made, first by the company commanders, then by the Battalion commanders, and finally the regimental commander looked things over. In addition to this we had a number of special inspectors, such as division inspectors for kitchens, sanitary inspectors for bathhouses and goodness knows what other sort of inspectors. After the inspection was finished my battalion commander, Major Taylor, gave me quite a 'raking over the coals,' telling me the colonel was not satisfied with conditions in the company, the company was the dirtiest in the division, that the equipment was not in good condition and many men were short of shoe-laces and other articles. Explaining to the major that I had been in command less than twenty-four hours, it was hardly reasonable to expect me to have the company meet the requirements in such short time. All to no effect, however. I simply had to stand there and take the call-down. Results are wanted in the army, not excuses. Criticism of conditions in the company was justified, they certainly were bad, but holding me personally responsible for them was rather far-fetched. From that day, until the company was mustered out of the United States service, sixteen months later, it was never again criticised as it was then.

Realizing the many changes taking place in infantry tactics I requested permission to attend the Division Musketry School. Orders were issued to this effect and on Monday, January 26th, I started the course for two weeks under the instruction of Captain Millard Tydings. The course covered every phase of modern infantry fighting, very much different from the methods used by the United States Army prior to our entry into the war. The course was valuable and I was glad I had made the application.

While attending the Musketry school I was keeping a watchful eye on the company and giving directions for its training and general tightening up all around. Efforts were being made to get the absentees back to the outfit. At the end of the course I felt that at least I could make a start, also believed the company was the equal of any in the division if given intelligent leadership. Its present condition was due to lack of proper supervision. Too many company officers had been assigned to duties away from the organization, as a result of which the men had fallen into a sloppy, careless, indifferent way of performing their duty.

On the Monday morning, following the end of the school, I took the company out for drill and from then on things began to happen. First, many of the non-commissioned officers were sent to the service schools and as their course was completed these men were used as instructors in the subjects they had learned at the schools. In turn other sergeants and corporals were sent to the schools, until each man had been to at least one, and in many cases had been through several schools. In this way a corps of instructors was built up covering every branch of infantry work. Close attention was given to the food and its preparation, clothing and equipment were examined and deficiencies corrected.

By degrees the organization came into shape. It was hard on both officers and men. Many nights I did not go to bed before two o'clock in the morning. Most of the paper work of the company, such as transfers, payrolls and other records of men and property, as well as the preparation of a schedule for the following day's work, all had to be attended to after the company had been 'tucked into its little feather bed' each night.

In the early part of 1918 the prospects of the 29th Division ever seeing France appeared very dim. Many divisions that had been in the service much less time than we had were already 'Over There.' We seemed to be in the same spot as in September 1917. The little progress made in the previous Autumn, together with the continual transfers of both men and officers, all tended to retard training. The transfers of the men, especially, was cutting down the numerical strength and general efficiency of the whole division. For a time it appeared to me as though the division was being used as a replacement unit; that is to train recruits and as they become somewhat proficient transfer them to combat units to replace battle casualties.

This was a most unsatisfactory condition and made the enforcing of discipline a hard proposition. No one was certain whether he would go across with his own outfit or suddenly find himself transferred to another organization. Each week saw orders coming in directing that men be sent to a base port, for immediate duty in France. One order called for fifteen men for duty as car builders. The men selected for this detail were those who had been carpenters in civil life, or at least knew something about tools. Another order directed a number of men be transferred to a Pioneer regiment. Again an order directed certain men, called for by name, be transferred to the Air Service, as mechanics. Some of these transfers were made by my orders, as a punishment, a few were made at the request of the soldier himself, who had some fancied grievance, and others with a desire to get to France as soon as possible.

In spite of all handicaps and disappointments the company was rounding into shape. I had been able to have the quarantine lifted, so the men were able to go into town. A number of the men on sentry duty had received citations for their appearance and efficiency from Colonel Stritzinger, and when you received a commendation from that soldier you could rest assured you were really performing one hundred per cent duty. He was very particular about whom he commended. We also moved from the bottom of the division list, in respect to kitchens, to close to the top. All of this caused the men to take a pride in themselves and their organization. The going had been hard but well worth the effort.

Washington's Birthday, February 22nd, having been declared a holiday for the division, all but the necessary routine tasks were suspended. In view of the improvement the company had made—the day would mark the end of my first month with them—I made arrangements for a special mess to be served. The Mess Sergeant and cooks spent the previous day and night preparing for the big meal. The mess hall was decorated with pine boughs, so that the appearance of the old army mess shack disappeared. Dinner in the middle of the day was the big event, the food being served to the men at the tables, instead of their having to fall in line, as usual. Those members of the company attending the Third Officers Training School were invited to join with their comrades.

The Company officers, for the occasion were permitted to take dinner in the mess hall with the company. In addition to myself there were Lieutenants R. C. McNally, Andrew Derrom and Luther Heathcote, who had been attached to the company.

Apparently everyone was enjoying himself and for once each soldier seemed to get enough to eat. As one man expressed himself after the dinner: "That was a great meal, looks like we were being fattened for the killing. I'll bet the 'Skipper' will drill 'hell' out of us to-morrow." Altogether quite a difference from the usual 'canned horse, gold fish, slum, bullets' etc. Between meals the regiment had planned various forms of entertainment. In the morning there were athletic events such as foot races, horse races, mule races; in the afternoon a dance was held in the canteen to which the men were permitted to bring their lady friends, and at night an entertainment was arranged.

The months of March, April and May showed a big improvement in the division. In the company changes had been taking place as they appeared necessary for the general good and gradually an improvement was noticeable.

Many times since the war ended former members of the company have told me what a driver I was and how cold and heartless I seemed. Usually they ended by telling me that now they can appreciate the necessity for the relentless discipline. The men were given no reason for any order, their task was merely to obey, regardless of any inconvenience or hardship imposed. As a result the men were in no position to know or understand what was taking place 'behind the scenes.' Later, especially in the battle area, they became more familiar with conditions and came to realize that generally, the strict disciplinarian was apt to be the better officer and more willing to share danger with his men, instead of ordering them into places of danger and then seeking shelter for himself in a dugout.

Major General Morton was recognized as one of the strictest disciplinarians in the army. Several years after the war ended, while addressing the Veterans of the 29th Division, in the course of his address he made the following remark, which is evidence that he recognised the hard conditions of our service: "You were disciplined and driven at Camp Mc-Clellan until you probably thought I was crazy; at times I wondered if I were crazy. If you had not been disciplined there you could not have stayed on the line when given a sector to hold, nor could you have succeeded in battle. One of the proudest things you accomplished was, when put to the test northwest of *Verdun,* all efforts of the best enemy Shock Troops could not drive you out. You never lost a position once captured."

During this same period the usual weekly 'hikes,' on Thursday, were continued. Company and battalion instruction in attack and defense, range firing with pistol, rifle, automatic rifles, grenades, etc., every phase of infantry work was executed in detail, until each soldier knew, not alone his own weapon, but also many others, so that in an emergency he would be qualified to attack with any weapon. Instruction in gas defense was continued, the men performing problems while wearing their gasmasks. Schools were being continued and the latest styles in 'modern kultur' passed on to the companies.

Every man in the division was required to lace his shoes in exactly the one uniform style adopted, his hair had to be trimmed to not more than one inch in length. We also adopted a distinctive style in wearing campaign hats, each man being required to wear the strap from the hat at a point just above the ears to the exact point of the chin, not a quarter of an inch above or below the chin, but exactly on the point. We became quite well known as the "Chin-Strap Division" and this was the cause of more than one 'fistic' battle. It was just too bad for any officer or man who neglected any one of these regulations. As for having a button off the uniform, or not fastened, or failing to have the hat cord sewed on at four points. Well! neglecting one of these things, apparently, was a bigger military offense than it would have been to shoot a general. The old battle cry of the 29th Division was: "Button! Button! Who's got the button?"

By a series of conferences and lectures, in addition to the regular course of instruction, the officers were being made to understand what was expected of them. I recall one such conference, held at division headquarters, with all officers of our brigade present. The conference was all one-sided, General Morton did all the conferring as usual. On this occasion the General laid down the law very thoroughly, telling us just what was expected and the things he wanted done to build up the division for overseas service. Some of the General's suggestions appeared rather severe, as viewed from our pre-war experiences. Undoubtedly the 'old man' guessed our thoughts and closed his remarks, thus: "Many of you gentlemen believe that having served on the Mexican Border for a few months you know something about war. Forget that service, it was nothing but a military picnic." He certainly did ride us. The officers were having just as rough a time as the enlisted men.

Several lectures were given by officers of the British Army, assisting in our training. These lectures were interesting, reciting actual conditions in France. As these were personal experiences of the lecturer they gave us a clearer understanding of what we would have to contend with. One lecture, accompanied by motion pictures, gave a good idea of health conditions among the foreign troops. Shortly before receiving orders for overseas, a British Lieutenant Colonel gave a talk that was the clearest description of conditions on the front lines I ever heard; there was none of the 'Bunkum' about the German soldiers having to be driven into the trenches by their officers, but he did tell of the cool, calculating, methodical and spirited aggression of the enemy. He told us of the machine guns, the gas, the flame throwers and artillery barrages that blotted out every living thing in range. He spoke for more than an hour and finished by telling us: "You gentlemen must finish the job; we have done everything possible to bring the war to a successful termination, but now, England is fight-

ing with her back to the wall and France is 'Bled White.' "
These lectures materially helped us to understand the reasons
for many, seemingly, unnecessary irritations we were being
subjected to. They gave a better and clearer knowledge of the
mission that lay in front of us.

About the middle of March, 1918, Major General Morton
was relieved of his command, due to physical disability. After
a trip to Washington he returned to us, evidently having convinced the War Department he was fit for duty. The 'Old
War Horse' usually got what he went after. We were willing
to admit he was fit for anything. He was a better man than
any of us.

Early in April the National Guard colonels, who had been
at the Service Schools, returned to the Division, relieving the
Regular Army officers who had commanded the regiments
since January. Colonel T. D. Landon, former commander of
the old Third N. J. Infantry, assumed command of the 114th
Infantry, relieving Colonel Fred. Stritzinger. While I had never
been what might be called 'chummy' with our even-tempered
and sweet-voiced colonel, yet in justice to him I must say he
was every inch a soldier, who thoroughly understood his pro-
fession and most certainly improved the efficiency and morale
of the regiment. For what reason he was relieved I do not
know but have always felt that if the regiment had been left
under his command we would have fared better in France
than we did. Criticism from Colonel Stritzinger was not
given in honeyed words. He was scathing, on the other hand.
A word of commendation really meant something. When a
soldier received a word of praise from him, the soldier knew
he had earned it.

April 22nd the 57th Brigade left camp for a practice march
to Gadsden, Alabama, about sixty miles. As our battalion was
to be the advance guard into, supposedly, enemy territory, it
was necessary for us to move out at 6 A.M., one hour before
the brigade moved. The point of the advance guard was Company A, under command of Captain Fred. Rohrbach; Company B, under my command, with Lieutenants McNally,

Derrom and Heathcote and ninety-seven men, being in the support. Companies C and D were in the advance guard reserve. That afternoon camp was made at Wellington, the first battalion taking up an outpost position to protect the front of the brigade during the night, just as if an enemy were in front of us, the battalion spread out, fan shape, over a radius of several miles. On the 23rd the 113th Infantry became the advance guard and our battalion the rear guard.

The organizations passing through our outpost position presented an opportunity for a close-up view of our 'Jersey' troops and what they looked like. The field efficiency of troops is best estimated when they are on a route march, such as this, rather than at a review or formal inspection. The troops are more natural and as they swing along present a stirring picture. The regiments made a fine-looking group, apparently capable of giving a good account of themselves in whatever might be facing them. I saw many old friends of the New Jersey Guard, many of whom, like myself, had been thrown into the discard and later had to be called back to command their former units and then commanded them until the war ended or until wounded or killed. Little did we realize how many of the 'Jersey Brigade' would give up their lives before many months had passed. Such is war.

The next camp was at Glencoe, from which town we continued the march to Gadsden on the 24th, camping just beyond the town. On the 25th a maneuver was held. During a downpour of rain on April 26th, the regiment broke camp at 3 A.M. and marched to Glencoe, on the return trip. On the 27th at 4.30 A.M. we started the long jump from Glencoe to Camp McClellan, reaching there about noon. The condition of the company as it reached camp was very good, tired of course, and dirty from the long 'hike.' After a bath and general cleaning up of personnel and equipment the balance of the day was a rest period. The next day, Sunday, the usual inspection was held. The company was in excellent condition; the long march had shown only a few weak spots.

Shortly after the Gadsden 'hike' we went in for training

that would be helpful in our wanderings in the forward areas of France. Battalion and regimental practice marches were made at night, with the strictest march discipline being enforced, no talking, no smoking at the rest periods, even the wagons and automobiles travelled without lights. The artillery practised firing at night. Hearing the guns firing at a distance gave us our first impression of what later became a common occurrence.

Governor Walter Edge, with officials from various municipalities in New Jersey visited the camp on May 22nd, and presented flags to the regiments from that State, also a sum of money being given to each company having men in it, from home. This money, raised by popular subscription, was pro-rated according to the number of men from New Jersey in each organization. Among the visiting officials there were none from our home station at Orange. It was noticeable, however, that when the election for City Commissioners was about to take place a few weeks before this time, the candidates for office could arrange to have a representative at the camp to solicit the soldier vote. It was unfortunate that the election had taken place before the money was presented. There might have been a difference in the vote from Camp McClellan.

Early in April a detail from the division was sent to Camp Dix, N. J. and Fort Slocum, N. Y., and returned with a number of replacements. These men had been in quarantine for about a month, separate from the division; we saw them only once during that time; on one occasion, while we were on the range for rifle practice, the recruits out for a 'hike' stopped at the range for a short time. Orders had been issued that there was to be no intermingling. As a result the recruits stayed at one point of the range and watched us on the firing line, each group sizing up the other and making a mental estimate of ability.

A detachment of the replacements was assigned to Company B on May 22nd, again bringing the company up to nearly its war strength. These men, coming from the National

Army, were 'rookies' in every sense of the word, not one of the men sent to me had any military experience. They had to be assigned to squads and platoons, records made out for them and then completely equipped. They had brought only a few personal articles other than the service uniform. Plans had been made in the company store-room to handle this situation, each man went in the front door, passed through the building, and out the rear entrance. By that time the recruit had everything a soldier is issued. As they reached the company street the corporal of each squad gathered up his own men, showed them how to assemble the equipment according to regulations, then came the meanest task of all, cleaning a new rifle that is literally plastered with thick cosmoline. I'll bet those men have never forgotten the first few hectic days with us, being pushed and hurried from one duty to another. Then to be placed in recruit squads, for special instruction, to bring them up to the standard attained by the older men in the company. It meant hard work for everyone, but it was necessary to have these men get into condition as soon as possible, so that the division would be in shape to go overseas, at the earliest possible moment. The sergeants and corporals of the company assigned to this instruction work did a thorough job and I was well pleased with the manner in which they handled the task.

One thing that has always been a mystery to me is by what standards the doctors of the draft boards passed these men for the army and how some were ever accepted for service. The majority were fine, healthy specimens of men, intelligent and willing to learn, but some of them were useless for an infantry company. As an example, one of the men had no right shoulder blade; he explained to me that it had been removed as the result of an accident several years earlier; he claimed that he had told the doctors of the local draft board but, fearing he would be accused of trying to evade military service, had not pressed his claim, so had been accepted and sent to do duty in a combat unit. He was unable to handle a rifle. I had this man examined by our regimental surgeons, who recommended that he be discharged as unfit for military service. Another man wore glasses, could not see without them, imagine what he was facing in a gas attack; another man was deaf in one ear. Both of these men remained with the company until we reached the trench area, where I finally got rid of them.

One of the men assigned was weak-minded, he did not know his age, where he was born, what State he lived in or other simple matters; about the only thing he knew was that he lived in Cook County, wherever that might have been. When this man was paid it was necessary to keep an eye on him to see that some wise agent of the company did not separate him from his hard-earned pay; his letters were written by another soldier, who was not particular about telling true facts. One letter written by this self-appointed secretary to the other soldier's mother stated "he would probably be a lieutenant in a short time because the captain liked him." This secretarial soldier must have had a very poor opinion of the intelligence required to be a lieutenant. Eventually this soldier was transferred, after considerable argument, and became an M. P., in the rear area.

The new men appeared to take army life very seriously. I had many a good laugh while watching these men become soldiers. Many questions were put to me, in all seriousness, which showed how little they understood what the army really was. Shortly after the replacements joined the company, while sitting in front of my tent one evening one of the new men came over giving me what he considered a real 'snappy' salute, explained his local draft board had given him to understand that when a man was accepted for the army he would be assigned to a branch of the service for which his civilian occupation fitted him; he further explained that having been in the clothing business he felt his proper place was in the quarter-master service, where he would be of more value to the government, especially as he knew nothing about infantry. After listening to this soldier for a few minutes I explained that the army had a habit of doing things without any apparent reason, but they usually knew what they were doing and for him not to worry. As for not knowing infantry, the company officers would see to it that he became thoroughly familiar with an infantry soldier's duty before they were through with him. This man became one of my best runners in the fighting, taking big risks, until finally he was badly smashed up trying to get a message through from me to battalion headquarters in the Verdun Sector. He learned infantry all right and made good. This soldier, although a young man, after years of suffering from his wounds, due to his loyalty and devotion to the infantry, is now dead.

While intensive training was continued without any let-up, some time was also being devoted to athletics and entertainment, in an effort to offset the old adage "All work and no play makes Jack a dull boy." The entertainment usually consisted of a burlesque show or motion picture in the regimental canteen. Some of the actors in the burlesques were so bad that the poor acting made up for what the show lacked in comedy. Then we had boxing bouts between 'pugs' from the different outfits. Some of the bouts were very good, while others, like the shows, were rotten. Athletics were under the supervision of the regimental chaplain, Father M. J. Corr, who developed a championship baseball team, on which were a number of men from Company B. Mass boxing was introduced, in which each man in the company put on boxing gloves, then one platoon faced another for a battle royal, another method of training that helped to harden the troops for 'Over There.'

Since taking command, in January, many changes had taken place among the officers in Company B. On February 2nd Lieutenant L. D. Walker, at his own request, had been transferred. May 3rd, Lieutenants R. C. McNally and L. Heathcote were transferred out of the company; on the same order transferred to Company B was Ist Lieutenant Grover P. Heinzmann, from Company A. At the time the assignment of Mr. Heinzmann was not to my liking as I believed the old attachment to Company A would be a drawback to his giving proper co-operation to me. I had known the lieutenant for a number of years, in the 5th N. J. Infantry, but had very little dealings with him, except in an official capacity. In this opinion I was wrong. At all times he gave me his most loyal support. We will hear more about him later. May 25th Lieutenant Stephen Sabol was assigned to the company and a few days later was transferred to Company M. Several new officers, from the Third Officers Training School, were assigned to the company on May 29th: Lieutenants F. W. Schultz, C. G. Cooley, and G. L. Bussey, these men were from the 115th Infantry. At the same time the men from Company B, having completed the course at the Training School, had been commissioned and assigned, some to the 58th Brigade and others to the National Army Divisions. From accounts I received later these men made good in their respective assignments.

With the assignment of these new officers the company now had a full complement of officers and almost a full war strength of enlisted men. In view of orders to prepare for overseas duty the training took on even a more intensive turn as everyone realized our time in the States would be short. The everlasting 'Squads Right,' or as the men called it 'Squads Wrong,' was continued without any let-up, the men always growling, which seems to be the special privilege of all soldiers. When they were grouching they were happy, when there was no complaining it was advisable to keep an eye on them, they were apt to be up to some mischief. Particular stress was laid on bayonet work, the men, with a grunt and fierce expression, cleaning out trenches, thrusting and jabbing at canvas bags, filled with straw. Apparently our British instructors believed a grunt and roar to be very necessary to scare the Germans; my opinion is that our recruits were more nervous, when some wild-eyed 'non-com' came at them with a bayonet, than they ever scared the enemy.

While on the subject of instructors it may be interesting to note a couple of their pet theories. The British were very enthusiastic about the bayonet; they evidently believed it to be the one weapon that would eventually win the war, possibly assisted by machine guns. On the other hand the French instructors were admirers of the hand grenade for trench fighting,

with the assistance of the one-pounder gun to knock out machine-gun nests. Neither of these nations seemed to consider
the infantry rifle as of any value, except as a longer handle for
the bayonet. In the United States Army the rifle has always
been considered the real weapon of the infantry, and all other
arms as mere auxiliaries to assist the infantry advance. There
was a story being circulated about this time that will serve to
explain the viewpoint of these two armies. It was said that a
British 'Tommy' in battle would chase 'Fritz' all over a ten-
acre field until near enough to stick a bayonet in the German's
hide. The Frenchman, likewise, would run the enemy all
around the lot until close enough to throw a grenade at him.
The American, being less disposed to exert himself would say
"Oh! hell! what's the use of wasting energy, shoot the beggar
and be done with it." There was no foundation for the story
but it does show the importance attached to special weapons
and methods by the different armies.

Instructions from General Pershing emphasized the necessity of effective rifle fire; his plan was for our army to drive
the enemy out of the trenches and then to keep him on the run
so there would be no more stalling. The old American principle of fire and movement. Battles are won and positions held
only when the infantry has attacked.

Another part of training was the construction of a trench
system by our engineers on the Jacksonville road. Each infantry battalion was assigned to a forty-eight hour tour of duty in
the trenches. All the usual routine of trench life was performed
just as if an active enemy confronted us, relieving other troops,
living in dugouts, raids and all the endless details of trench
warfare. Although kept busy in there we did manage to get
some 'kick' out of the trip. One morning, at dawn 'stand to,'
while lying on the parapet watching the front of our line for a
possible 'enemy' raid, a 'fierce' battle started in the trench, just
below me. A raiding party of one officer and about ten men
from the Snipers' School, who were the 'enemy,' had managed
to get into our trenches, from the flank, and captured a few
men. The enemy were having a delightful time cleaning out

my lines. The officer leading the patrol, an old friend and former officer of the company, was very keen about getting prisoners. After watching the proceeding for a few seconds, unobserved, I rolled off the parapet and onto the lieutenant's neck, he must have thought a house landed on him. He became my prisoner and that ended his raid.

Towards the end of May orders were issued to prepare for immediate departure for overseas. These orders were very welcome. It had begun to appear as though Camp McClellan was to be our home for the duration of the war. The usual training continued, company commanders were directed to remain in the regimental area with a detail to rush the final preparations; company mechanics made regulation boxes, painted them with the various emblems, understood by the initiated but supposedly unintelligible to outsiders—the Blue and Gray emblem of the division, the triangle of the American Expeditionary Forces, the regimental letter 'D' and our company number, '2.' All personal baggage had the same insignia in addition to the owner's name, rank and organization. All surplus personal property was disposed of, only strictly regulation equipment and a few personal effects being allowed. It was amusing to note the things a soldier would want to take with him, how he would growl when ordered to get rid of some piece of property that could be of no earthly value to him. Later on he reached a point where he would 'chuck' everything he owned, except what he wore, if not continually watched.

In preparing for foreign service one of the things requiring considerable attention was the state of each soldier's financial obligations to the United States Government. There had been so many over-lapping deductions that many of the men had not drawn any pay for months, in fact the longer they remained in the service, the deeper they became indebted to their "Uncle Samuel." Eventually this muddle was straightened out. You can appreciate the old army song "All we do is sign the payroll and never get a gosh-hanged cent." Much has been said about the American soldier being the highest paid of any army. So that there may be a clearer understanding of just how much a soldier actually drew in cash, let us pause for a moment and figure out what became of his pay.

At the outbreak of the war, a private was paid fifteen dollars a month with no deductions, except possibly a voluntary allotment to his family. In the summer of 1917 the rate of pay was raised to thirty dollars per month. This looked like big money, there were visions of suddenly becoming wealthy, but soon there appeared a method of separating the soldier from this additional wealth. In the fall the government agreed to contribute ten dollars per month to dependents, on condition that the soldier allot fifteen dollars each month to his family; then later came the Liberty Bonds. Each soldier was induced, by various methods, to buy at least one of each series. As some of the wise ones remarked: "We have the pleasure of fighting the war and then paying for it." In the spring of 1918 a drive was made to have every man take out government insurance, the premiums, averaging about five dollars per month, to be deducted from his pay. Another form of contribution, some large and others not so big, was a court-martial fine, the result of an unauthorized vacation from the army; each company had a few men who donated to this form of entertainment. If there was anything left the soldier could draw canteen books at one dollar each, not more than four a month, again deducted from the pay. I have heard that these books were sometimes used in a game called 'craps,' probably used as score books. If, by chance he still had a few cents left, the soldier could send his laundry out, instead of washing it himself.

To be a successful company commander a captain needed to be a banker, broker, clothing and shoe merchant, grocer and butcher as well as an expert in firearms, tactics and military strategy. Any error that could not be traced directly to the individual soldier had to be paid for out of the captain's salary; never a change of the government being 'gypped.' First, last and all the time the soldier pays, even as the disabled veterans are paying today. If anyone desires to acquire gray hair in a hurry I suggest trying to command a company, war strength.

It is guaranteed to give you many a headache and plenty of gray hairs.

At last the eventful day arrived. June 6th, at 1.30 P.M., the command "squads right" was given for the last time in the company street. I believe most of us felt a little pang at leaving there; we had seen some hard times, many disappointments, but after all it had been our home. Looking at Company B I was proud of them. They were a fine appearing body of troops, a straight, clean-limbed, sturdy-looking bunch of youngsters that could 'lick their weight in wild cats'; they were my men, I had trained them. Whatever might befall us in the future I felt they would give a good account of themselves. The lieutenants were dependable and efficient. I believed the company had confidence in me as I had confidence in them.

A short march to the railroad siding, then boarding day coaches at 3 P.M. we pulled out, bidding farewell to Camp Mc-Clellan; no patriotic crowds to bid us Godspeed, just plain military efficiency. Orders were given and executed with the precision and snap of regulars. Au revoir, Camp McClellan! With all your hardships, the time was to come when we would look back and think of you and wish for the peace and safety of your hills.

The trip to Newport News, Va., was uneventful, reaching Camp Stuart about noon on the 8th. From then until the 12th the time was spent issuing overseas equipment. It seemed to me that most of the property was issued between midnight and reveille. Very few succeeded in getting into Newport News. I managed to get into town for one more good American meal, and to wire farewell to my family.

So closes our peaceful training. From here we are to know that we are at war, always in danger from the enemy, until death or the end of the war shall write FINIS.

## Chapter V

## GOING OVERSEAS

JUNE 14TH, 1918, at 7 A.M., the First Battalion was formed and marched from Camp Stuart to the C. & O. R. R. Docks, Pier 5. There we saw the transport that was to take us across, the *U.S.S. Pastores,* all decked out in camouflage, a United Fruit Line steamer, withdrawn from the South American trade for transport service. Luckily we had been assigned to an American ship manned by a U. S. Naval crew. As I heard later troops crossing on ships of our allies did not fare as well as those crossing on our own boats.

When it came time to go aboard, about ten o'clock, the company was reformed, the officers first, then the First Sergeant followed by the main body of the company arranged alphabetically, according to the passenger lists which had been made up several days previously. I remained on the dock with the company clerk during the embarkation, checking each man as he went on board. Reaching the deck, each soldier was handed a ticket by a sailor, showing the location and number of his berth, the deck it was on, the lifeboat or raft he was assigned to and other routine information. The embarkation was handled very expeditiously and without confusion.

On the *Pastores,* in addition to our battalion, were the Supply Company 114th Infantry, 29th Division Headquarters Troop, and of all the luck, we were picked to have the pleasure of making the trip across with the 29th Division Staff as traveling companions, and above all we had the 'honor' of having Major-General Charles G. Morton as one of our 'guests.' Was it possible our beloved Division Commander was so distrustful

of the 'Jersey' Troops that he was afraid to allow us to make
the trip alone? Did he consider it good policy to keep us under
his watchful eye at all times, even in the middle of the Atlantic
Ocean? Some of his later orders would seem to indicate that
he was somewhat suspicious and lacked confidence in us. He
had many and good reasons to be doubtful of the loyalty to
him of the 57th Brigade.

Shortly after all were on board details of various kinds were
made up, and men assigned to duties for the entire trip; arrangements were made to have some of the men from Company B assigned to the kitchen, or as the sailors called it "the
cook's galley." In this way I was sure the company would have
plenty to eat. Past experience had taught me always to have
some of our men in the kitchen whenever it was necessary to
depend on other people to feed the company. I was assigned as
assistant to the police officer, Major Taylor, who was in charge
of all police regulations for the army on our transport. Other
officers and some of the non-coms were placed as lookouts. Assignments were made to lifeboats and life-rafts, etc., life preservers were issued and orders given to wear them at all times.
Every provision was made to get us off the boat without loss of
life, if we should run into a submarine or a mine. The U. S.
Navy deserves great credit for the manner in which they transferred the army to France through a sea full of hidden dangers.

The *Pastores* lay at the dock until shortly after midnight
and then moved out to midstream, remaining there until about
noon. The troops were kept below decks until we sailed and
were out of sight of land, when they were allowed up on deck.
As assistant police officer I had been inspecting the ship during
the morning. At sailing time, being on one of the upper decks,
under cover of a ladder, I had a chance to see what was taking
place. There was no excitement, either on ship or the shore, a
few sailors and soldiers waving to us, also a few civilians. As
we dropped below the city and into the bay, I saw a lady standing near the water edge, intently watching us go out. With
the aid of my field glasses I was able to recognize the lady as
the wife of one of our officers on board. This incident con-

vinced me that the order barring relatives from seeing us off
was for the best, the parting would have been too hard on both
the soldiers and their families. From various points of vantage
other men were stealing a look at our United States and wondering if we would ever see it again. There was a lump in
many a throat and for very good reasons there was no desire to
talk, each man was busy with his own thoughts. In reading
accounts of other wars, and troops leaving the country, it is
always described as a sort of jollification, bands playing, cheering between ship and shore, waving of flags and handkerchiefs,
etc., but not so in this case; only a quietness that was almost
depressing and plain naval efficiency. This war was different
in many ways.

> "Good-bye Uncle Sam! We'll do the best we can, if we
> don't come back. Well! So Long!"

\*       \*       \*       \*       \*       \*       \*

Before proceeding with the ocean voyage and service in
France let us review our stay in Camp McClellan; this whole
period was one grand picnic and the much-quoted reorganization was the biggest tangle of all. Instead of being called a reorganization it should be known as a disorganization. Nothing
I have ever experienced could possibly equal the complete dis-
ruption that took place at this time. Later on battalions, with
approximately sixty percent battle casualties, were in better organized condition than they were at that time. It was not until
the early spring of 1918 that these conditions commenced to be
ironed out and a semblance of progressive training and discipline started.

Another serious handicap to which I have referred was the
continual transfers of officers and men that kept up until March,
1918. When Companies H and K, of the 5th N. J. Infantry,
were consolidated in October the strength of the new Company B was nearly two hundred sixty men and six officers. Six
months later, due to these transfers, the company had dwin-
dled to one hundred twenty-five men and three officers. This

Quarters of Company B.

certainly did not tend to help the morale or to aid in training. Then one month before we receive orders to go across the company is filled up with a group of replacements that are in every sense just plain 'rookies.' These recruits from the National Army had to be trained and brought up to the standard of men who had been in the army for more than a year. Remember that each time any considerable number of recruits are received the training starts all over again from the beginning, for the entire unit.

It is my opinion that the National Guard should have been kept intact and the organizations brought up to war strength by filling in with men from the new draft army, using the men from the same locality as the home station of a guard company. Faster progress would have been made and divisions could have been ready for overseas service six months earlier than they were if some such plan of filling up the old established organizations of the Regular Army and the National Guard had been worked out. It would have eliminated the necessity of forming an entirely new and untrained army.

The statement will be made that to have the men of the National Guard and the National Army in the same unit would have been the cause of friction. Such a statement is a reflection on our men, who were in the service for one purpose only, to finish a disagreeable job at the earliest possible moment. Many of the men who came under my command, as replacements, were from New Jersey, and I never saw any serious differences, no more than is usual where a crowd of men are suddenly thrown together, merely an adjustment, each man to his proper place. Repeatedly I was requested by men from the 78th Division to have them transferred to my company, so that they might be with friends from home. On several occasions in France men purposely 'lost' their outfits, then attached themselves to us. There is an old saying appropriate to this subject, "Misery loves company."

The breaking up of the National Guard regiments was poor business in more ways than one, especially among the officers. Many officers who were efficient in their own special line were let out for no apparent reason other than that they did not belong to the 'clique.' I knew one particular case of an officer, a successful business man at home, who had made a study of ordnance property and handled it for some years. When the reorganization took place this man was left 'out in the cold.' He became so disgusted with conditions that he resigned a month or so later. Instead of allowing this officer to resign, he should have been transferred to some ordnance depot where his knowledge of property would have been of real value to the government; however, that was not the way things were being done. This officer had been patriotic enough to allow his business to suffer while he served his country for six months on the Mexican Border as an Ordnance Officer, and then again for eight months in the World War. At the end of that time he was 'eased' out of the service as undesirable. Yet, all over the country at arsenals, munitions and ordnance depots, young 'whipper-snappers,' who did not know the difference between a pistol and an army mule, were being commissioned and given charge of important supplies.

Dissatisfaction and discord was just as prevalent among the enlisted men as it was with the officers. While in the 54th Depot Brigade many times I was requested to help or to suggest a way for men to get out of the new organizations where conditions were very unsatisfactory. When assigned to the command of Company B, in January, one thing which particularly impressed me was the absence of so many sergeants and corporals who had served in the Guard for a considerable time; also a number of good soldiers were missing from the company. Many of these men had been transferred to other companies of the regiment to make up the new Third Battalion.

The entire situation was very discouraging. The blame cannot be placed on any one man's shoulders; every man with a little authority had his own pet theory of how to win the war and no two theories were alike, and as a result little was accomplished. The whole situation was due to lack of preparation for any such calamity as we found ourselves in.

Even at the risk of becoming tiresome, it is necessary to continually refer to the much discussed reorganization, if only to have my readers thoroughly understand the reason for so much of our hardship and the extremely heavy loss of life on the battle fields around *Verdun*. This reorganization was responsible for a great deal of inefficiency, many officers selected to command units were picked through political connections, or favoritism, rather than for their ability to command. It was evident very early in our career that the real power of the New Jersey troops lay not in Camp McClellan but in our home state, or in a representative near the camp who was the go-between.

From October, 1917, up to the time we were ready to go across certain high officials of the State of New Jersey, or their representatives, were in Anniston, and many were the conferences and 'pow-wows' these politicians and their satellites, among the officers in camp, held at the Anniston hotels. This group of political soldiers had their nerve with them all the time. In the fall of 1917, each officer in the 29th Division, from New Jersey was notified that a reception was to be held for His Excellency the Governor of New Jersey, at the Anniston Inn. The assessment would be three dollars and it was expected that the officers would meet the assessment and attend the reception under the penalty of arousing someone's displeasure. Of all the castiron nerve this was the beat of all. That notice was sent to all, even including those of us who had been 'kicked out' as inefficient at the reorganization. Like every one else I was simple enough to pay the assessment and to make my appearance for a very short time at the reception. If I had only known then, what I learned later, or could have even surmised all the heartaches plainly attributable to this same group, I would have seen them all in the lower regions before being foolish enough to even pay the assessment, let alone attend the reception.

Of what use were these politicians to us? We were no longer New Jersey National Guard, we were now soldiers of the United States. There was nothing the officials of New Jersey could, officially, do for us. Were they endeavoring to ascertain why so many officers were resigning, being relieved, transferred or discharged? That cannot be the reason, because most of these changes were in our brigade, either at the direction of the commanding general of the brigade, or at least with his knowledge. No, those were not the reasons. The real reason for these politicians 'hanging' around Camp McClellan was an effort to take care of their friends, and in the event of the division commander 'falling by the wayside,' to have one of the 'Jersey' officers to command the 29th Division. The Lord help us! if such a thing happened. They were not missing a trick, looking well into the future and preparing, as far as possible, for any and every eventuality.

I had no great love for Major General Morton, but in fairness we must admit that he made soldiers out of us and as hard as conditions were under his command he toughened us to meet battle conditions. If the plans of this other group had succeeded we would never have been sent to France. General Morton knew that politics were being played, he refers to it in his "Recollections of the 29th Division." It played a big part, not alone in the reorganization, but also throughout the entire service of the command. The General had his own troubles, even as the lowliest in the ranks.

When the Federal Government requires its men to go to war it is only fair that politics be kept out, and the lives and interests of men shall not be made the plaything of self-seeking politicians, in or out of the service, whose only interest is simple personal selfishness. It should not be necessary to keep one eye on the enemy of the country in front of us, and the other eye on more deadly enemies in the rear, who are the cause of untold misery, hardship and suffering, yes even the loss of lives, as well as the loss of rewards won by honest, tireless effort.

Another injustice to all concerned was the transfer or promotion of officers on the staffs to command combat units. My experience is that, generally, a good staff officer makes a poor line officer or a good line officer is of little value in an office. On more than one occasion I have found it necessary to recommend that officers with troops, under my command, be transferred to staff duty, where they made good. Command of

troops requires an understanding of men, a natural leadership
that will cause soldiers to follow their officers through the
worst kind of fire, regardless of the price to be paid. Troop
leadership cannot be drilled into some men, it cannot be
learned from books, it cannot be bought, and who you know,
politically, is of no value when guns are blazing and shrapnel
is singing around and over your head. I have often noticed
that an officer is made or broken the first few hours he is with
troops. Let an officer handle a company of old soldiers for
one hour and they will have his 'number.' They will know
just what to expect and how to behave. The comment will be
"He is an easy mark" or "Better keep an eye on this officer,
he knows his soldiers" and they will act accordingly.

More will be heard of this leadership. As time goes on we
will see the natural leaders commanding troops in action, the
others being eliminated or transferred to departments where
they could not sacrifice lives. The one sure test of all soldiers
is battle. What will we do when we get in it?

\*        \*        \*        \*        \*        \*        \*

After fifteen months in the Federal Service we are just beginning to get into the war. I often wonder what would have
happened if the United States alone had been engaged in a
war against one of the Central Powers? Could we have waited
all this time to get troops ready for action? Most decidedly
not. The enemy would have been on our shores long before
we were ready. The men would have gone over the first
month they were in the service, if ordered. The General Staff,
apparently, did everything possible after war was declared, but
the country had not been prepared for any such gigantic un-
dertaking as this. The fault lay with those smug, complacent
citizens who, as late as 1916, had cried from the house-tops
"We will never have another war, the people of this country
are too intelligent to enter a war, we have too many interests
in foreign countries. Even if Europe is at war, we will not be
in it." These same ones were now doing the flag-waving and
making speeches, patriotically demanding that every man and

every ounce of (somebody else's) strength be expended to win, but personally they made no effort to bring the war to a successful and speedy termination by getting into a uniform, or if they did get into the service they arranged to be placed in an office position, as far away from the front lines as possible. Well! Here we go. The National Guard, 'the Tin Soldier,' is going into it. When it is over, what then?

\*       \*       \*       \*       \*       \*       \*

Proceeding out to sea the convoy was picked up by a destroyer escort and some "S" boats. In addition to the *Pastores,* in our convoy we had the balance of the 57th Brigade on board the *S.S. Wilhelmina, Princess Matoika, Lenape* and a number of other vessels carrying other organizations of the division. Overhead planes were flying on the lookout for submarines. It was all strange to us. On land we could take care of ourselves, but out there on the water the army was helpless and there was nothing we could do about it. We were at the mercy of the Almighty and the United States Navy. However, we had confidence in both, so all was well.

Sunday morning, June 16, about 8 o'clock, we had our first contact with the enemy. I had just reached deck after breakfast when the most weird shriek was let go from one of the destroyers; all over our ship bells were ringing the alarm, horns blowing, sailors dashing to their stations, soldiers pouring up from below decks and falling into ranks ready to take to the life-boats, if necessary. All the troopships crowded on steam and spread out in different directions. It seemed to me that the *Pastores* just stood on her rear end in an effort to make a sudden and sharp turn to the left. The naval gunners opened fire. This appeared to lessen the tension as we all became interested in the shooting. It was surprising how little excitement there was among the soldiers, in fact everybody seemed to be enjoying the show, all sorts of remarks coming from the men. When a shot was fired some wise gentleman would yell: "Here you are 'Fritz,' catch this one." Or "Here comes your breakfast," or "Kaiser 'Bill,' count your men, some are missing." Also other remarks that were not so refined.

While the firing was going on the destroyers had gone toward the rear of the convoy, searching for the 'U' boat. Finally one of them signalled the others and then started forward, smoke pouring from her funnels. I watched her with my glasses as she threw something into the air, which looked like a big ash can. It went up a short distance and then fell back into the water. In a few seconds a pillar of water rose in the air. This was repeated several times. Gradually things quieted down and the usual routine was continued. Talking with a naval officer about an hour later, he told me that a 'U' boat had been sighted and the destroyer had sunk her with depth bombs. From the reports, this incident occurred about one hundred fifty miles east of Atlantic City, New Jersey. The enemy must have been taking us home to bury us.

Shortly before noon on Sunday, the balance of the 29th Division Infantry joined the convoy, they had sailed from New York on Saturday. Our southern troops sailed from a northern port and our northern troops from a southern port, Newport News. Not a bad idea; a good way to prevent last minute farewells and 'French leave.' Major General Morton never missed a trick. He knew his soldiers.

Life on board ship was comparatively easy. We had a calisthenic drill each morning, then a short drill with the rifles; the crowded condition of the boats made it impossible to do any drilling that required moving around. Other than these exercises, guard and the routine details, there was nothing to do but sit around and read, smoke, watch the porpoises jumping around, play cards or maybe a little game of 'galloping dominoes.' Smoking was permitted during the day but forbidden after sundown; there were no lights on the boat that might be visible from the sea. Every care was taken to prevent enemy submarines from seeing us. The hour for attack was usually about daybreak.

Instead of taking a direct route to Europe, the convoy zig-zagged all over the Atlantic Ocean. For a short time we would travel east, then a change of direction and sail north, then east again, then south, but all the time heading in the general direction of France. The trip across was very pleasant and all hands enjoyed the rest after the strenuous times at Camp McClellan. The weather was good and with a smooth sea we had comparatively little sea-sickness, which was strange considering the number of men on board. Only a very few of whom had ever crossed the ocean before they came aboard the transport, many of the men had never even seen the ocean before this trip. To my mind one of the most forlorn individuals in the world is a sea-sick soldier. He is willing to call the war off and go home. He gets about as much sympathy from his comrades as a man with a black eye caused by bumping into a door. He receives all sorts of advice on how to cure the 'disease,' such as being offered a piece of nice fat salt pork and advised to swallow it. In many cases the mere odor of food being cooked below decks was enough to send men rushing for the rails. Life ran very smoothly, with but little excitement. As might be expected we had many incidents of both a serious and humorous turn that served to make the time pass rapidly.

One of my routine duties was the daily inspection of our guards, in company with a naval officer. Among the points inspected was the door to the ship's magazine, at which point we always had a sentry on duty. On one of our inspections the naval officer asked the guard what his orders were, to which the soldier replied: "To keep this door closed." The officer replied: "That is right. Remember, that under all circumstances you must close that door, in an emergency, such as a fire or even if we should be torpedoed. You must close and fasten that door before you attempt to save yourself." As the magazine was at the bottom of the ship it is easy to imagine what that man's thoughts were when the guns opened fire or the alarm sounded. No doubt he was glad he had taken out insurance. He might even have visualized his beneficiaries enjoying spending it.

'Stand To' at daybreak each morning was a weird affair.

About one-half hour before dawn all troops were formed on the decks ready to abandon ship. Many a morning standing in front of the company, all of us wearing raincoats, with the life preservers over them, the sea mist spraying over us, in total darkness, not a light anywhere, rather a 'spooky' feeling would creep over me, wondering what the sea had in store for us, then watching the daylight creep over the horizon and expecting each moment to hear that awful cry from the lookouts, "SUBMARINE!" The command 'Stand Down,' which meant that we had once again passed through danger, was always welcome; it seemed to lift a load from our shoulders and to relieve the mental strain.

The lieutenants of the company had been assigned to stand lookout with the naval personnel, and their task was not an easy one. In addition to the strain of continually being on watch for submarines they also had the pleasant feeling of climbing up to the 'crow's-nest' and then being tossed around as the ship pitched and rolled.

After a few days at sea the morning assembly became rather routine and created a tendency to arrive at the assembly point on the last minute. In one room three of our officers slept. One of the officers had an alarm clock with him and decided to set the alarm but failed to mention the fact to the others in the room. All went well until that alarm clock 'sounded off' at 3.30 A.M. One of the sleepers, always having the 'U' boats on his mind, made a flying leap over two beds and was just going out of the door, dressed in pajamas, when he was stopped. The alarm on that little clock sounded to him the same as the ship's alarm to abandon ship. Were we jumpy? Oh! no! We were perfect little heroes, maybe.

Other pastimes were the abandon ship, fire and collision drills. In these exercises several of the army officers had been assigned to command lifeboats. I had been given command of a boat up on the top deck; at an alarm it was my job to make a dash for that boat and await further orders. This boat swung from davits. Occasionally the command would be given to man the boat. That was all right as I was over the deck. One morning the order came to swing the boats out while we were in them; this was not so good to my way of thinking. All that kept the boat up in the air were a couple of vicious looking sailors holding on to the ropes, who appeared as though they would enjoy nothing more than to give this poor army officer a free, speedy ride down and then a ducking in the ocean. I decided right then and there that I was never meant to be a sailor, both the enemy and the water are against you. In the army only the enemy is opposed to you.

As if the risk of trusting myself to one of these 'tubs' was not enough I was given the 'privilege' of having Major General Morton assigned to my boat. Of all the life rafts and boats on the *Pastores* it was my luck to have him along to worry about. I would have enough to do in an emergency to look out for myself and keep a whole hide, without having him to tell me that my shoes were not laced properly or that my chin strap was not in the right place. After one of these drills I heard one of the soldiers remark to his pal: "Did you know that General Morton is assigned to the captain's lifeboat? Imagine that." The other soldier replied: "That's all right, if we have to abandon ship the captain is sitting pretty. All he has to do is save the 'Old Man' and the general will make a colonel of him. If the captain will only see to it that the 'Old Man' is drowned I would be willing to start a subscription to buy a medal for the 'Skipper.'"

All was not fun, however. There were serious moments as well. One evening, while at supper, the alarm suddenly sounded and the ship's guns commenced firing. In the ward room, at the time, were practically all of the army officers and most of the naval officers seated at mess. When the alarm sounded we all left the tables and started for our posts. At the ladder going up there was a slight block, delaying the exit. I felt someone shoving and pushing behind me, evidently in a hurry to get on deck. Turning to see what was the cause of the disturbance I had my first view of shell-shock; one of our officers was just about ready to collapse from fright, or ready to fight his way up the ladder. The strain was beginning to tell. When I finally reached the deck the men were pouring up the ladders and hurrying to their posts; some excitement which was easily controlled, due to all hands being at supper, below decks, when the alarm sounded.

After the fuss and excitement had died down the cause of all the trouble was discovered to be a barrel, at first supposed to be the periscope of a submarine. It became quite a joke when we learned about the barrel, but it was better than all the theoretical instruction we could get. It caught all of us off our guard. It taught us that the real thing was liable to happen at any time, night or day and when least expected.

The last few days at sea were considered the most dangerous period of the entire trip. The waters adjacent to England and France were full of submarines and mines planted by the enemy. Life preservers, that had been discarded for a few days in midocean were again worn, canteens filled and carried on the belts at all times. As we neared the French coast the convoy was met by additional sub-chasers, aeroplanes and a couple of 'Blimps,' to escort us through the mine fields and to the shore. Every precaution was taken for our safety. As mentioned previously, the navy deserves a great deal of credit for the thoroughness with which they transported the army overseas and without loss. They did not get up to the big front, but they had a front of their own that required a lot of nerve and the United States Navy had plenty of that.

And so the voyage ended, June 27th. About noon land was sighted and in the afternoon the pilot came aboard. That night we lay in the *Loire River*. Passing through the locks early next morning the *Pastores* tide up to the dock in *St. Nazaire*. The troops disembarked about eleven o'clock A.M. on June 28, 1918.

At last we are here. What now?

## CHAPTER VI

## IN FRANCE

### "GOING UP"

As the ship was warped into the dock we had our first view of France. On the dock, in addition to the U.S.Q.M. Detachment, in charge of the debarkation, were quite a number of natives. One of the first things to impress me was the number of crippled and maimed men, in addition to many others wearing bandages. We were greeted with a polite, welcoming smile, yelling "Bon American" or "Vive l'Amerique." We had considerable fun with the French 'kids' on the dock. Walking along as we were being tied in they would yell up "Mister gimme Penny" or 'Souvenir,' holding out their hands for us to drop coins. It was laughable to hear the comments of our men when they heard the youngsters talking French. One soldier asked one of them a question and the little fellow started out with a string of French. The question was repeated and again the rapid-fire French. Finally the 'kid' gave it up with a shrug of his shoulders. Our American soldier exclaimed in astonishment—"Damn it, that kid can't talk English."

During the training in the States we had been told about the wonderful discipline of the foreign soldiers, particularly of the smart appearance of the French army. Well, one look at the uniformed men on the dock caused the remark to be made —"So these are the smart French soldiers." Almost all the men were in uniform, one kind or another, many of the older men wearing uniforms that apparently had been worn during the Franco-Prussian war. Only a few soldiers were in French Blue as we knew it later. Nearly all wore a medal of some kind, of which they were very proud. There were many

'Croix de Guerres,' won for bravery in action. One soldier wore the French Legion of Honor, had three wound stripes on his sleeve and at this time his head was bandaged. There was something about these people that made us realize they had put up a good fight and needed our help. The women, almost all of them, were dressed in black, a sad, weary look on their faces. It had been a long war and even then the prospects of success were not any too bright. The Central Powers were giving the Allies a rough handling. It seemed as though the U. S. had entered the war too late to be of any value. Up to this time, fifteen months after we declared war, only small detachments of our army had met the enemy in battle. The French had suffered a lot, but were keeping up a wonderful spirit. They would not admit the possibility of defeat.

At last we were on the dock and how good we felt to have our 'dogs' on solid ground once again. Ships are all right for a sailor, but an infantryman needs solid ground under his feet and then everything is rosy.

After all troops were off the boat, we swung out for Camp No. 1. At last we were really in the A.E.F.—the Almighty alone knew what was before us.

The First Battalion marched through the streets of *St. Nazaire* out to the rest camp. Why it was called a rest camp I could never understand, the only thing missing in the camp was REST. Every time you turned around there was more work to do. Each night a detail went down to unload ships; during the day we kept busy building roads in the camp, in addition to the regular routine of guard duty and making our own camp. As might be expected, some men, at the first opportunity, sampled the 'Vin Rouge' and as a result were introduced to the guard house by the military police. The second night in camp, a Marine M.P. came to me, as Officer of the Day, and reported he had an officer of the regiment, who had been picked up in town with a good load of cognac on board, and it was necessary for them to turn him over to me. I had the officer put to bed and sent for one of our doctors and told him this was a case of sickness. The doctor examined the patient, looked at me with a grin, and re-marked, "He will be very sick in the morning." He was.

While at this camp I went into town a few times and had quite a time trying to procure a meal, in the restaurants or hotels. Trying to make any purchase was a real problem. The easiest way to buy anything was to select what you wanted, hold it in one hand and with the other hand hold out a fistful of change and let the storekeeper take what he wanted. If we were over charged we never knew it. While on the subject of inability to speak the language I am reminded of one of our officers who had remarked many times that he would have no trouble with the natives as he had learned to speak French while at college. He even gave a few lessons to help us. Unfortunately the natives could not understand his brand of French. He might have passed a creditable examination in French while at college, but he was unable to buy anything to eat in France.

The first time in to *St. Nazaire* another captain and myself going into a restaurant tried to make the waiter understand that we wanted to get a steak and fried potatoes, but it was a case of 'pas comprez.' Then we tried to get some ham and eggs but that was just as bad. The outlook for getting any eats was not good until a soldier who had been in France for some time came in. I asked him if he could speak French; could he help us get something to eat? Oh, yes, he could speak the language and in the celebrated French of the A.E.F. he ordered a meal for us; ham and eggs, fried potatoes, coffee etc. Altogether we fared very well.

\*    \*    \*    \*    \*    \*    \*    \*    \*    \*    \*

While at *St. Nazaire* we saw German soldiers for the first time, prisoners of war, a truck loaded with them returning from work. There was a camp for them here. The prisoners seemed to be contented and appeared glad to be out of the fighting. One thing impressing itself on me was the open hatred of the French for the Germans. As the prisoners passed many of the natives would cry out "le Bosch," and then spit after them. This hatred was fanatical, the feeling never seemed to decrease, up to the time we left France, a year later. The peasants never mentioned Germany without some expression of hate. It appeared to be burnt into their very soul.

Another very noticeable thing was the number of women doing what we considered a man's work, in all kinds of stores and shops, even driving wagons, and, as we saw later, doing all the work on a farm. There was no complaint, simply an intense determination to whip the 'Bosch' at any cost. I believe, if the French government would have allowed it, these women would have gone into the front line trenches with their men. I have often thought of these people and the little they lived on, in comparison with conditions in the United States. So far as could be seen there was no profiteering, no fabulous prices for foodstuff, all prices set by the French government. Except for the fact that so many men were in uniform the American people did not seem to realize we had a war on our hands. I wish they could have seen conditions in France.

During our stay here there were many laughable incidents. On one occasion two United States colored soldiers were trying to be friendly with two French colonial soldiers, also colored. The American boys were talking at a great rate, laughing and trying to make the French soldiers understand, but the Frenchmen listened for a time and then started talking to each other in French. Finally our men gave up the task in disgust. One story heard was about an American 'darkey' who had just landed. He was walking through the streets of *Brest* all alone and rather down in the mouth on account of his inability to make himself understood. Finally he spied another colored man coming towards him. He walked up to the other chap and asked if he could tell him where he could get something to eat. Unfortunately the other soldier, an officer of French colonial troops, could not understand English; our American turned from him in disgust, muttering "Ain't dat boy high-hatted?"

In the cafes it was noticeable the ease with which men and women sat at the same tables drinking their wine. There was none of that modesty to which we were accustomed at home. If a woman wanted some wine she simply went into the cafe and bought it. Another difference between the French and Americans is that the Frenchman will sit for an hour sipping his glass of wine. The American takes his cognac at one gulp, at the end of the hour he is in fine shape, knows he can lick the German army all alone. The Frenchman simply takes another sip of wine and politely inquires what all the excitement is about.

Any member of the A.E.F. who was in *St. Nazaire* will never forget the old sea-going hacks that traveled between the town and camp. It was not uncommon to see those carriages going out to camp with two or three buck privates sitting in them and enjoying life thoroughly. The sea-going hacks were an old fashioned, open barouche, drawn by one horse that had no value for military purposes, with an old Frenchman driving, sitting on a high seat, everlastingly crying to his horse, "Allez! Allez!" As one man remarked "Even the damned horses talk French." How well these same men learned to talk French to the horses up front.

While at the port the officers were directed to purchase the 'Sam Browne,' or as sometimes called the Liberty, belt and overseas cap. Wearing the belt made me feel like a 'Blooming Limey' but when I appeared in front of the company wearing the cap I felt like an idiot. Lieutenant Heinzmann claimed to have had the same feeling.

Another interesting feature was the French system of time. Starting at midnight and going through the full twenty-four hours there is no A.M. or P.M. 9 A.M., our time, is just 9 o'clock, 2 P.M. is 14 o'clock in French time, 10 P.M. would be 22 o'clock, etc. To avoid errors and confusion, in military orders, time was always quoted in both styles as 7.10 P.M. (19.10 o'clock). For military purposes, I believe the French system creates less possibility of error.

During the afternoon of July 3rd we left Camp No. 1, and

marched through *St. Nazaire* to the railroad station, where the troops entrained, and our wanderings through France commenced. What shoe leather would be worn out, what changes in the organization would take place and who of us there now would ever see the Atlantic ocean again, or would come into that depot?

Before proceeding with the journey let me pause to give a limited description of our means of transportation, the same being used throughout France for troop movements by rail. Each time we traveled we had the same conditions. The narration must be meager. It would take someone other than a mere soldier to properly describe a French troop train and the really pompous railroad employees. The depot master with his little tin whistle is the acme of officiousness. Many of us had traveled on troop trains to the Mexican border and back again, then made trips to Camp McClellan and Newport News, in day coaches, each man having a seat, a place to wash, water to drink and stops made along the line for hot coffee; then to bump into a French troop train, the shock was enough to make any man 'dizzy.' All there was to travel in were old, dirty, third class coaches, or 'dinky' little box cars, setting up on iron wheels. On the side of each car was painted 40 Hommes or 8 chevaux (40 men or 8 horses). One soldier aptly remarked "Forty of us in that car? I'd rather be a horse, we would have only eight in there." Then the little bit of a steam engine, they looked like the small tin trains, seen in toy store windows at home. Heinzmann swore that if he could steal one he would send it home to his daughter for a Christmas present.

Into each box car forty men were crowded, along with the rations necessary for the trip, such things as canned corn beef, salmon, beans, tomatoes, hard bread, etc. Once the train started there were no scheduled stops, you ate on the fly. The only place to sit was on the floor, or on the pack. Every man in the car could not sit down at the same time. The choice seat was around the door where four men could sit down and hang their feet out the door. Sleep was almost impossible unless you stood up; forty eight hours on one of these trips was enough to make a man twist a wounded lion's tail.

After going forward and backing up for a couple of hours, or until it seemed as if each railroad employee in the yard had blown his tin whistle, in addition to a few extra toots from the contraption called an engine, we started off with a jump, as though the engineer was determined to get us up to the big front that night or 'bust a lung' trying.

Leaving the city yards we went through very pretty country. As the sun was shining for a change we all enjoyed the scenery, it gave us an opportunity to see what 'Sunny France' looked like when the sun WAS shining. Passing through we found the natives very friendly. Smiling and waving, they appeared glad to see us. A short time after the trip commenced we reached one of our military hospitals, *Saveney.* As our train came to a stop in the yards, there standing on the depot was a neighbor from home, Sergeant T. Mooney of the U. S. Engineers. He was with the detachment building the hospital. It was a pleasant meeting, even though for only a few minutes. The train moved out again in a short time.

Shortly before dawn, July 6th, the train pulled into *Vaux de Aubigney,* from here we 'hiked' to *Courcelles-val-des-Esnoms-par-Parthouy,* reaching the town about 6.30 A.M. The march through the little towns and villages was uneventful. At this early hour we met only a few people and they gave us the usual salutation "bon jour." We also became acquainted with the metric system, as used by the French, distance being measured in kilometers instead of miles. We were not long in learning to sing out to the natives "combien kilomets?"

*Courcelles* gave us our first experience of billeting or quartering troops, entirely different from anything we had been accustomed to. For a time we all felt like apologizing for being around. However, we soon got used to it and became as hardened as any European troops. Marching into the town we were met by a detail from our regiment that had been sent on ahead of us, and then started to put one squad in a barn, a platoon in a hayloft, a couple of squads in a shed, etc., until the entire company was using some kind of a building as a home, for such time as we might stay in the town. Another room was assigned as a company P.C.; the company officers were given quarters in private homes throughout the town. For a time this new situation was embarrassing to us though it did not appear to bother the inhabitants. Like everything else they accepted this inconvenience as part of the war.

My billet was the so-called best room of a farm house, in which were the usual furnishings of this type of home, a table, several chairs, family photos, bric-a-brac, etc. The most interesting piece of furniture was the bed and its covers; in addition to the usual covers, and on top, was what appeared to be a big comforter, about the size of the bed and reaching to the pillows. In reality it was a cover made of a soft material and stuffed to the thickness of about ten inches. During the year we remained in France, I was never able to have that thing stay on the bed while I was under it. Every officer I knew had the same complaint. You would put the cover over you on retiring but you could bet 'all the tea in China' the cussed thing would be on the floor the next morning. Several years after the war, with my family, I made a trip to Canada. Rather than stay in city hotels we boarded at farm houses along the country side. The homes in Canada could easily have been the billets we had slept in in France. Even the stuffed covers were there, so I felt right at home.

After the billeting was completed we had an opportunity to see the sights and look the town over. The first thing that struck our eyes, and our nose, was the well-advertised manure pile. No self-respecting French town or village is complete without them, always directly in front of the house, some piles large and others not so large. It was the opinion among us 'A.E.Fers' that the size of the pile denoted the owner's importance, the largest pile being in front of the mayor's house.

*Courcelles* was like all small towns and villages that we encountered; the usual small stone houses, wooden buildings were rarely ever seen, clustered around a common center. The farms were around the outside of the village, small but inten-

sively worked by women and children, aided by a few old men
or men disqualified for military service. Each town had its
pump and cafe, both of which provided considerable amusement for us, the pump as the community washing center for all
manner of things and persons from the baby to the horse; the
cafe being the main point of attraction, especially as the natives used water for washing purposes only. Another interesting person was the 'Village Crier.' Every time I saw one of
them he appeared to me as a revival of the old picture books
of the middle ages. These men, with a snare drum slung
around the neck, stood in the center of the village beating a
few taps on the drum to attract attention. The natives would
gather around to hear the latest news. This was the French
method of distributing news in the remote small places, the
same as we would get from our daily papers at home, without
quite as much scandal or detail. The village crier was the
bearer of all kinds of news, always official—news of the original 'call to the colors' in 1914, news of the varying fortunes of
war, of the battles, news of the United States entry into the
war, news of every conceivable kind, that applied to the people as a whole. During the enemy drive in the summer of 1918
it was pitiful to see the effect of this news on the native women,
knowing that their husbands and sons were in the thick of it.
Many times I have seen these old men giving out the news with
tears streaming down their cheeks.

The children were a source of much amusement to all of
us, especially the boys wearing their socks and short knee-pants,
with a smock or apron over the suit and practically all of them
wearing an overseas cap, either French blue or 'Yankee' olive
drab. These youngsters made great friends of the American
doughboy. The ease with which our army learned to make
itself understood, I hesitate to say that we learned to speak
French, was due to this friendship. A soldier would not hesitate to ask a child the name of an article or would even try
to speak the language to them, but would feel embarrassed
trying to make himself understood with an older person. It
was not unusual to see a doughboy with a group of these

youngsters around him while cleaning equipment, or perhaps sharing his mess with the 'kids.' These friendships were often the open door to a good meal, or as often happened a soldier sick with a cold would be taken in from a cold, damp billet, put into a warm, dry bed and taken care of by an old French mother, who more than likely had a son up where we were going.

We often argued and bickered with the French people about some soldier pilfering wood or perhaps 'swiping' vegetables from their farms. Many of these arguments were caused by our own carelessness or recklessness, we did not understand these people and the necessity for economy as they did. Despite our arguments we did respect the wonderful fight they had made, the enormous losses sustained by them uncomplainingly and their sincerity in winning the war. As we came to understand them all of us appreciated their patience with us.

Arriving at *Courcelles* on Saturday morning, the balance of the day and Sunday were spent in getting settled. Early Monday morning we started on our regular training schedule. Having done very little in preparation for the real task since leaving the States, the first week was given over to whipping the company back into its proper shape. It may have been the climate but it was surprising how quickly we rounded into shape; the fact that we were getting closer to the real thing gave us an interest that had been missing at Camp McClellan. It was much easier to assume that a feed bag, filled with straw, was a big, fat, juicy 'kraut'. You could put real feeling into a bayonet thrust. In many places we had cards painted with the pictures of "Kaiser Bill," von Hindenburg, the Crown Prince or other enemy leaders and used the cards as targets. It was surprising how much the interest increased in rifle shooting with this method.

Many schemes were devised to speed up the training and to promote accuracy, also to accustom the men to making rapid changes from one subject to another. For instance, while the men were at bayonet drill, grenade firing or other training, suddenly and without warning the command "Gas" would be given. Each man would instantly stop whatever he was doing, get into his gas mask and then continue on with his work, until the order to remove the mask was given. Rifle firing was also practised while wearing the gas mask. Competition of all kinds was encouraged between the squads and platoons; football, baseball, boxing, running, gas mask drill, taking apart and reassembling automatic rifles, any idea that would speed up was applied. The rivalry between units became very keen, thus creating a company spirit that produced gratifying results. This system was used at all times when we were out of the front line positions.

Since arriving in France many orders and memoranda had been issued, impressing us with the necessity of building up and preserving a cordial feeling between our Allies and us. The officers particularly were instructed to watch for any careless slip on their own part or the men under their command. Captains were directed to lecture their companies, explaining why we were in the war, what the Allies had accomplished, the need for co-operation to bring about a speedy and successful termination to the fighting. In compliance with these instructions I assembled the company and talked to the men, cautioning them to be tactful in dealings with the people they came in contact with. Any careless or thoughtless act on our part would be looked upon as the general conduct of the American Expeditionary Forces instead of as an individual act. They were to remember they were representatives of the United States and to keep in mind that by their actions, both in and out of the fighting, they were making United States history.

Supper, on the day above referred to, was not very attractive. Rations had failed to arrive, as a result of which we were compelled to use the supplies on hand. The manner in which this meal had been prepared was not very enticing. I had a short and forceful talk with the lieutenant who had charge of the mess and plainly told him what I thought of him and his kitchen detail and directed that he clean out the kitchen crew. While eating, one of my corporals, with his mess gear in his left hand, came up and saluted. When asked what he wanted, he replied: "This afternoon the Captain said we were making history." I replied: "Yes, what about it?" The corporal shoved his mess pans towards me, containing the same food I was eating, and asked, "How can a man make history on that stuff?" In more than twenty years in the military service, I cannot recall any other occasion on which an enlisted man had been able to 'take the wind out of my sails' as this man did. For a few minutes the corporal had me 'groggy'; all I could say was "I'll take care of it." Many years have passed since that occasion, but whenever I meet Corporal McGuirk the scene is brought back to mind and gives me a good laugh. He certainly must have been sore when he was willing to take a chance on what action might be taken. Withal I admired his nerve, the training was beginning to take effect.

On Thursday our battalion went on a practice march, joining with the rest of the regiment for a small brigade maneuver. This was the first time the 114th Infantry had been together since leaving Newport News; it was good to see them again. We had many friends in the regiment and looked upon the other units as comrades with whom we would go through many dangers. We also had reached the point where we could make an estimate of each other's value and what to expect in the big show.

On this 'hike' we discovered that the same regimental and brigade commanders were with us, and as usual we were in for a few more harsh words; always constant criticism, never a word of commendation or even constructive criticism, always a growl, and with some of the higher officers we had, who lacked the backbone to protect their junior officers, life soon became a misery. We had traveled across the ocean and from *St. Nazaire* to *Courcelles* without complaints and seemed to fare very well. It always appeared to me to be a case of bluff, trying, on one hand, to impress the junior officers with their importance and on the other hand endeavoring to demonstrate their own efficiency to the division commander, but failing in both cases. As a matter of fact a feeling of dissatisfaction and discontent was created that was not relieved until several important changes were made in the brigade. Later we did get officers who knew how to obtain results, without this everlasting nagging, and although the later officers were strict disciplinarians, still they had a sense of fairness and justice as well as appreciation for the work being done by the juniors.

After supper, July 13th, orders were received directing me, in addition to a number of other company commanders of the division, to proceed to *Chatillon-sur-Seine,* for a four weeks' course of instruction at the Second Corps school. The order specified I was to leave within an hour, which meant that I had to pack my equipment, etc., and turn the company over to my second in command, Lieutenant Heinzmann. Such is army life. All set for a good rest, after a strenuous week, and instead of rest I was to be on the go for the next six weeks. Saturday night I stayed at regimental headquarters; Sunday morning I left there and reached *Chaumont,* General Pershing's headquarters, at noon, arriving at the school 11 P.M. Sunday.

Bright and early Monday morning we started on a course of instruction that kept the student officers busy every minute of their waking hours. We were formed into platoons and handled the same as a regular line company; all rank was dropped among the students. In one class the instructor was an American corporal. I could name some corporals in Company B who would have given anything to be in that instructor's shoes and to have me in their class. The bayonet class was conducted by a British sergeant. He was a fanatic on the use of the bayonet; we had to stand in front of him and ward off his attacks with a bayonet. If we failed to turn his weapon aside and block his attack we were due for a rap on the knuckles or to be shoved off our balance with the butt of his rifle. That sergeant was really good with his weapon. His ambition seemed to be to have gore dripping from his bayonet every minute. There was no playing at that school; the instructors, both officers and enlisted men, were experts in their special subject; they were very thorough and each believed that his particular weapon would eventually win the war.

The course covered every weapon used in an infantry company. In addition we had demonstrations by all supporting weapons, such as machine guns, trench mortars, one pounders, field artillery, etc. Then lectures by officers of the Allied armies, giving us the latest ideas in modern 'kultur.' It was very necessary to keep in style in this war; obsolete methods were liable to be costly. In all of these lectures there was one point continually left with me. The Allies had apparently reached a stalemate and had become bedded in their trenches. They seemed to be making very little effort to get the enemy out of the trench system and into the open, where a decision could be reached. "Out in the open." General Pershing's plan, our entire system of training was based on the idea of open warfare.

One lecture especially showed how deep-rooted was the trench idea in the mind of the allied soldier. A British officer, who had been in the war from the beginning, gave us a lecture on trench fighting. He explained very thoroughly the various lines of trenches and how each line was to be held; the first line, nearest the enemy, to be held lightly with a limited number of men, principally as lookouts; the second line to be more strongly held and the third line as the main line of defense. He further explained that in the event of an enemy attack our men on the front line should pour a heavy, rapid fire into the enemy and then drop back to the second line where a more determined and organized defense would be made to break the attack. If the enemy still continued to be successful, then we were supposed to retire, through the communicating trenches, to the third line, there to make the 'do or die' defense, at all costs. He explained that by this time our reserves, from the rear, would have arrived. His whole lecture was just as if learned from a manual. This officer was very emphatic about counter-attacking immediately the enemy was stopped, and then recapturing the lost ground. Completing the lecture, he inquired if there were any questions. A lieutenant of the class stood up and asked the question that was probably in each officer's mind. "If it is necessary to counterattack to drive an enemy from a captured third line position why not make the front line the main line of resistance and keep the enemy out of there?" No doubt the question was somewhat out of order as there were times when 'Jerry' simply would not be beaten; however, it probably sums up the difference between our army methods and those of our allies. Whenever our troops were attacked the enemy had a real fight on his hands. The attitude of our men was, "If we have got to have a fight let us have it here. Why the hell run back a half mile and then have to chase 'Fritz' back again into his own hole?"

The course was strenuous, also very instructive. We learned many things that were of real value to us in battle later. During the period at school we were kept informed of the work being done by our army, in the form of official communications, issued each day. They gave us a good idea of the fighting. We had very little information about our own division; there were rumors around that the 29th Division had gone into the lines, but where we did not know.

As the end of the course approached all of us became anxious to rejoin our organizations. Although satisfied that if my company had gone into the trenches they were fully capable of giving a good account of themselves, yet felt that I was missing a great deal in not being with the organization I had trained. When the school ended we started back for the division, at 4 A.M. August 12th. I rejoined Company B shortly after noon on the 13th, at Retzwiller, Belfort area, in Alsace. Lieutenant Heinzmann informed me that our battalion was to take over a trench sector the same night. Company B had been assigned to a front-line position.

Back again to the old outfit, what had I stepped into? Seventeen months after entering the Federal service we were, at last, going into actual war. All the stories we had read of the war, all the lectures we had listened to, all the horrible stories of the allied soldiers, had created a picture that appeared impossible; now we were to know by our own experience just what war really was. No more make believe, no more assumed situations, from here to the end it was to be the real thing where men would be wounded and killed. When a soldier looked through the sights of his rifle he would see a human target in field gray of the enemy; no more jabbing bayonets into straw filled sacks, now he would jab them into human bodies; no more false gas alarms, when that cry was sounded it would mean getting into a gas-mask immediately and staying in it until the call 'all clear.' All the years of training in the National Guard armories and schools, at the Sea Girt, N. J., camp, Federal maneuvers, Mexican Border, Camp McClellan and all the other places that had helped us to gain a little knowledge about the business of war was to be put to practical use. Now everything was in the lap of the God of war. It was up to us to apply the lessons we had learned and if the lesson had not been well learned someone was going to be the sufferer, perhaps ourselves, or in the case of inefficient officers, the lack of proper training would show in the casualty lists among the men under their command. What will the answer be? From here I leave you to be the judge and jury.

## Chapter VII

# THE WESTERN FRONT

### RELIEF, OCCUPATION AND LIFE IN TRENCHES

In the 114th Infantry, one thing always made a sure bet. Upon returning after an absence from the regiment, we were certain to find there had been more changes among the officers. On this occasion the commanding officer of the regiment, Colonel T. D. Landon, former colonel of the Third N. J. Infantry, had been relieved. He was succeeded by Lieutenant Colonel George Buttle of the old First N. J. Infantry. I wondered how soon we would have still another commander. It was evident the division commander would not be satisfied until he was rid of almost all the field officers of the former New Jersey National Guard. Major General Morton had too much respect for political affiliations to allow these gentlemen to remain with the division any longer than absolutely necessary.

This everlasting changing of officers was raising the devil with the morale of those who remained. We were never sure of our status. Undoubtedly these changes were intended to keep us on our toes, all the time, but unfortunately they had the opposite effect. Many of us would have preferred a transfer to another division where service conditions were more agreeable. Officers would be relieved of their command and not know the reason until they appeared before the reclassification board, there to be informed of the cause. Many officers after being tried were assigned to other combat organizations where they made good records.

We were never told, officially, for what reason a man was relieved, but by the usual system of army rumors we had a fair idea of what was taking place. One report had it that a battalion commander, while his command was in the trenches, had been relieved because he appeared out of his dugout without his spurs. Charge: improperly dressed. Was it possible that he was expected to ride his horse across 'No-man's land'?, probably waving a flag. This officer was considered as above the average in efficiency.

On another occasion we heard of a machine gun commander being relieved because a private in his company had violated some minor sanitary regulation. When you consider that a machine gun company in a holding sector is divided into small units all over the battalion area, each little detachment in charge of a non-commissioned officer, the impossibility of a company commander having his men under his eyes at all times is apparent.

While these were only rumors, it gives a fair idea of the conditions and the picayune reasons that caused so much dissatisfaction and unrest. Officers were being transferred for the most trivial things, yet others were being retained who should have been relieved. Even at this early stage, these latter were showing signs of weakness that would mean disaster later on. Some of the earlier assignments, made apparently for reasons other than military efficiency, were falling down. Bluff might work in a training camp, but you couldn't 'Bluff' the 'Heinies.'

August 13th, about 8.30 P.M., the First Battalion, started up to the trenches, through *Manspach,* in which town the P.C. of the 114th Infantry was located, then through *Dannemarie* to *Hagenbach* the location of the battalion P.C. with Company D, our battalion support. Company A, Captain Fred. A. Rohrbach, in the lead; Company B, in the center; Company C, Captain Harry Doremus, at the rear of the column we continued the march to the trenches where each unit was met by a guide, who led us to our respective sectors. Company B arrived in sub-sector *Schoenholz,* at the company P.C. designated as 'Moroc,' about one o'clock. The relief was completed about 3 o'clock, at which time the command of the sub-sector passed into my hands. At last we were actually facing the enemy and responsible for a small piece of France.

Since the end of the war the question has often been asked

as to how we felt when we finally found ourselves on the front line? The men appeared to take it all as a matter of routine, something for the officers to worry about. They were much more interested in finding a place to sleep and the possibilities of making themselves comfortably at home for their period of trench duty. The fact that a part of the German army was in front of them, less than four hundred yards away, was of little importance for the moment. They were more interested in getting the heavy pack off their back and resting after the long 'hike.' When told that the enemy was only a short distance away they would take a look over the parapet and not seeing any movement would look at you as much as to say "stop kidding me."

In my own case, for a time after relieving the officer who preceded me I was busy organizing my headquarters. When finally I had a few minutes to realize existing conditions, it was just breaking day, with me standing on top of my dugout for 'Stand to.' Watching the night fade into day and appreciating the responsibility of my position, yet I could not seem to feel any heroics or a deep feeling of patriotism or a determination to die for my country or to liberate France from under the heel of the invader, as we had heard and read about so many times since entering the war. As it became brighter I could see that we were in a fairly good defensive position and if our playful enemy 'Fritz' made any attack, he was in for a rough crossing of the low ground, in front of us.

The enemy had a decided advantage over us. Having been in the war for four years he knew all the tricks of the game, and there is no place where experience counts for as much as in war. He also was more familiar with the terrain than we were for the moment. To offset these enemy advantages, I had every confidence in Company B. The junior officers were loyal and dependable. My second in command, Heinzmann, I believed to be competent to 'carry on' in the event that he should suddenly be thrust into command of the company. The lieutenants of the company, Chester H. Elms, Chas. G. Cooley, and George L. Bussey, also the sergeants and corporals were a good set of men, intelligent, active and good leaders. The men in the ranks were a young, active crew taking whatever came as a matter of course and not worrying about the enemy until they met him. As a whole I felt that Company B was capable of taking good care of any mission assigned to it.

Observations and service with the 114th Infantry led me to believe that the majority of the company officers were a conscientious lot, efficient and fully aware of their responsibilities, intelligent men who were perfectly willing to give all they had, even life itself, to win the war. It was too bad some of the officers of the staffs and the regiment lacked these same qualities and failed to realize that the old militia days had passed, that we were now in a real war, with an efficient enemy in front of us. We will see that a few of our militia officers still remained to torment us, a menace not alone to themselves but much more so to the rest of us.

My personal feelings when the line was reached may be summed up as follows: Almost fourteen years from the day I enlisted as a private in Company H, Fifth Infantry, New Jersey National Guard, on August 20th 1904, I was in command of more than two hundred men and officers, as fine a body of men as any officer could wish to command, in charge of a sector that had been German territory from 1871 to 1914. I believe that at the moment I was prouder than at any other time in my life and so far as I was concerned Company B would hold that sector until relieved or dead. What success was to be ours from this point on would be told in the reports of our commanders as the war progressed.

\*　　\*　　\*　　\*　　\*　　\*　　\*

On taking over the sector the platoon commanders had been directed to have the men avoid exposing themselves, to make no demonstration that would indicate to the enemy a new organization on their front. Needless to say, if 'Jerry' had known that a green unit was holding the lines he would have made life a misery for us. More than likely we would have been favored with one of their 'Flying Circuses' or raids. My plan was to have the company become acquainted with trench routine, to get used to shells dropping around, to hearing the whine of rifle bullets as well as the sudden bursts of machine gun fire. They had been well grounded in the theory of war; this was to be a sort of post-graduate course before tackling the real work of chasing 'Fritz' back to the Fatherland.

Shortly after daybreak I made an inspection tour of the position and found the men keen and alert, watching the enemy position through the trench periscopes and loop holes in the sand bags. The men on lookout were well placed and able to observe what was going on in front without exposing themselves; they appeared to know what was required of them. The corporals had taken shots at the enemy position and had made range cards so that in event of an attack our men would be able to set their rifle sights for effective fire. Altogether I was satisfied; quite a difference between this and the guard duty at Camp McClellan, where it had been a task to have the men know even their general orders; there was a reason here they could understand and appreciate.

The sector occupied by my company was on a slope of ground dropping down to a flat stretch about 300 yards wide, running to the Rhine-Rhone canal with the enemy barbed wire and trenches across the canal from us. Our own trenches were divided into three small sub-sectors across the front, designated as 56— 57— and 58 from our left to right. 58 had a small section of front and then bent back up a ravine. Each sector was divided into parallel lines, known as A, front line observation, and B a second line, our defense position to be held in case of attack. Each of these sectors was held by a platoon. The front line 'A' usually had a thin line of sentries, changed each day, the main body of the platoon being in the second line 'B,' where the men could get some rest and be used for working parties as required. Three platoons occupied the front lines and one platoon served as support, near the company P.C. This platoon was used to supply necessary details, and in case of an attack could be moved up front to support any threatened point. Each platoon was given a tour on the front line and then relieved to come back to the support; by this system each platoon became familiar with all phases of duty. There was always repairs to be made, sections of the trenches being blown out by artillery, replacing sidewalls of trenches that were continually falling, due to wet weather, mending 'duck boards,' etc. The supports also furnished the main patrols for 'No-man's land.'

Soon after entering the trenches I discovered one form of 'entertainment' that was about as exciting as having a shell explode alongside of us. The floors of trenches that had been occupied for any length of time had been covered with a wooden walk, 'duck-boards,' usually about three feet wide, built in six foot sections, of timbers for sleepers, and slats laid crossways at intervals. As the trench bottoms were always damp, even in good weather, these platforms were supposed to be an aid in walking. They were a help in dry weather, but after a real French rainy spell these boards were mostly 'duck,' that is when you stepped on one end the boards 'ducked out' from under the feet. If lucky you landed on your feet, if unlucky? Well! You were all wet.

During daylight hours only work imperative for protection was done, usually an emergency, or work out of sight of the enemy. When night came the real work of the trenches began. Patrols were sent outside of the line to repair wire entanglements, other patrols went out and beyond our wire to protect the working parties and to discourage enemy patrols from cutting our barbed wire or possibly making openings in our defenses for a future raid.

After the second night in the lines orders were received from the battalion P.C., to have patrols go out on various missions; some were sent across 'No-man's land' to the canal bank, others would leave from 56 A, scout well to the front and return through 58 B. It was not expected that these patrols would do much damage to the enemy but it did give us experience in covering strange country in the dark without getting lost. All of us learned to travel without making a sound, to keep our eyes open for the enemy, to see all of value to us without being seen by the enemy; on more than one occasion I have been within a very short distance of an enemy patrol and by the simple expedient of lying flat and noiseless, had them pass by without discovering me. We also became used to the flares, similar to a sky rocket, throwing a calcium light suspended by a small parachute. This light will illuminate the surrounding area like day, while it is burning. We knew that machine guns were trained out to the front, ready to fire at the first thing that moved. We were always on watch for the few sparks falling from the rocket as it went up, then we dropped, no matter where, and with face and hands buried in the mud we stayed down, without moving a muscle, until the flare died out. The first trip into 'No-man's land' at night was a hair-raising experience, every tree stump and bush looked like an enemy, a fallen tree took on the shape of a man lying down. Everything assumed an unusual form, many a patrol opened fire with rifles, automatic rifles and grenades on what later proved to be an inoffensive tree stump.

The men took to patrolling very well and appeared to enjoy the work, especially if they had a chance to stir up 'Heinie.' To use a common trench expression, "he was their meat." The men were cool and went about their work with the offensive spirit to win; the non-commissioned officers surprised me by their leadership, they had reached a stage where their rank really meant something and in leading their men on patrol they showed plenty of initiative. Many of the men were showing special aptitude in patrolling alone; other men were developing into wonderful snipers and were causing the enemy some losses. Altogether I was well satisfied with their work. When the former members of my old command read this they will probably remark: "and he was always growling that we would never make soldiers if we lived to be a hundred years old." When orders were received to take over a sector I felt a little nervous as to how the men would react. Within 48 hours

I lost that nervousness for all time; we were masters of our front and retained it every time we landed on the lines, whether it was in a quiet sector or on the big fronts during the major operations.

In a very short time the true feelings of all began to appear. By actions alone it was very easy to understand our troops. The majority of men that I observed seemed to take the war as a sporting proposition, the enemy fired at us and we returned the compliment, usually the quickest and best shot won, or they tried some 'stunt' on us and we returned it with a little added interest. If the enemy raided us it was our opportunity to convince our naughty little playmate that if he played with fire, he was due to have his 'tootsies' burned.

While describing conditions in the sector, please understand that the enemy was not asleep by any means; although things, generally, were quiet, with very little visible activity, there was, however, a charged atmosphere apparent at all times. It was plain to be seen that everyone was expecting something to happen at any moment. The tension was due of course to the possibility of an artillery barrage or a trench raid, either one or both of which might drop down on us at any minute, day or night. I recall one morning a heavy shelling was placed on the right of the 29th Division Area, lasting about 45 minutes and falling on the French sector. We could see nothing of the action. During the bombardment every man was on the alert, wondering what was taking place and who was to be raided. It was possible that 'Jerry,' while shelling one part of the line, and keeping our attentiton centered on the barrage, might slip over and raid some point in another sector.

Company B had one particularly bad spot, on our right flank at G. C. 58. The section bent back from the front up a ravine ending in a dense woods. Across the ravine from us, about 150 yards, was Company C. At the head of this ravine there were no troops or contact of any kind between the two companies, this condition was a standing invitation for enemy raiding parties to crawl up the ravine during the night and attack at their own sweet pleasure. As a matter of fact this section of trench was raided while occupied by Company L, 3rd Battalion, of our regiment a few days before we went in. During the raid the enemy put down a barrage, boxed in this point with artillery fire so that reinforcements could not get through and then proceeded to clean out the trench, killing and wounding a number of men and taking some prisoners. The raid was for the purpose of taking prisoners so the enemy would know what organizations were occupying the line in front of them.

These raids were short, sharp and cruel affairs, both sides using the same general plan and every means possible to gain their objective, the artillery preparation, in each instance, smashing down on the point to be raided and driving everyone under cover. During the barrage the attacking party works its way up to the enemy lines, close behind the barrage, and at a prearranged time the curtain of fire is lifted, throwing shells around and boxing in three sides of the sector to be raided; at the same moment the raiding party dashes into the trench and proceeds to capture or kill everyone in sight. Hand grenades are thrown into the dugouts to kill any who might have taken cover.

In preparation for these raids each soldier who is to take part is thoroughly trained, in a special class, on a 'dummy' trench that is an exact duplicate of the trench to be raided. When a raid is planned these men may rehearse for several weeks until each one is thoroughly familiar with the special task he is to perform. The success of a raid depends principally on surprise, speed and accuracy; surprise, so that the enemy is caught without warning; speed, to prevent reinforcements reaching the attack and then to get away before artillery can cut off a retreat when the raid is completed; accuracy, so that the object for which the raid was staged shall be accomplished, whether it be to capture prisoners, to destroy strong points or to demoralize an enemy. This last is especially effective when used against green troops. Trench raids are by far the worst type of fighting. Each side reverts to the primitive man. It is all done at close quarters, using bayonets, trench knives, revolvers, grenades, and clubs, in addition to kicking, biting, clawing, scratching—everything is fair in a trench raid. Rifle fire is of little use at such close range. In a well-planned raid the attacking party generally outnumbers the enemy at least two to one.

A raiding party, going out at night, is a wicked looking crew. All have their hands and faces blackened, not a word is spoken, the equipment they carry is so arranged that there is no danger of rattle. Usually each man carries a pistol and trench knife; some carry hand grenades and others carry trench clubs; these clubs are made from the thick end of a pick handle, about twenty inches long, with spikes driven through the butt end so that the spike point comes through and then barbed wire is wound around the club between the spikes, at the thin end of the club a wrist strap is attached, making a very effective persuader for any enemy who might be disposed to argue about being taken prisoner.

On this tour of duty the 29th Division was under the direct command of the 40th Corps of the Seventh French Army, for training. They kept a close watch on us to see that we made no serious mistakes. On duty with our battalion, as a councillor, was a French officer, Lieutenant Monier, a very fine chap who had seen a lot of service. He had a wealth of experience and was thoroughly familiar with the Alsace front; he gave us many valuable tips on stabilized warfare. Like most of the French officers we came in contact with he was very particular about trench conduct; they had become so accustomed to this type of duty that every detail was executed by rule of thumb. This method did not appeal to the American soldier. We had been trained according to General Pershing's plan to attack and keep on attacking until the enemy was ready to quit. In view of this training we were continually harassing the enemy, sending patrols out at night, cutting enemy barbed wire, throwing grenades into his trenches, and so far as possible annoying him.

Whenever our mentor, Lieutenant Monier, spoke of the

enemy it was with the deepest contempt and venom; like most of the French he had a deep hatred for anything that even resembled a German. The lieutenant was continually telling about the number of times he had fought the enemy, also about his trips on raiding parties, scouting patrols, etc., until I felt that a tone of superiority over us was noticeable. I may have been mistaken, but failed to see that the men under my command were less aggressive than any I had seen in the French army. Even with our limited experience I felt we could give 'Jerry' more to worry about, while opposite him, than the French. As I found out later the enemy had very little respect for the French, so that made the feeling mutual.

On one occasion while making an inspection, accompanied by Monier, he continued this brag about crossing 'No-Man's land,' telling of a trip he had made as a spy, inside the German lines to *Mulhausen* and drinking beer in a cafe there. The same superior tone was always apparent, until I was fed up on it and could stand no more, without at least showing this Frenchman that what he could do a United States soldier could do better.

At the time there were six of us in the party, Monier, four runners from the company and myself. We had reached a point at 58 A, occupied by a section of my second platoon under the command of Sergeant Sampson Horrocks, on what had been a main highway in peacetime, both sides of the road lined with brush. Of course the road between the lines was almost wiped out by artillery fire, trees lying across the road afforded good cover. As we reached this point I was about filled up with Monier's story and ready to do almost anything to shut him up, so remarked to him:

"Well, lieutenant, I am going out and have a look at 'Jerry's' line. Do you want to come along?"

Directing Sergeant Horrocks to pass the word along the line that we were out front and for him to cover the patrol, without further comment I jumped over the parapet and ran into the bushes for about 25 yards, my four runners right behind me and the Frenchman coming along, chattering at a great rate, getting his French and English all mixed in an effort to tell me I was crazy and that the Germans would see us. The most to be made out of his chatter was *la boche* and then pointing to the enemy trenches. Once out front no more attention was paid to him. He might be our instructor while in the trenches, but out there I was 'boss' and intended to handle the patrol in my own way. If he wanted to stay with us he would have to obey orders. He stayed with us.

While acting on impulse when first going out, there was no intention of letting the patrol be captured or sacrificed. But as long as we had started I decided to do some scouting and satisfy myself on a few points that would be useful. One thing interesting me was how my trenches appeared to the enemy. Another was to get a close-up view of 'Jerry's' wire in daylight, especially noting the openings in his wire. I organized the patrol and started across 'No-man's land.' Several points of value were found, that patrols out at night would have missed. One point especially was the location of a small footbridge, about 12 inches below the surface of the water, evidently used by the enemy as a means of crossing the canal in his trips to our side of the line. Up to this time I had not been informed of the existence of this bridge or how the enemy was getting across. No attempt was made to get on the enemy side of the bridge. We were able to see all that was necessary without exposing the patrol. After looking things over for a time we started the return trip. On the way back we stopped at a point from which our front line was visible, thus giving me a picture of our defenses as they appeared to the enemy. After spending about an hour in 'No-man's land' we returned to our own lines. "All's well that ends well," and that Frenchman made no further comments on his personal bravery.

Life in the trenches was much the same each time we went in, so that the foregoing description will suffice for the general routine, the major events being recorded as they occur.

Our first trench tour came to an end early on the morning of August 20th, we being relieved during the night by Company F, 113th Infantry, 29th Division. Marching back through

*Hagenbach* to *Manspach* we were bivouacked in a field for the day. After dark the same night we resumed the 'hike' to *Montreux-Chateau,* arriving about 4 o'clock in the morning of the 21st.

While on trench duty our guardian angels must have been watching over us. We had no casualties, but less than 24 hours after we left 'Fritz' again became playful and put over a raid on Company H, 113th Infantry, killing and wounding a number of their men. The 'Jersey Guard' was learning. Although suffering heavy casualties these 'militia men' drove the enemy back and across 'No-man's land' into their own lines. The 113th Infantry probably would have chased the Germans out of their own trenches if orders had not been issued recalling them.

## CHAPTER VIII

## OUT FOR REST

### MONTREUX-CHATEAU

LITTLE of what had been transpiring in the division was heard while in the trenches. At *Montreux-Chateau* we were able to get an inkling of what had been taking place. As usual there had been several changes and more officers relieved. This was nothing new; every few days or week we heard of someone being sent back for reclassification; in fact these changes came to be quite routine, the same as going out for drill at a specified hour each day, or going to meals or standing 'retreat' each night.

On this particular occasion the news was a big relief to many of us, as though a heavy load had been lifted from the shoulders. Orders had been issued relieving the Commander of the 57th Infantry Brigade. This relief of our Brigadier General seemed to give a new lease of life to all, as well as a desire to accomplish something more than mere routine duty. With all respect to the General's military ability and with no intention of casting reflection on his record, which I understand was excellent while in the Regular army, yet, I have always felt he was too well acquainted with the political element in the New Jersey Guard, which was responsible for so much of our trouble in the division and for Major General Morton's suspicion of the officers in our infantry regiments. In conversations then, and since the end of the war, with other officers, they have expressed the same opinion about this political machine that had been working for its own special benefit ever since the beginning of the war.

The division commander, undoubtedly, had many and good

reasons to believe that in the 57th Brigade there existed a powerful political group, but when he imagined all of us in the same class then General Morton was wrong. The big majority of the officers in our brigade were a hard-working, conscientious group, interested in their responsibilities and work, desiring nothing more than the privilege of performing their duty, perfectly willing to take whatever came their way, be it death, wounds or promotion, without fear or favoritism: unfortunately for us, the line officers who were trying to do our duty rarely ever came into contact with the division commander. The men that he saw were the battalion, regimental and brigade commanders and their staffs. That was where the real politics was being played.

Upon the relief of our Brigade Commander, Colonel Milton A. Reckord, of the 115th Infantry, 58th Brigade, was assigned to the temporary command of our brigade. Oftentimes I have wondered if Colonel Reckord's assignment was another indication of General Morton's lack of confidence in his New Jersey Troops? Why was it necessary to go into the other brigade to get a commander for a period of a few weeks? Were there no field officers among the 'Jersey' troops in the 29th Division capable of a temporary brigade command? Another thing, taking Colonel Reckord away from his own regiment and passing command of that organization to a junior officer, a major, while it was in a forward area would seem to indicate either a surplus of good field officers in the 58th Brigade, or else that conditions in our brigade were pretty rotten. It may have been a little of both reasons.

While on the subject of this assignment, let us consider a few kitchen rumors floating around and the effect on the junior officers and troops. In the 'Jersey' organizations a feeling existed, possibly unwarranted, that the commanding officer of the division was more partial to the 58th Brigade than he was to us, whom he suspected of playing politics to obtain control of the division. It will be recalled that Major General Morton was examined, about March, 1918, and declared physically unfit for foreign service. The 'Jersey' political element was given credit for this trick, so that a new Commanding General would be appointed for the division. It was common rumor that if the trick could be worked it was hoped to have the new commander selected from among the New Jersey troops, several prominent names being mentioned for the position. If this part of the trick had materialized, there would have been some double-crossing among the political soldiers themselves. Several officers, each working his own strings, were hoping for the job as commander.

After a trip to Washington, D. C., another examination was given the "Old Man," and as the story goes, assisted by a little help from friends of the 58th Brigade, who were supposed to have some influence at the national capital, Major General Morton returned to confound these schemers and to upset the plans of our political soldiers from home. Is it any wonder that the division commander, knowing these conditions, was convinced the 57th Brigade was seething with politics and that the 58th Brigade was really giving him their whole-hearted support? Is it any wonder he showed his lack of confidence in us at the first opportunity, by placing an officer of the other brigade in command of us, instead of giving the temporary command to the senior officer of either the 113th or 114th Infantry, as is the usual procedure in such cases?

With a condition such as this what chance did we have to make any headway or to accomplish results? Our best efforts were being blocked, or used for political purposes continually. You will understand that at the time of which I write we were unable to do or say anything. All we could do was to watch the game and when 'Jersey' lost, we all took the same medicine, even though we, individually, were not in the game.

I had known of Colonel Reckord at the time I was attached to the 112th Machine Gun Batalion. He impressed me as a good officer, capable and efficient, who treated his junior officers as men. He could censure a man when necessary without making him feel like a 'whipped dog.' As far as I was concerned the change seemed to offer possibilities of a more peaceful future. Ever since joining the regiment I had noticed a feeling of fear and depression, as though each man was afraid of some unknown disaster about to fall on him with no way to protect himself.  A short time after this change in commanders took place this depression seemed to vanish, to be replaced by a feeling of security and confidence, as well as a desire to stay with the 29th Division and particularly to prove that the New Jersey National Guard was equal to the best when properly commanded.  Even yet it would take considerable time and more transfers before all the elements of 'Jersey' politics were eliminated, but at least the machine was showing signs of cracking.

    *       *       *       *       *       *       *

*Montreaux-Chateau* was an old billeting grounds for Company B.  They had been here for a short time just before going into the trenches.  For me, of course, it was new, having been at school while the company was here.  However I was getting used to making my home wherever my hat hung.  Another thing, one of my sergeants who served on the detail that preceded the company to a new area always saw to it that I had the best billet possible.  In this town he had picked out a comfortable room which was appreciated after a trench dugout.

A tour of duty in the trenches creates a let-up in personal cleanliness as well as care of equipment, also in the snap and precision of troops.  One of the first things taken up in a rest area is a thorough cleansing of personnel and equipment and then an inspection to see that things are up to standard.  These inspections are usually the hardest of all.  They are as nearly perfect as human beings can make them, in an effort to pull the men back from the groundhog they became while in the trenches to a human being.  This was followed by a period of close order drill until we commenced to look like soldiers once more; then on to the battle formations, for attack and defense, scouting, patrolling, and all the hundred and one things the modern infantryman must know.  Schools for officers and 'non-coms' were held each evening, always studying and learning the lessons of war.  Never for one minute were we allowed to forget just why we were in France. Is it any wonder the men were unable to settle back into their civil occupations as soon as they were discharged from the service? Or that some of them imbibed a little too freely in the bottle that kept the summary court officer busy? I often thought I would like to get away from the whole thing for a time, if only for a few days, and so forget war, at least temporarily; but no such luck was possible at the time.

The stay in this town lasted about two weeks with the usual drills and problems, both day and night; close attention was paid to equipment, food and rest. The town was fairly good-sized and as usual provided certain forms of liquid refreshment that had a habit of getting some men into trouble. I recall one night about 11 o'clock on my way to battalion headquarters, proceeding along the dark road. In the distance I heard three voices proclaiming to the world at large the charms of 'Sweet Adeline' and 'Mademoiselle from Armentiers' as well as trying to sing 'Keep your head down, Fritzie boy.' One of the singers had a charming melodious voice that had been considerably enriched by a few drinks of 'vin rouge' but still had a distinct Gaelic accent. Not recognizing me as they arrived closer a melodious voice 'piped up' "Who the hell are you?" I replied, "I'll damn soon show you who I am if you don't get into your billets." Then a yell from one of the trio, "Gee! it's the 'Skipper.'" Three soldiers disappeared off that road like a flash. Those three men were kept in suspense for a few days; very likely, every time I appeared in their vicinity, they expected a 'raking over the coals.' There had been no harm done so I forgot it. I wonder if those soldiers still remember?

Some distance outside of *Montreux-Chateau* there was a trench system partially constructed, in most places about four feet deep and known to us as reserve trenches. Whether this was intended as a training system or with the thought that it could be developed into a real front line trench if the enemy managed to break through I never knew. After a few days in billets we were introduced to these trenches, being taken out there and required to man them just as if an enemy was in front of us, following the usual routine of front line relief, with all the details, each squad and platoon occupying its proper position, establishing communication to the right, left and to the company P.C. in the rear. When everything was in position in my area I would send a runner back to the battalion P.C. with a message that relief had been made, and liaison with the companies on the right and left established.

The first time we went out there I took it as a matter of instruction and gave close attention to the smallest details, but when we went to the same place a couple of days later and did the same things in exactly the same manner, with the same troops occupying the same positions as on their first trip, and then did the same thing a third time it became a joke to try and make the men believe that they were going out to stop an enemy attack. The commanding officer of our battalion would call his company commanders to the P.C., usually at night, and inform us that the enemy had broken through the front line and we were to take up a position in the reserve trenches, prepared to stop the drive. We would be ordered to start in one hour. Each company was to occupy the usual position, Company A on the left, B in the center, and C company on the right, with Company D as battalion reserve. On these occasions the usual battle orders were not issued, no provisions made for feeding the troops or other details necessary when troops go into the line at any time. Rolling kitchens, water carts, and company wagons were to stay at *Montreux-Chateau*. The major probably thought we believed him, but if he could have heard the swearing when the captains left him he would have understood that we knew a little more than he gave us credit for. The usual procedure on these occasions was to leave town about 11 o'clock at night, 23 o'clock French time, march out to the trenches, take up a position, report when ready and then stay there until 6 or 7 o'clock the next morning when we would march back to billets, tired out, then rest for the balance of the day. Some higher ups were taking their positions quite seriously, almost bending backwards in an effort to impress superior officers with their own importance and efficiency. Wait until we reach the 'big show' and see what will happen. Writing reports will not win battles. At this point it is well to note the close attention paid to minor details, such as the liaison, in these practice trenches. When we reach the major battles note the lack of attention to these same details.

While stationed in this town we had our initial experience with aerial bombing. About two o'clock one morning when things were quiet and all of us asleep, we were awakened by the roar of aeroplane motors directly overhead, and the terrific crash of bombs exploding about the town, the bombardment lasting about fifteen minutes. When the bombing started the men quickly and quietly took advantage of available cover. There was nothing we could do about the raid, except to keep out of the danger zone. Infantry rifles are of no use against aerial attack. With the other officers a check-up was made to see that the men were safely under cover and find the extent of possible casualties. Again we were lucky, there were no casualties in the company. Most of the damage being on the outskirts of the town.

One very noticeable thing, during this air raid, was the self-control of the civilians. There was little excitement, but like the military they had taken cover until the raid was over. In the towns and villages up near the front the natives seemed to consider such things as air raids, long range shelling or gas as part of their everyday life. The old men working in the fields, the women around the homes and farms, all had gas-masks at hand in case of a gas bombardment. Even the children, going to and from school, had their book-bag slung over one shoulder and a gas-mask carried over the other. The smallest tot, able to walk, had a mask. I have often thought that the French civilians were less excited about these raids than we were. Of course they had been on the receiving end of the game for four years and were getting used to it. In talking with the natives about these raids, they would shrug their shoulders and exclaim "C'est la guerre" (it is war). This was civilized warfare—shelling, bombing and gassing innocent women and children. Such conduct would be expected in the old Indian fighting days in our west, but among so-called civilized, modern nations I had always understood that non-combatants were to be spared.

War has its comical sides just as well as the more serious. Many little incidents occurred that gave us a laugh, usually it would be a soldier caught trying to get away with some stunt or other. Having been an enlisted man in my earlier days I was somewhat familiar with the usual tricks of a soldier. Many times I cautioned the company about doing things they should not do, generally telling them that any trick they might think up I had probably worked years before. An incident occurred here that shows the usual tricks they were up to—foolish stunts that got them into trouble. One Sunday afternoon, with two other officers, while taking a walk through the outskirts of the town, we passed a field of growing potatoes. A couple of men were seen crawling through the field. Without stopping I told the officers what I had seen and directed that we keep on the road until opposite the men and then by approaching from different directions we would cut them off. The men evidently saw us, for as we approached they lay down among the potatoes, hoping we would miss them. They nearly succeeded, but unfortunately for them our eyes were good and we finally spotted them. Each one had his cap full of potatoes. I had these men walk into town in front of us carrying their 'loot.' They were both men from my own company and I was 'sore' and intended to severely punish them. However, when we reached the billets a number of the company men on the streets started to work on these culprits and my desire to punish them disappeared. The 'razzing' these men received from the outfit, not for stealing the potatoes, but for being caught, made them feel rather foolish. I decided they were punished enough. One of the culprits is now a prominent citizen in his own community and holding a responsible public office in Essex County. It is all right with me. I won't 'squeal.'

The stay in *Montreux-Chateau* was enjoyed by all of us. We caught up on a little rest and again were in shape to tackle the more strenuous life up front. While here we had the first casualty in the company. One Sunday morning a corporal and his detail of Company B who had been on special duty were returning to their billets just as mess call sounded at noon. They dropped their arms and equipment on the bunks and went for mess. Returning the corporal lifted his pack from the bunk intending to hang it on the wall. As he picked it up, his pistol in the holster was discharged in some manner, the bullet passing under the bed, striking the corporal in the leg, a nasty wound but not serious. He was immediately placed in care of the battalion surgeons, Lieutenant Leslie T. Bolton and Lieutenant John J. Halnan who administered first aid, and he was then transferred to the base hospital. A very unfortunate accident and I was sorry to lose Corporal Robertson; incidentally the corporal was returned to us about a month later, in time to take part in the heavy fighting where he was again wounded.

Since arriving in France several changes in the company personnel had been made, some men and non-commissioned officers had been transferred to other companies; we had reached the stage where personal likes and dislikes did not count. Naturally there were men in the company who did not like my methods and failed to give me their loyal support. As soon as I found this condition arrangements were made for their transfer to other companies, where they did good work. From here on we would need co-operation, there would be no place for anything but soldiering. On a number of occasions since the war several of these men have expressed their regret at not staying in Company B and playing the game.

A very tempting offer was made while at *Montreux-Chateau,* that of Postmaster for the 29th Division, A.P.O. 765, the offer being made by an officer friend of mine, who, knowing my family, was trying to do me a favor by getting an assignment that would have been a nice soft spot, out of danger. He was very much upset when the offer was declined. He insisted I take the position voluntarily or he would see that orders were issued assigning me to the job. I told him that having trained Company B, I intended to stay with the men from home and take part with them in the fighting. Nothing more was said about the post office and eventually another officer was detailed to the position. Some weeks later, after one of the hard battles near Verdun my friend remarked, "Don't you wish you had taken the post-office job, it is a little less strenuous than up here?" Maybe he was right, but there was a lot of satisfaction in leading Company B into battle.

About 8 P.M. (20 o'clock), September 7th, our battalion left *Montreux-Chateau* bound for the trenches again. Hiking to *Manspach* we arrived shortly before midnight in a terrific rainstorm, everyone of us soaking wet. Trench coats and raincoats were of no value in that storm. Any man who made the 'hike' never forgot it. Even now, years after the war, whenever a few of the survivors get together they still talk about it. It was an inky black night, no lights, the battalion marching in column of twos, Company A leading, march 50 minutes and rest for ten minutes with no place to sit when the rest period arrived, just stand there in the rain. We seemed like an army of ghosts, not a word spoken except that eternal command of the officers "close up." A case of keeping the head down and 'bucking the storm,' no use grouching, just a soldier's luck. I was marching with one of my sergeants at the head of the company, trying to follow the connecting file to Company A. At times we could see him, then merely a black shadow who would fade and become lost in the darkness. Finally strapping my wrist watch, with a luminous dial, onto the pack of my sergeant I directed him to keep in touch with the preceding connecting file. Many times all I could see was that illuminated dial 'bobbing' up and down as he marched along. Several times the light would stumble and I knew the sergeant had stepped into a hole. Altogether the 'hike' was a nightmare.

As remarked before, even the serious and unpleasant happenings have their humorous angles, so this 'hike' has given me many a good laugh, although for a time I thought there would be trouble for me. On our trip out from the trenches, two weeks before this, we had spent one day at *Manspach,* at that time Company B had bivouacked in a field. Being a clear day in August it was no hardship, we merely made shelter-tent camp and went to sleep. On this march into *Manspach* we had the rain. Shortly before reaching the town I went to the head of the column and asked the battalion commander where my company was to billet. His reply was "each company will take the same billets they had when here the last time." The old story over again, if you do a thing once do it the next time you are here. It saved any mental effort on the part of the staff, poor fellows, they worked so hard trying to avoid real work. Explaining to the major that my company had been camped on an open field, and with everything soaking wet, it would be an unnecessary hardship to have the men open their wet packs and try to make a shelter-tent camp. I suggested the possibility of having my company double up with the other companies of the battalion. The only satisfaction I received was "Captain, you have your orders, obey them." Not a thing in the world for me to do about it. Like a soldier 'I had to take it and like it.' Being a soldier is a great game if you can stand it.

Dropping back to the company, the first sergeant was given the necessary instructions to make camp. Right away he started to explain about wet grounds, etc. Cutting him short I told him to obey orders. To say he was mad would be putting it mildly; he knew and so did I that he had his task cut out for him when he told the men to pitch tents; they would probably want to know if they were soldiers or sailors; and if sailors where were the boats. However, he merely saluted and said "The Captain's orders will be obeyed," and as he turned to leave I said to him "Sergeant, if needed you will find me in my billet; I will be out on the field in the morning at 7 o'clock." I thought a smile was noticeable on his face as he left me. Like all good soldiers the men would look out for their own comfort, if left alone. About 6 o'clock next morning I went out to the field to see how the men were. There was not a sign of a soldier on the field, it had me guessing where they had gone to. Looking around I noticed many of the old barns and sheds had animals tied outside. The company was soon located; when they had reached the field, instead of pitching camp they had gone into the sheds, and made themselves at home, tying the animals outside. The men were sleeping all over the place, on the floors, in the stalls, on wagons and under them. One man was sleeping in a hay rack, over a cow chained in a stall. This soldier had evidently been unable to get the cow out so he went to sleep in the rack.

I was reprimanded by the major for failing to have my men obey orders and told what would happen to me if it should be repeated. The reprimand did not have the effect expected by the major. He had slept in a dry bed that night. So had I, even though there were eight men sleeping in my room with me, four of us in one bed and five more on the floor. Some officers could see only one side of an order. I have always insisted that an order be obeyed to the letter, but I also believe that common sense should be used when issuing orders. Officers are supposed to show the use of a little common sense at times.

CHAPTER IX

# IN AGAIN

SECOND TRENCH TOUR IN SCHOENHOLZ

SUNDAY, September 8th, about 8.30 P.M., the battalion left *Manspach* and marched to the trenches, relieving Company L, 113th Infantry. We 'took over' the same sector we occupied on our previous tour. When we left the trenches we had been relieved by Company F, 113th. Upon returning, two weeks later, we found another company in the lines. There had evidently been a relief of companies and battalions within the 113th. This was the proper method, not as we were doing, having troops always occupy the same position. Varied sectors presented varied problems of defense and provided greater experience. Emphasis on this point is made to show the slipshod manner in which things were being done in our battalion.

When orders were issued to prepare for a return trip to the trenches and companies were assigned to occupy the same positions as on the first tour, Captains Fred Rohrbach, Harry Doremus and myself requested the battalion commander to rearrange the assignments so that each company would have a different sector to defend, it would have been simple enough to have the companies 'swap' sectors. The only change made was to replace Company C on my right, with Company D from the reserve. These two companies merely exchanged places. A and B companies went into their old positions. This was an early indication that those two companies were to be given the front-line position, for attack or defense, whenever the First Battalion was on the front. This is not intended as a reflection on our comrades of Company D, whose work I had many opportunities to observe and always found it equal to the best, but it was an indication of the indifference and shiftlessness that existed at battalion headquarters. Apparently too much effort and exertion would have been required to issue orders necessary to change companies around into positions other than those occupied during the first tour of duty.

While the occupation of front-line positions in quiet sectors, such as the *Alsace* area, imposed certain dangers and responsibilities, it was primarily an advance training period that gave us an opportunity to try out the various lessons and theories we had learned in the training camp and service schools. A new series of positions would give us new conditions to cope with, new ground to protect and hold, or new enemies to combat. For instance: Company A had a bridge over the canal in their sector; in my position we had a ravine cutting back from 'No-man's land' into our lines on the right. Each company had its own local conditions that presented a variety of problems. As the companies went back into the lines, each was familiar with its own terrain, but unfamiliar with its neighbors' problems. My thought was that a change would benefit all of us by varying our experience. As we found out later, experience is a much better teacher than theory; for some reason lessons of war experience are never forgotten.

The relief of Company L was completed in regular routine about one o'clock. There had been no change in the sector while we were in rest area. I was informed that the enemy had been rather quiet during the period, which might mean that we had green troops in front of us or 'Jerry' might be planning some future entertainment for us. However there was nothing to do about it at the moment, except to keep an eye on him and so far as possible be prepared to break up his playful pranks whenever he was disposed to come over. Early in the morning I made an inspection of the front line and found everything secure, the men making themselves comfortable and at home, all hands trying to get as much rest as possible. Except for the men on lookout, who of necessity kept watching the enemy line, we might have been in the practice trenches at Camp McClellan.

Trench routine is a drab, monotonous existence, although the rats and 'cooties' made life quite entertaining at times. 'Cooties' were everywhere. No matter how clean a soldier tried to keep himself, these pests would be on his clothes within 24 hours after getting into the trenches, then came the everlasting 'shirt reading.' Rats were everywhere, in the dugouts, in the trenches, out in 'No-man's land.' It was common for a sentry hearing a noise in the wire to fire and then discover it was only a rat. We had a lieutenant in the company afraid of nothing excepting a rat. One night while the lieutenant was trying to steal forty winks of sleep on a bench in the dugout a rat landed on the table alongside of the sleeper. Just to see the excitement I tossed a paper at the rat who promptly jumped from the table onto the lieutenant's chest. The noise had wakened my friend just as the rat landed on his chest; he let out a mighty roar and tumbled off the bench. I never saw a man move as fast as the lieutenant did in trying to get rid of the rat. These pests were all over, in our trenches one night and over in 'Heinie's' the next. They were doing considerable destruction as well as carrying disease.

A few days after 'taking over' the position our battalion commander visited my P.C. with the new commanding general of the 57th Brigade, Brigadier General Leroy Upton, who was making a tour of the battalion sector and meeting the company commanders, the general having just been assigned to the division to replace the former brigade commander. General Upton was an officer from the regular army who had commanded an infantry regiment in the 2nd Division at the Battle of Chateau-Thierry, and had been promoted for his work there. This assignment relieved Colonel Reckord, 115th Infantry, who had been in temporary command of the brigade.

My first meeting with General Upton was rather a startling one. He and the battalion commander arrived at the dugout about 1 P.M. I had just finished shaving when one of my runners came racing into the dugout all excited, exclaiming: "The major is upstairs and has a general with him." No wonder the runner was excited, when he saw a general so far up front.

I was surprised and due for many surprises from this gentleman, as I met him in many unexpected and dangerous places later on. He was the kind of officer who believed in seeing things for himself. Hurriedly slipping on my equipment, I ran upstairs, adjusting my gas-mask as I reach the officers.

Major Taylor introduced me to the general, explaining that I was the commander of Company B and in command of the sector. The brigade commander meanwhile was sizing me up from head to foot. He remarked: "As you came up you were adjusting your gas-mask, do you always wear it?" I explained that I had just finished shaving as he arrived and for that reason had removed the mask. He replied: "There is not much gas up here, you hardly need your mask, do you?" I replied that it was not for me to decide as orders were very specific that gas-masks were to be worn at the 'alert' position at all times in the forward areas. The General knew that, as well as I did; he was merely sizing me up. I noticed that he had his mask slung in place while talking.

There was another surprise in store for me when the General snapped, "There is a lot of politics being played in this brigade, isn't there, Captain?" To which I replied, "I do not know" and was promptly 'called' for making such a reply and warned not to make that kind of an answer again. He then repeated his question and asked if it was not so? To which I replied, "I am paid by the United States Government to fight its battles, and to train soldiers for the same purpose. As part of that duty a section of France has been assigned to me to hold, and the job is keeping me fairly busy, and left no time to bother with any other interests." This reply, undoubtedly, was more than he expected and with some officers it might have led to serious results for me, but I was 'fed up' on this everlasting political game that was rampant in the brigade, and particularly so in our regiment. I wanted General Upton to understand that there were a few officers, at least, who were trying to do their duty as soldiers without considering political results. As the General was leaving he shook hands, wished me luck and remarked, "I am told that this brigade is rotten with politics. I'll break it up if I have to relieve half of the officers to do it."

Certainly General Upton had been told that politics were being played. General Morton, the division commander, knew exactly the political ring, and as soon as possible he started relieving from command officers against whom action while in Camp McClellan would have brought down some very powerful pressure. After all the United States Senate was a power to be reckoned with. General Officers of the army, you know, are appointed with the consent of the Senate. When the 29th Division reached France this influence lost much of its power. General Pershing had a war on his hands that he wanted to win, and he needed officers who could win the war and leave politics out of it, at least until the war was over.

While on the subject of changes I might remark that again a new colonel had been assigned to the regiment, lasted a few days and was then relieved. I never saw this officer. Officers were coming and going so fast these days that a secretary would be needed to keep track of them. Another colonel came to the regiment and after a few days visited the company P.C. At the time of the visit I was down on the front line. Lieutenant Heinzmann explained I was making an inspection and asked the colonel if he would like to have a guide to take him down to the Front. The colonel decided he had a headache, that there was no need for him to go down as long as I was there. Another colonel I never met.

As previously stated trench life is very much routine in a quiet sector. The French authorities, under whom we were serving, were very careful about stirring up any activity in the *Alsace* sector. They had it all figured out that *Alsace-Lorraine* would be theirs when the war ended and they wanted it in good condition, not blown to pieces like other parts of France. For that reason we were not allowed to stir up things without permission of the French command. It was more or less a case of, if we left the German alone he would not annoy us but if we shot at him too much he would return the compliment, usually giving us more than we sent over. This 'status quo' was sometimes broken, especially by the so-called specialists who brought up their various weapons and contraptions to annoy 'Fritz,' then would pull out before the return bombardment started, leaving the infantry to take the punishment. How we would 'cuss' these special troops, usually winding up by telling them to go and enlist in the army and learn to be real soldiers.

About noon one day one of the runners came in and asked where he could get a few sandbags. Immediately I had visions of some part of our line having been blown out. Artillery on both sides was continually shelling around, usually without much damage. Asking the orderly who wanted the sandbags he told me that a sergeant from our regimental one-pounder platoon was upstairs and about to shell the enemy; the runner was quite tickled at the thought of having a grandstand seat while watching the enemy being shelled. Upstairs the sergeant and detail had his gun set up, right on top of my dugout, all ready to shell German machine-gun nests. I promptly told that sergeant to take his detail and gun to the hottest place he could find and get off my 'home'. The sergeant replied that he had orders from the brigade commander to break up those nests. Of course I could not question orders from the General. I could and did insist that he get that gun off my dugout and to take it any place he liked, but the farther he got that gun away from my sector the better I would like him and his detail. He finally moved his gun a short distance into the woods, fired about a dozen shots at the enemy position, then packed up and 'beat it' for headquarters. A few minutes later the German artillery opened up on us, and as usual the infantry had the pleasure of being on the receiving end. The firing continued for about a half hour and was quite heavy, searching the woods for the gun. One shell took the corner out of a trench a short distance from my P.C.

During this tour of duty we had some very wet weather, showers three or four times a day keeping the trench bottoms a sea of mud. Trench sides caving in making repairs necessary. Attempting to keep clean was a problem, everything we touched was covered with mud. The officers with several changes of clothing and partially dry dugouts were kept busy trying to keep clean and dry. How the enlisted men were able to remain as clean as they did was a surprise to me. Inspections seldom showed any serious violations of sanitary regulations. It was my experience that trenches taken over by American troops from the French were much cleaner and in better condition when we left them than when we moved in.

About midnight, September 13th, an artillery bombardment of considerable intensity was laid on our lines by the enemy and continued until 4 o'clock in the morning. I never learned the reason for this demonstration, but there was no attempt at raiding by the enemy. To protect our front I had several patrols out in front of the wire, but they were unable to make any contact with the enemy. It may have been that 'Jerry' thought a relief was in progress and laid down the barrage to intimidate any green troops who might be coming in. If so, he simply wasted ammunition and did no damage.

Early on the morning of the 15th Company B had its first casualty as a result of enemy activity. Corporal Fred Jurgens, in charge of front line post at 56A, had a sentry on duty in a listening post. About one o'clock the soldier heard a noise outside our wire but could see nothing. He challenged by using a prearranged signal but received no reply to his challenge. A short time later the sentry again heard something moving. Knowing that patrols from our own lines were operating out in front he hesitated to fire. He signalled again and still received no reply. As he brought his rifle into position to fire he became the target for several grenades, 'potato masher' type. The sentry immediately opened fire although severely wounded. Corporal Jurgens, in the post at the time, was also slightly wounded in the lower back with a piece of grenade. The sentry had five wounds. My thought is that an enemy patrol was moving in front of our wire and when challenged the first time they simply played 'dead' until certain that our man was not going to fire. Then making a noise to attract his attention they heard him signal the second time, thus locating his position. Immediately they let fly with a few bombs and started back for home and mother.

At the company P.C. we heard the firing, but as it was only a short burst among considerable sniping we paid no attention to it. About a half hour later a messenger came in to report that one of our men had been wounded and requested that a litter and medical orderly be sent down to attend the wounded man. Several attempts were made to bring him back to the first-aid station but his condition was such that shortly before daylight I sent a runner back requesting that a medical officer be sent down to us. Lieutenant Leslie T. Bolton reported to me about five A.M. Taking four of the biggest men in the company as litter-bearers we finally reached the wounded man. He was resting well but in considerable pain. Dr. Bolton gave first-aid treatment and then tried to get him back through the trenches. It was impossible to get a stretcher through them. We were unable to carry it level in making the turns. The doctor was anxious to get the soldier into the hospital as soon as possible, but there was only one way to get the patient back and that was by taking him over the top of the trench. This would be dangerous but as there was no other way out of the difficulty, when I told this to the detail, they did not hesitate. With a comrade needing help personal considerations were not thought of. I led the party back, taking advantage of all the available cover finally reaching my P.C. without any additional casualties. It was not until we reached company headquarters that I noticed Corporal Jurgens had been wounded. He had not mentioned it for more than six hours. From this point Lieutenant Bolton and the medical detail took both men back to the dressing station and later sent them down to the Base Hospital. As these were our first casualties we considered we had been fortunate thus far. From here on we had many men wounded, and were unable to give them the care and attention as in this case, much as we would have liked to. Later they came too thick and fast, and many a soldier risked his own life to give aid, or even a drink of water, to a wounded 'buddy.'

During the day of September 16th an order came down

from the Battalion Commander directing me to send a patrol
out that night, the patrol to consist of one sergeant and four
men from Company B and one sergeant and four men from
the battalion scouts. The patrol was to be under the command
of the sergeant from my company and to leave about 9 P.M.
from 56 A, work out to the enemy line, patrol along their front
and return through 58 B at 1.30 A.M. This would have the
patrol moving from the left of my front, across and back into
the ravine on our right. The mission of the patrol was to destroy or capture any small enemy detachments that might be
working out front.

To command this patrol Sergeant Joseph Fachet, a man in
whom I had much confidence, was selected. The sergeant had
made several trips into 'No-man's land' and was thoroughly familiar with the ground to be covered. He was a good leader
and cool in danger. Before the patrol started I called the sergeant's attention to a shed about midway between the enemy
lines and ours and somewhat over towards Company D sector,
opposite the ravine on our right. I directed him to take a look
at this shed on his way back and see if it appeared to have been
used.

Prior to the patrol leaving I made an inspection of them
and they were as fine a looking gang of young murderers as
you could find anywhere. They were stripped down to fighting trim, each carrying a rifle or automatic rifle, trench knife
and hand grenades, and some of them had trench clubs. Each
man had blackened his face, hands and arms so there would be
no light reflected if caught in the burst of a flare. Altogether
they looked wild enough to frighten an enemy to death without firing a shot. Having seen the patrol get out of the trench
and on its way I returned to the company P.C. to care for the
usual routine of night work as well as to be in a position to
handle whatever might turn up. The evening passed in a quiet
way, no excitement other than the usual exchange of artillery
fire, enemy shells going well to the rear and our shells sailing
overhead searching out the enemy position. As long as they
kept away from us we gave them no attention.

All was uneventful until about one o'clock. While standing on top of the P.C. from which a fairly good view of our sector was possible, talking with Lieutenant Heinzmann, I remarked to him: "I wish that patrol was in and then me for the haypile," to which he replied: "You woke me when you spoke, I was asleep standing here." We were all dead tired, never turning in until patrols were back and then for only a couple of hours' sleep, in our clothes, on a bench. There were wire bunks in the dugout but they had so many cooties in them that there was no room for us without crowding the cooties, so we slept on the benches.

While talking to the lieutenant a few shots broke out in the direction of 58 A, then 'hell' broke loose, rifle fire, grenades and automatics all popping at once. Whatever was going on was a peach of a scrap. For a short time there was little to worry about, as there was no artillery fire, which we would have had from the enemy if it was a raid. It might be a small fight between two patrols. I was not alarmed about it. An excellent officer was in command at that point, Lieutenant Chester A. Elms, capable of handling the situation. If it became serious he would send a runner back to me. In the event that it developed into a real fight he would use a signal rocket. A captain's duty is to command the entire sector, and up to a certain point to allow the junior officers to run their own show.

Lieutenant Elms was not long in calling for help. After the firing had continued for two or three minutes he shot up a red rocket, calling for an artillery barrage in front of his position. When taking over the sector a map had been supplied showing the barrage lines to be laid down when called for. At the first burst of firing Heinzmann had jumped down into the trench below me, and had his signal rockets ready if called for. As soon as Elm's rocket burst I directed Heinzmann to fire the rocket covering the endangered point. This should have brought down our barrage about 150 yards in front of Elm's position and boxed his front so that an enemy could not escape unless they went through the curtain of fire. The support platoon was also ordered to report to me.

To understand this rocket signal, let me explain that a system of relays is used. As in this particular case a point in danger fires a rocket which is seen at the company P.C. Lookouts are watching for these rockets at all times. As the company sentries see the front line rocket they in turn send up another rocket which should be seen at the relay station, several hundred yards to the rear. They in turn send up another rocket which the P.C. of the artillery would see; the color of the rocket designates the sector to be covered. We also had a telephone line back to the artillery position, which was kept sealed at all times and orders were not to use the 'phone except as a last resort.

Rockets were still being fired from the front, Heinzmann was also sending rockets, but when after ten minutes we had no reply from the supporting artillery, I directed the lieutenant to remain at the P.C., while I took the company support platoon down to the front. He was to break the seal on the telephone and try to get word to the artillery in that way. As he told me later, when he tried to use the telephone it was dead. Probably the line was shot out.

Ordering the support to follow me, we started above ground, by the shortest route, to get to the aid of Lieutenant Elms. At this time I had no knowledge what had caused all the firing, which still continued and apparently was in about the same position as at the start. In a short time we reached the lieutenant who reported that Sergeant Fachet and his patrol were fighting their way in, evidently falling back from a strong enemy patrol or raiding party. After a hurried conference with Elms it was decided to cut around to the left of Sergeant Fachet and try to drive the enemy up the ravine, where we would be able to capture them. As we started out the sergeant was again forced back, fighting as pretty a rear guard action as you would want to see. This was no time to think of prisoners, the enemy was making a determined effort and pushing their attack vigorously to prevent our patrol from getting into the trenches. Without further delay I ordered the support platoon to attack and drive the enemy back from Fachet and to hold until our men were in the trench.

When I reached the sergeant he impressed me as rather enjoying the affair. He was as cool as could be and perfectly self-controlled, even bringing in two wounded men, Sergeant Lambert of the Scout platoon and Private Madigan of Company B, both men had been shot through the leg and had to be assisted. The other men of the patrol were acting well, firing and endeavoring to keep the enemy off until assistance reached them. As soon as we had the wounded in I ordered Fachet with the support platoon to make a scout out in front of the lines, to search for any enemy wounded that might be lying out there. We were unable to find any. They had evidently decided to get back to their lines when our reinforcements appeared. We could hear them going back. Another thing causing me to stay close to my own lines instead of following the enemy across 'No-man's land' was the possibility of the French artillery waking up at any minute and dropping a barrage on our heads. You will understand that a friendly shell causes death just as quickly as an enemy shell.

About the time I met Fachet a shell landed out in front of us followed by several others. They had been fired by a detail from the trench mortar section, Headquarters Company of our regiment. The detail under the command of Corporal Chris. Hamilton had seen our signals. Although under orders not to open fire unless masked by artillery, Hamilton realizing something was wrong with the supporting artillery, and that we needed his gun, disregarded his orders and fired over us. This undoubtedly influenced 'Fritz' to call the war off and go home. On the way back we were agreeably surprised to note that the artillery had finally decided there was a war on, and started to throw a few 'spitballs' out front. The first shell landed 26 minutes after we had sent up our first rocket. How was that for close co-operation between the artillery and infantry? In the war between the States, General Sherman remarked "War is hell." The A.E.F. had its own expression—"This is a hell of a war."

So ended that little fracas. The patrol upon its return appeared to be in good spirits, somewhat pleased with themselves at being able to beat off a strong enemy party and avoid capture. From all accounts the attacking force was about 40 strong. While inspecting the patrol I discovered the assistant company clerk, Corporal Malcolm C. Murray, who should have been at the company P.C. taking care of records. When I asked what he was doing there he replied: "I wanted to go out on the patrol. I knew the Captain would not give me permission, so went out without permission." I called him all kinds of a fool and remarked "It is too bad they did not shoot your fool head off." The reason for mentioning this incident is that it typifies the feeling of the men of the company who were quite willing to get into contact with the enemy at all times.

Sergeant Fachet, the patrol commander, gave me the following account of his experience: "After leaving our trenches we worked over to the left a short distance, placing two men in front of the patrol, as scouts, with the rest of the men following at about 25 yards, each man separated by about five yards. This formation was used until the canal was reached. We then lay there hoping to capture an enemy party. After a time we moved back about 25 yards and at that distance moved parallel to the canal, at about each 75 yards we halted and sent scouts to the flank and rear to look for enemy patrols. All was quiet, no sight of the enemy. About 12.30 A.M. we had reached a point opposite the ravine on our right, between Co. B and Co. D, and started to work back towards our lines and over to the shed. There was a light fog and some gas in the low ground. While making a reconnaisance around the shed one of the patrol coughed. He tried to muffle it. I cautioned the man but he was unable to control it and coughed the second time. Then a shot was fired by the enemy. We swung to face them and from their volume of fire it was evident we were outnumbered. I ordered the patrol to fall back toward our trenches and to prevent the enemy from getting around us. While dropping back to our lines Sergeant Lambert and Private Madigan were hit; I got them in back of the patrol and assisted them as much as possible. I believe there were about forty men in the enemy party; we had not seen them until they fired on us."

Except for the fact our supporting artillery had failed to answer our signals, thereby missing a fine opportunity to trap this enemy party, the scrap had been well handled and Sergeant Fachet had shown excellent leadership in getting out of a nasty place and bringing his wounded back with him. Altogether I was satisfied with the men. Their training was beginning to show results.

My opinion is that the enemy was planning a raid on 58, up the ravine. They had probably gotten into the ravine with the intention of raiding Lieutenant Elms' position sometime during the night. The fact that our patrol met no enemy during the time they were in the vicinity of their wire leads me to believe that all enemy patrols were kept in to avoid having us too alert. Very likely the only enemy out was this party that Fachet met. When the member of our patrol coughed and the sergeant spoke it naturally made them nervous to find an American patrol between themselves and their lines. They opened fire to get themselves out of what appeared to them as a nasty position and with the hope of capturing one or two of our men, which would have answered the same purpose as a raid.

In my report to the battalion commander, describing the fight, credit was given to Sergeant Fachet for his masterly handling of a very ticklish situation and to the men of his patrol for their coolness under fire. In recognition of his ability recommendation was made that the sergeant be promoted to the rank of Second Lieutenant. Provision is made in Army Regulations for such promotions. The following morning the battalion commander came up to the P.C. After discussing the night's events he suggested the report be changed as Sergeant Fachet could not be promoted as recommended. When asked if there was any reason why the sergeant could not be promoted, as provided for in regulations, the major informed me that he lacked the necessary scholastic base. Such an excuse was ridiculous and I informed the major I preferred to have my report stand as submitted, that in my opinion the regiment needed officers of this type, men who were showing military ability first, and college degrees afterwards.

This was a real war in which men were being killed and wounded and not the sham battles of our training camps. The men who were winning battles were those who could use military common sense, men who would stand up and fight alongside of their men, even when the odds were against them. Theory was valuable only so far as it gave a leader something as a guide. Initiative, aggression and a willingness to get into hand-to-hand combat with the enemy, captured machine-gun nests and trenches—not theory.

I am reminded of a regular army officer who had been detailed as an instructor during our tour of duty on the Mexican Border in 1916. He was supposed to assist us with the details of military matters, the little things we had not used during our National Guard days. Whenever this instructor was asked to explain a point he would reach into his hip pocket for the regulations, then read the section in question with no practical explanation. We did not need him to read it to us, we had regulations and could do that ourselves. What we wanted was the simple direct method, not theory. Evidently that was the type of officer our major desired, at least his attitude so indicated.

All patrols that went out did not have the same excitement as the one just mentioned. Most patrols had rather a quiet time, usually nothing more exciting than dodging star shells or possibly exchanging a few shots with 'Jerry,' and in general learning the more serious lessons of active service. There were some occasions however that for a time looked as though they might develop into something serious but later proved to be quite the opposite.

On one occasion while out with a small patrol, about three o'clock in the afternoon, looking over the front of our trench line, and the condition of the barbed wire, we worked along the front and up to the center of the ravine on the right of 58. As mentioned previously this ravine was a danger threat and required a constant watch on it to guard against enemy raiding parties coming in on us. There were a number of broken-down and disused trenches here that provided good cover for small detachments. Whenever out front I always made it a point to look over the ravine closely. On this trip as we were scouting among the old trenches voices were heard. Knowing we had no men near that point I signalled the patrol to get under cover and remain quiet, also for First Sergeant V. J. Marriott, who was out with us, to follow me. Working my way up to the point from which the voices had come I waited for further sounds, lying flat on the outer parapet, with a grenade in hand, and the sergeant a short distance to my right ready to go to work with revolver and grenades. After waiting a short time several men were heard walking, and talking in English.

For a moment I was at a loss to figure the thing out, none of my men were out near there. These trenches were not being used and the ends of the trenches near our lines were blocked with barbed wire. To suddenly jump up would mean that whoever was there would certainly open fire, without waiting to find out who we were. For us to heave our bombs into the trench might injure some of our own men who had gotten into the trenches. There also was the possibility of the whole thing being a nice little trap for us. It had me puzzled for a time. Due to the artillery fire I was unable to hear what was being said. Sergeant Marriott had remained close to the ground watching me for signals. I signalled him to have the remainder of the patrol move up quietly. Wormed my way up a short distance until able to see into the trench and then nearly passed out. Without them seeing me I called to the party to stand where they were, as we were coming in. When sure the trench occupants understood, I dropped into the trench, followed by the remainder of the patrol, and certainly received the shock of my life. The men heard talking were five men dressed in the uniforms of the Y.M.C.A. Questioning brought out the fact that four of the party were a quartet of Princeton college men who had come to France to entertain the A.E.F. They were being guided through the trenches for a look at the front lines by a somewhat older 'Y' secretary. When I told them where they were, showed them 'No-man's-land' and the enemy lines, their desire to see any more of the lines was at an end.

The patrol and the 'Y' men started back through the trenches to the company P.C. On the way I asked how they got out there and why they had not reported to my dugout. The reply was they had come up through the woods until they reached the trenches and believed they were still inside of our lines. Somewhere along the line they had managed to get hold of a few 'Citron-Grenades,' as they supposed for their protection. I hate to think of what would have happened, if they had tried to use these grenades. They would have caused more damage to themselves than to the enemy. Our men always got rid of this type of grenade at the earliest possible moment, they were too tricky.

Speaking of patrolling calls to mind an incident that occurred after one of our patrols had been out. In talking with one of the men who had been in a small scrap while out front, I asked him what he thought of going out on patrol, also if he liked the work. This soldier, a young Jewish boy from New York City, replied: "Captain, if you will let me go home now, I won't ask for any car-fare." This I believe, expressed the feelings of most of us. We had seen war in a small way and if what we had already experienced was any indication of what the heavy fighting was to be, then it was easy to realize we were going into something that would require all the knowledge of war possible, all the stamina we could muster. Even at this early stage we were seeing men and officers cracking under the strain. One captain of the regiment had asked to be relieved from command, frankly admitting he could not stand the strain. The strain on all was tremendous.

The long, intensive training in the United States, in the rear areas in France, then actual contact with the enemy in the trenches, had created a jumpy, nervous condition that had tended to break down some of the more high-strung men. On the other hand this very system had developed many men into wonderful leaders. It was plain to see that the majority of the company could be depended on in any emergency. Apparently it was a survival of the fittest, the weaklings were gradually eliminating themselves. Several men received offers of positions in the rear lines, positions of safety and comparative comfort but refused the offers in order to remain with the company.

During this tour of duty in the trenches the company had been reduced approximately 20% by the following assignments of officers and enlisted men to schools and special duty of various kinds.

1st Lieut. Fred. W. Schultz, at the Staff School.
1st Lieut. Henry E. Bateman, on special duty as Battalion Scout Officer.
2nd Lieut. Chas. G. Cooley, at the Infantry School.
2nd Lieut. Geo. L. Bussy, on special duty as Battalion Gas Officer.
2nd Lieut. Henry Averill, attached to Company B, away from the company on special duty.
21 men on special duty as Battalion Scouts.
6 "   "   "   "   in Battalion Intelligence Section.
2 "   "   "   "   at Division Ammunition Dump.
2 "   "   "   "   at Division Post Office, A.P.O. 765.
1 man "   "   "   at Regimental Post Office.
1 "   "   "   "   as mess orderly at Division Headquarters.
1 "   "   "   "   at Infantry Specialists School.
1 sergeant on special duty at Battalion Combat Train.
1 man on special duty as Battalion Interpreter.
2 men sick in Base Hospital.
1 sergeant and 6 men on duty in company kitchen.

A total of five lieutenants and 45 men were away from the company, leaving for actual line duty about 190 men, myself in command with 1st Lieutenant Grover P. Heinzmann and 2nd Lieutenant Chester H. Elms, attached, for duty.

About September 20th a detachment of officers and noncommissioned officers from the 88th United States Division made a personal reconnaisance of our position supposedly to relieve us. For some reason this relief was never accomplished. I was informed that this division lacked equipment necessary for front-line duty. During the night of the 22nd and 23rd we were relieved by a company of French Algerians, who were very methodical in making a relief. In and out of trenches so many times they could make a relief with their eyes closed. Taking over a new sector was merely a case of moving from one home to another. Having moved in they made themselves comfortable; such a little thing as an enemy in front never bothered them in the least.

As each platoon was relieved it was marched to a point in rear of the area by the senior N.C.O. Assembly of the company, on the road to *Hagenbach* was completed about midnight and the hike back was started, everybody in good humor at going out again, as we thought, for a rest, after two weeks of strenuous work. All of us were very tired and looked forward to a good wash, a hot meal and then sleep; what a grand and glorious prospect. A soldier should never anticipate what is in store for him, he has too many people who control his destiny. Our dreams of rest were quickly and rudely shattered upon reaching *Hagenbach.* Company B, with the balance of the battalion, was marched to *Dannemarie.* At that town we were loaded on trucks about 4.30 A.M. and taken to *Chavonne-sur-le-Tang.*

The trucks were commanded by one of my former officers in Company H, 5th N. J. Infantry, but now with the 104th Motor Supply Train. Duties had prevented our seeing each other for some time. Both of us coming from the same home town, we spent the time during the trip exchanging news from home. The lieutenant informed me that the reason for being moved in trucks was that a new drive on a large scale was about to open and our division was to be in it. Just where the attack was to take place he did not know. Some place called the *Argonne Forest,* wherever that was.

Any time we were taken for a ride, instead of being compelled to 'hike,' was a good time to keep a weather eye open for some trick. Any undue consideration for our comfort made me suspicious; in this case it indicated that we were needed at another sector. We would be given possibly a few hours' sleep and then move on again. The prospects of getting rest were about to be rudely upset. If a move was contemplated we would be kept busy with orders and instructions for the movement.

We arrived at *Chavonne-sur-le-Tang* about six o'clock in the morning and billeted around the town. I turned in for a few hours' sleep, but as expected, after about two hours, a runner informed me that I was wanted at battalion headquarters. This continued practically all day. We were directed to be ready to leave town about 6 P.M. and march to *Movillars* to entrain for a destination kept secret from us.

At last we had completed our training. According to plans of the General Staff our course of instruction to fit us for duty as combat troops was finished when we came through the trench training in a quiet sector, such as we had just left. Certainly we had received every type of instruction that would fit us for battle. Apparently everything possible had been provided in the way of equipment and instruction that would make us the equal of the enemy. We had been in the service eighteen months, the training had been hard and had wiped out the physically unfit, the weaklings and most of those temperamentally unfitted for this sort of work. The men in the regiment were hard as nails, confident of their ability to meet and defeat any enemy.

I had absolute confidence in Company B and would not have hesitated to lead them into any fight. During the trench service they had demonstrated their fitness. Lieutenants Heinzmann and Elms had proven their ability. A few more lieutenants for duty with the company would have been helpful, however my sergeants were capable and fully able to handle the platoons—in fact, more so than many officers I knew. This was true throughout the regiment. All the companies were in good shape and as separate units were the equal of the best, but unfortunately the battalions, as organizations, were simply not functioning. The battalion staff was merely a higher command who 'passed the buck,' down to the companies, without a thought of results. Results were demanded from the company officers and heaven help us if we failed. At no time during the period of active operations did I receive any constructive help from the battalion. The whole attitude was one of bluff. No matter what was requested by higher authority, no matter how impossible the orders issued, it was always a case of "satisfy the colonel or don't displease the general." If an order was issued to stand on our heads while on trench duty we were expected to carry out the order, not for any good military reason, but simply do it so that the colonel or general would be happy. This is probably the reason why necessary changes were not made earlier. The type of officers referred to were tricky enough to make the brigade commander believe they were efficient. My candid opinion is that these officers were in a 'blue funk' continually, between fear of the enemy and fear of the brigade or division commander. They lacked the intelligence to protect their own rights. Then again, so many colonels had been in command of the regiment, and they were being changed so rapidly, that no attention was paid to the battalions. In every case that I recall orders issued by regimental or higher command were passed to the companies in our battalion exactly as issued. For example, the order placing troops in an open field, for a one night bivouac, during a steady rain. Another order directing a P.C. to take position at a specifically designated point, evidently figured from a map, without any personal knowledge of actual conditions at that point. If the order had been carried out that P.C. would have been placed in an open field, in plain view of the enemy, who would promptly have wiped us out with artillery and machine guns. I understand that orders issued are to be obeyed, but it is also understood that orders are issued for the accomplishment of some military mission. Sensible orders are so formulated that tasks are completed with the least possible losses and without causing a useless sacrifice of troops.

The conditions up to this time had been exasperating and

annoying more than anything else, and could have been over-looked if it was not for the fact they had created a system that worked to our disadvantage in the coming battles. In the trenches there was an opportunity to observe, and then make a decision for almost every event that occurred. From here on important decisions of life or death would have to be made instantaneously and intelligently.

War is no child's game and in itself imposes hardships that are unavoidable. Death, wounds, sickness—these we expected and were willing to take chances with; but sufferings brought about through greed and selfishness were something entirely different.

If I seem to be critical, or to keep repeating about conditions, it is only to emphasize things as they existed and to show the handicaps we were working under. It will also prepare my readers to understand a number of almost unbelievable incidents that occurred later. In conversations with other officers of the regiment at that time and since the end of the war they have expressed the same opinions. In view of what we were now going into conditions with us were not of the best. Politics and inefficiency had "raised hell" with the regiment.

## CHAPTER X

## "GOING UP"

### PREPARATION FOR THE BIG PUSH

ABOUT 6 P.M., September 23rd, the battalion left *Chavonne-sur-le-Tang* and marched to *Movillars,* arriving about midnight. Troops were immediately loaded on our old friends 40 and 8, boxcars, and about an hour later started for "somewhere in France." Where we were going we did not know. One thing noticeable in these changes of station was the lack of any particular interest, on the part of the men, as to possible destination. They might ask where we were going. If the answer was vague it never made any difference. Even on this trip, though it was generally known that we were going into something big, there was no excitement and no great interest in the destination. The only thing of interest to the men was the hope that we would not be on the train very long, because any rest in crowded freight cars was out of the question.

The battalion rode all the next day, detraining at *Revigney* at 11.30 P.M. After unloading the train we moved away about 1.30 A.M. on the 25th, arriving at *Laimont* at 3.30 A.M. where we billeted for the day. At 6.30 P.M. we again moved out and arrived at *Rembercourt* at 11.30 P.M., remained in billets until 9 P.M. on the 26th, then moved out of billets and bivouacked in the field. From this point on we were very much like a 'barnstorming' circus making one or two day stands, marching at night with such sleep as we could snatch during daylight hours, touring France via 'hob-nailed express.' Long before this, even in Camp McClellan, we had been 'dubbed' as 'Morton's Circus.' Now we were a real circus.

By the time of arrival at *Rembercourt* we had a general idea of what was about to take place. We heard that a general push was coming, along the entire front, in order to give the enemy no opportunity to mass his forces in any particular place. The United States forces were to be used as a distinct Field Army under direct command of its own officers. The point selected for this attack was in the region of the *Argonne Forest.* The *Argonne* has been described so many times it would be useless for me to make any other comments, except that it was admitted to be "the toughest spot" along the entire front and was given to the United States Army because we were fresher and in better physical condition than our Allies, who were about worn out.

The stay in this vicinity was notable particularly by the opening of the *Meuse-Argonne offensive,* and the terrific artillery bombardment prior to the 'jump off' and during the early stages of the battle. So far as I know of history, the world had never seen, or heard, of such an annihilating fire. Guns of all calibres, large and small, kept up an incessant barrage day and night. How those gunners kept their guns in action has always been a puzzle to me. Bivouacked as we were in the fields it was impossible to rest. The firing of the artillery seemed to keep the earth in a continuous tremble that made sleep impossible. What it was doing to us was as nothing compared to its effect on the enemy. Both German and Austrian prisoners told me that our artillery simply blotted their trenches out of all shape and for the first few days it was 'nip and tuck' with death every minute.

The 29th Division was one of three divisions assigned as reserves for the First Field Army, to be used at any part of our line needing additional pressure. Parked on the road, alongside of our bivouac, was a train of motor trucks, each in charge of a Hindo-Chinese driver and assistant, ready to move us to any point of danger that might appear. For three days we kept our eyes longingly on those trucks hoping we would get a ride instead of 'hiking,' but again we were S.O.L. When it was time for us to move we 'hit the trail via the hob-nail express'; in plain English we 'hiked' and the trucks moved up empty. As the French say 'C'est la guerre.'

The period spent in the field was somewhat monotonous, while waiting for something to happen, to rest and grow fat, and be ready to pile into those trucks at a moment's notice. The first twenty-four hours we were not allowed to even unroll the packs. During the remainder of the time we did manage to put up some shelter tents. The weather was very bad, raining quite a little and very cold at night. Many of the men were developing severe colds which later necessitated sending them to the base hospitals, from which some never returned. They paid the price without the excitement of battle.

The mention of cold nights recalls to mind an incident that often brings a smile. The first night alongside of the trucks, between the roar of the artillery barrages, the cold and no blanket, sleep was impossible for me. I tried lying on the ground but in a short time the cold and dampness would penetrate the trench coat and uniform until my blood seemed to be an icicle. Then it was a case of up and exercise to get warm again, usually taking a short fast walk along the road. You may wonder why I did not get into one of the trucks. That would have been comfortable but unfortunately orders were that no one be allowed to sleep in them. This was reasonable when you realize all of the men would be unable to stretch out in the trucks; they were intended for us to stand up in, not to lie down. During one of the trips up the road a Dodge touring car was discovered and no one in it. If I had had a blanket everything would have been rosy. A short time later another figure appeared on the road. It looked like an Indian, but developed to be a friend, Chaplain A. N. Smith of our regiment, and of all things he had a blanket wrapped around him. He was complaining of the cold and dampness. I generously offered to show him a dry place to sleep if he would share his blanket. The deal being made I led him to the Dodge car where we both wrapped in the blanket, curled up, and went to sleep in the rear seat. All was well until either of us wanted to turn over, in which case one had to nudge the other and then the army would turn over. You can imagine the nice comfortable sleep when you visualize my six feet and the Chaplain's five feet six.  We were bent around that back seat like a couple of cork-screws.

Since leaving the *Alsace* sector, the 114th Infantry had not been together as a whole.  The battalions generally were located at some little distance from each other for the sake of cover against enemy observation, but always near enough to be formed into a unit within a short time.  As a result of this separation and continual movement, I did not know for some time who was in command of the regiment.  Rumors were around that a new colonel had been assigned, but they came and went so fast I sometimes thought they were like rations, issued every 24 hours.  This particular change, however, was to be very interesting as it had considerable bearing on my work later on.

The new commander of the 114th Infantry, Lieutenant Colonel Hobart B. Brown, entered the war as a major in command of the First Squadron Cavalry, N.J.N.G.  This outfit later was split up and transferred, some to the Field Artillery and others to the 29th Division Military Police.  Given promotion and assigned to us, Colonel Brown came at a time when the regiment most certainly needed intelligent leadership if it was ever to amount to anything more than 'cannon fodder.' Having known the Colonel for a number of years in the 'Jersey Guard' I had come to have considerable respect for him and to appreciate his ability, and felt his appointment would assure us of decent treatment and that the junior officers would be treated as men and not as heretofore, like something to be walked on.  My one fear was that Colonel Brown's assignment came too late for his influence to be felt before going into battle.  Time alone would tell.

The promotion and assignment of Colonel Brown was by direction of the 29th Division Commander, Major General Charles G. Morton, who, after his many years experience in the regular army certainly should have been well qualified to know the type of officer needed to command troops about to enter battle.  It has always been my thought that General Morton made this assignment believing Colonel Brown to be

"In the Alsace Trenches." Eleven of the men in this picture were either killed or wounded during the fighting.

1. Company P.C. in the woods near Hagenbach. "The Skipper" seated at entrance.

2. The runners of Company B. These messengers had an exceedingly dangerous duty.

3. 1st Lieut. G. P. Heinzmann, second in command of Company B.

1. Pontoon Bridge over the Meuse River between Regneville and Samogneux, our regiment crossed here on the evening of October 10th, 1918.

2. Wagon trains of 113th Inf. and 111th M.G. Battalion in "Death Valley" near Haumont-pres-Samogneux. Enemy artillery shelled the ravine shortly after the picture was taken.

3. Road from Brabant towards Etraye Ridge under Gas. Clouds in background are enemy gas.

one officer from New Jersey who was not a part of the political machine that had been the source of so much trouble to him. Another thing, Colonel Brown had moved up the ladder quite rapidly. In 1916 he went to the Mexican Border as a first lieutenant. About the middle of September, 1916, upon the resignation of Major Bryant, Lieutenant Brown was elected Major of the Squadron, then to the Military Police and finally to command an infantry regiment. In addition to this another point tending to create a feeling of dissatisfaction was the question of seniority. Seniority in the army is a very ticklish thing, and the cause of much petty jealousy, although basically it is good and very necessary. In the 114th Infantry were many men who had been senior officers to Colonel Brown during 1916, 1917 and early 1918 and most of these officers were still holding their same low rank. In a regiment such as ours where so much reliance had been placed on political affiliations to gain promotion, a condition of this kind had a tendency to create some discontent. Had an unknown, strange officer been sent to command the regiment this condition could not have prevailed. Altogether the situation was unfair to Colonel Brown. In view of his quiet, gentlemanly demeanor, I believe he had his hands full getting the effective wholehearted co-operation necessary. When he was assigned to the regiment the battalion commanders should have been transferred or relieved, so that the battalions would have the leadership so badly needed. It would have been better if majors from other regiments had been given command of our battalions.

The battalion remained in the fields until September 29th, 4 P.M. then hiked to *Rembercourt* in about one hour. Being assigned billets we thought that at last we would get a good night's sleep, but "soldier proposes and a higher officer disposes." Shortly after midnight we were routed out of bed and at two o'clock in the morning took another stroll arriving at *Nubercourt* about six A.M. Monday and billeted among the natives, as usual in the various barns and sheds around town.

Late the same afternoon, shortly before leaving this town,

Brigadier General Upton came to me. From his looks I surmised that something had gone wrong, he certainly was mad. Without hesitation he stated that he was not satisfied with conditions in our battalion; that he had gone looking for the battalion commander and had found him asleep. He said I was to be prepared to take command when he gave the order. Explaining to the General that I was not the senior captain in the First Battalion, General Upton replied: "I want officers in command of units that I can depend on. You will be ready to take command when I order it." This was very much of a surprise to me. There were several captains in the regiment senior to me and until now, what little thought had been given to such matters, was that the senior officers would move up first. With all his experience General Upton did not seem to realize just how strong the political element was in the division, and that recommendations for promotion could be side-tracked for the benefit of others in the machine. We will see more of this later.

Leaving *Nubercourt* about 7 o'clock Monday evening we marched to *Vadelaincourt,* arriving around 10 P.M. and bivouacked in the woods. We had now passed beyond any civilian settlements. From here on everything was a shambles, hardly anything standing above ground except an occasional woods, mostly shellholes and trenches. During this period the 'hikes' were usually short, just moving up in rear, as the attacking divisions pressed forward. We remained at *Vadelaincourt* until 7 P.M., October 4th, and then moved to the *Bois de Sartelles,* arriving at 11.30 P.M. We pitched tents in the woods which was large enough for the entire regiment. No effort was made to establish company streets; each two men pitched their tents on the best available spot, companies keeping in the same locality.

On one of our stops near this point, about the time we were ready to put up tents, one of my corporals, who had been scouting around, informed me that he had located some portable barracks a short distance in the woods. They were not occupied and he thought they had bunks in them. Naturally

I was interested. I followed the corporal to the barracks. Sure enough here were several brand new buildings that had never been used. The question was, how to get into them. Over the door was a transom. Giving the corporal, a slim youngster, a 'boost' he worked his way through the opening and unfastened the door on the inside. About this time a French soldier appeared and tried to keep us out, yelling "Allez! Allez!" Funny how stupid we became all at once. We had completely forgotten every word of French we had picked up and simply disregarded him until he finally rushed away. Sending the N.C.O. back for Lieutenant Heinzmann and the company I took possession of the barracks. About the time the company was comfortably settled in their bunks, some other soldiers came along and decided they were going to bunk in with us. This produced a fine little scrap. Our French friend also came back with more 'poilus,' so that a real fracas was going in a few minutes. One man in particular insisted that he was going to sleep in one of the bunks if he had to fight for it. First Sergeant Fachet soon had the situation under control and the company had thrown out the invaders, including the 'Frogs.' Talk about fighting for a home, the men were so full of 'scrap' they did not wait to get at the common enemy, they even fought among themselves. If they couldn't do any better they jumped the 'Frogs.'

Around the first of October a memorandum reached battalion P.C. directing that the name of a lieutenant, interested in athletics, be forwarded to headquarters. The battalion adjutant, Lieutenant Frank Fisher, noticed one of my lieutenants exercising in front of his tent. Fisher, thinking this was another case of headquarters wanting an officer for extra duty immediately sent in the name of the 2nd Lieutenant Charles G. Cooley, of Company B. A short time later Fisher told me he had sent in Cooley's name and more than likely some form of athletics was about to be introduced into the battalion. He appeared to take the thing as a joke and thought he was 'putting one over' on Cooley. The real joke came out a few days later when Lieutenant Cooley was relieved from duty with our

regiment and ordered to proceed to a base port, where he
would be promoted to a First Lieutenant, then proceed to the
United States to assist in the training of a new division. This
was one time that Lieutenant Fisher missed a trick. He acted
a little too fast. It would have been a nice assignment for himself, much safer than the front lines. When he found that
Cooley was going back home he was sick.

Bivouac in *Bois de Sartelles* gave us considerable rest, which
we needed, having been in the trenches from September 8th
to the 24th and then on the move almost every night. Personally I was rather tired. In addition to routine duties with
the company I had made a reconnaisance up front, in the
vicinity of *Forges,* the night the *Argonne Drive* opened,
for the purpose of locating a possible crossing of the *Meuse
River*. This patrol was made by orders of General Upton,
and Colonel Brown directed me to make the trip. On another
occasion I was called back to 29th Division P.C. to testify
at the trial of one of our captains who had been relieved.
Several other officers of the battalion were also at the trial, as
witnesses. None of us was keen about testifying against the
defendant and as far as possible tried to be generous, but the
colonel of the trial board would stand for no evasive answers
or half truths. Questions were framed in such manner that
yes or no was the only answer we could give. It was made
very plain that we would be doing an injustice to the men
under our command as well as to ourselves if we evaded the
truth as we knew it. After this trial I began to realize that
if all officers played the game we would get results. I learned
too that Major General Morton was relieving officers for any
reason, be it politics or inefficiency, as fast as he discovered
them. At this point we were about five kilometers west of
*Verdun*.

Sunday, October 6th, was rather an eventful day. Starting
in the morning Father Michael J. Corr, our Catholic chaplain,
sent out a notice that he would say mass in a shed in the woods.
Many times since the war I have attended services at which
Chaplain Corr has been the celebrant. Seeing him in his

vestments always brings back the memory of that Sunday in *Bois de Sartelles*. I always expect to see some part of a uniform showing through his vestments as they did that morning. After mass the chaplain preached a very impressive sermon, telling us that within a few days probably we would be going into action. He urged each man to make peace with The Almighty, and for each one to write home to the folks. Then directing all to kneel, according to the rites of the Roman Catholic Church, he gave General Absolution.

Picture if you can a dense woods, aeroplanes, and artillery shells passing overhead in both directions, expecting a shell to drop on us at any minute; then a shed with probably a thousand or more men in and around the building, all kneeling, heads bowed in devout prayer and the chaplain at the altar giving his blessing. You cynics and worldly-wise individuals scoff if you will, call it childishness if you like, but under fire you will again become a little child, afraid of the darkness of uncertainty. I have seen many sights during my military experience that have been impressive, some things were ghastly, others demonstrative, spectacular, some very pathetic; but nothing I ever experienced impressed me so much as that scene. It was so very sincere; each of us appreciated exactly what we were about to go up against and were asking Almighty God, not to spare our lives but to forgive, to give us strength to accept whatever might befall us. It certainly made all feel stronger and ready to face the next few weeks with more fortitude.

In the afternoon the regiment was assembled and services conducted by Chaplain A. N. Smith, at which time he introduced Mr. Homer Rodeheaver, the celebrated cornetist, campanion of the Evangelist 'Billy' Sunday. Mr. Rodeheaver, overseas with the Y.M.C.A., played several religious selections for us. After this we were addressed by Brigadier General Upton. He urged us to be ready for the battle we would be in within a few days, calling attention to the breaking up of the Central Powers, and urged that when we got into action we drive through and keep on driving, giving the enemy no rest, until all resistance ceased. General Upton called attention to the fact that he commanded the 9th Infantry at *Chateau Thierry* and in that battle had lost better than 40% of his men and 50% of his officers. In the coming engagements he expected even greater losses. Nice, sociable, even-tempered General we had for a boss. He made us think he drank T.N.T. instead of coffee with his meals. Later events proved that his expectations were justified.

Sunday night 2nd Lieutenant Robert L. Mitchell reported to me for duty with the company. I assigned him to command the second platoon. Lieutenant Mitchell was a former member of the North Carolina National Guard and had served with the 30th Division as a non-commissioned officer. He was then sent to the Officers' Training School and upon graduation sent to me. Like most young officers, newly commissioned, he was full of enthusiasm and energy and entered upon his duties in a way that gave indications of accomplishing results. He was a quiet, likable sort of a fellow. I took rather a liking to him.

After the address of the brigade commander the chief topic of conversation for the remainder of the evening naturally was a discussion of the impending battle and our probable point of attack. A study of a map of France, west of *Verdun,* will show by the towns mentioned that the advance of the 29th Division was generally north and east, towards the *Meuse River.* This was necessary as the 33rd U. S. Division was on the extreme right of the American attacking line, with its right against the river, near *Forges.* As the Allied attack progressed, after September 26th, the 33rd had to continually stretch itself to conform to the general advance. Across the river, on the east bank, was the old German position of the 1916 attack around *Verdun,* from which the enemy kept hammering the right of the 33rd. For this reason our division was kept close to the west bank of the river as reserve in case the enemy should make an attempt to cross and curl up the American right flank.

On the east bank of the *Meuse,* opposing the German and

Austrian troops, was the 17th French Army Corps with their 18th Infantry Division near the river and their 26th Infantry Division on the right of the 17th Corps. Since the beginning of the drive there had been no particular effort required on the part of the French, their task being to keep 'Jerry' in his trenches, and as far as possible to prevent him from becoming too much of a nuisance to the American right. Incidentally the majority of the enemy facing the French were Austrian Troops who were ready to quit at the first opportunity.

Just where the 29th Division would go into action, on the west or east bank of the river, was unknown to us at the time. One thing was uncertain however. No matter where the attack was staged it would be something to write home about, if we lived long enough or were able to write when it was over. The country we had been traveling over was generally rolling with some fair-sized hills and pretty much wooded. The roads were in poor condition due to shell fire and the enormous amount of traffic going over them. Artillery and all supplies for the troops up front had to be moved by auto truck at night, the roads being deserted in daylight hours. A march on these roads at night was a delirium; trucks, wagons, staff cars, motorcycles and columns of infantry moving in and out. It was a madhouse, but somehow we managed to get through and under cover before daylight.

On the evening of October 7th the regiment again moved a short distance to *Bois Bourres,* near *Germonville.* At this point we had dugouts for a change. They were dry and very comfortable. The dugouts, constructed by the French, were in good condition, evidently built as reserve depot for troops in the rear of the front line as it existed prior to the *Argonne Drive.*

Early on the morning of the 8th an order from the battalion commander directed me to report to the regimental P.C., in light field equipment. Reporting to the regimental commander I was directed to make a reconnaisance along the west bank of the *Meuse River* as far north as *Regneville,* in an effort to locate any possible points that could be utilized by the regiment to make a crossing. Two lieutenants were assigned to accompany me on the patrol. Colonel Brown also informed me that the 58th Brigade had gone 'over the top' soon after daybreak and were attacking on the east bank of the river, from the vicinity of *Samogneux,* opposite *Regneville.* I was to gather as much information as possible about the heavily shelled roads and exposed positions. Proceeding to *Charny* we followed the west bank of the river looking for fords, shallow spots or some kind of a footbridge that could be used for a crossing. Nothing was located except an old wooden bridge that might possibly have been used after some repairs, especially planking, but this would have taken considerable time. Even then I doubted that it would stand the strain of a regiment passing over it; certainly the wagon train could not use is, so decided the bridge was of no use to us. Scouting along the river, under considerable shell fire, we finally reached *Regneville* where a pontoon bridge had been thrown across. This was the only means of crossing the *Meuse River.* The bridge was in plain view of the enemy and getting across without casualties was going to be a real job. Crossing to the east bank we located the *Canal de l'Est,* north branch. It was dry and our 104th Engineers were filling in the canal with debris from the destroyed buildings nearby. At this point I met several men who had been in the old 'Jersey Guard' with me at home, all of them now members of the Engineers.

While on the patrol considerable data was obtained from various sources along the way. One artillery major especially gave valuable information about the system of enemy shelling, the points along the roads that were being subjected to special attention from 'Boche' artillery, also indicating, on his maps, points that were under direct observation from the German lines. This information was very valuable in moving the 114th up in the next few days and undoubtedly saved us from running into barrages.

Upon completion of the original mission I directed one of the lieutenants to return to the regimental P.C. and give the information we had obtained to Colonel Brown, also to inform the Colonel that I was remaining for a time in the vicinity between *Samogneux* and *Brabant-sur-Meuse,* with the other lieutenant, for the purpose of gaining first-hand knowledge of the battle in progress in that vicinity, as our 115th and 116th Infantry were driving through towards *Mal-brouck Hill.*

The 58th Brigade was having considerable success and reasonably easy going. The enemy in front of them were about filled up with the war and from what I saw of the Austrian prisoners being sent back by the 58th Brigade they were glad when captured. It meant the end of the war for them. As prisoners they could reasonably expect at some future date to be released and returned to their native land; as combat soldiers their chances of even being alive at the end of the war were very slim. It was better to be prisoners of war, especially when they fell into the hands of the Americans; they did not like to be captured by the French. The machine gun and artillery fire was causing considerable casualties to our Southern comrades but the advance was steady. The 33rd Division had been keeping watch on our regiments and as we made progress one regiment of that division made a crossing of the *Meuse River* at the towns of *Brabant-sur-Meuse* and *Consenvoye* and then connected up with our 58th Brigade.

After scouting around in the rear of *Brabant* gathering more information we started back for the regiment late in the afternoon. All this area was being heavily shelled. Getting back to the bridge without becoming a casualty was quite a task. Just as we crossed the pontoon bridge several enemy shells landed in the water near the west shore, on each side of the bridge. When the shells exploded we were close enough for the splash of water to reach us; rather close but the old saying still held good "a miss is as good as a mile." However we did not let any grass grow under our feet. We just traveled and when I say traveled I mean we really were running.

From the west end of the bridge a road slightly rising led back over an open space for about 700 yards—not a particle of cover—under direct observation and fire from the enemy lines. It was a very unhealthy place for troops to be caught in daylight. About half way over this open road I met a machine gun platoon under the command of Sergeant A. Broskie, a young soldier I had known in Company I, 5th N. J. Infantry at home. The sergeant was taking his platoon over the river to get into action. It was good to meet him but would rather have met him in some more healthy spot. I did not envy him the task of getting across that bridge. Giving such information as might help, I wished him luck and watched him approach the bridge. He got across without any casualties. Continuing the return we arrived at the P.C. of the 114th Infantry about 5 P.M. I found my company had been moved to the north edge of the woods.

During the evening a large number of prisoners of war, Austrian, passed our bivouac. Most of them were boys about 16 or 17 years old or men around 40 years. Very few were young men such as our troops, ranging in age from 19 to 25 years. The comments of our men were quite interesting, but showed no enmity. Rather the contrary, the attitude was more like that seen at a ball game at home, the victor merely 'kidding' the loser for not being a better player.

October 8th about 6.30 P.M., we moved to *Cumieres* only a short march, but owing to road congestion we were delayed and did not reach the bivouac on *Dead Man's Hill* until 11 o'clock. From our position on the easterly slope of the hill we looked across the flats towards the *Meuse River* and to the east beyond. We had been informed that the 114th Infantry was to go into action on the east side of the river. The time or place of the battle was not given, we only knew that we were to attack in conjunction with the 18th Division, 17th French Army Corps.

The stay at *Cumieres* was marked by one incident providing excitement a little out of the ordinary and for which we had ringside seats. From the vicinity of the bivouac several observation balloons were sent up each morning to watch over the enemy lines. One morning two balloons had risen to position and a third balloon was being raised, when out of a clear sky a German aeroplane made a dive for the bag farthest north, promptly opening fire with his machine guns, using tracer bullets. As soon as the German plane dove the balloon observer tumbled out of it, like a ball, dropped a couple of hundred feet and then opened his parachute. As soon as it was evident that the first balloon was coming down in flames the 'Heinie' aviator turned for the second balloon, but the observer in that bag had no business with that plane and promptly bailed out. Both balloons came down in flames near the river. No one can blame the observers in the balloons for jumping. To be caught in one of those flaming shrouds was certain death. Our anti-aircraft batteries opened up on the plane, but as usual shot at everything on the map except the 'Heinie,' who merely circled around a few times until sure the balloons were going down, then made a couple of dips for our benefit. It appeared to me as though he was thumbing his nose at us. Then he departed for the Fatherland. The third balloon, only up about two hundred feet, was in a nasty place if the enemy plane had come after him. He was up just far enough so that the observer's parachute would have been of no use to him if compelled to jump. He was hauled back to the ground. Aviators and balloon observers can go up in the air, I'll take my chances in the infantry. I don't mind playing soldier when one foot is on the ground.

While at this place we were visited by a party of Y.M.C.A. entertainers, the principal attraction being the celebrated American actress, Elsie Janis, all decked out in a 'tin hat' (trench helmet). The entertainment was good and much appreciated, but it was too spectacular and exceedingly dangerous with shelling going on all the time. It was extremely dangerous for groups to gather at any time. What if a shell landed in the crowd? Miss Janis and her party were probably farther forward on the front than any entertainers; they were certainly under fire that time.

On Dead Man's Hill the time was spent getting some rest and checking over the company equipment in preparation for the coming battle. No matter how many times the organizations were inspected some men had always lost part of their equipment or reserve rations. This was not a serious matter up here; there was always so much discarded equipment laying around that a soldier could pick up almost any pieces to replace lost articles. In the matter of the reserve rations, carried by each soldier and not to be used except by order of an officer or in an emergency such as being cut off from the regular source of supply, the men were always short, especially the hard bread. Many a time I have reprimanded a soldier for being short of his 'iron rations,' accusing him of eating the hard tack without orders; yet I have been just as guilty for I have done the same thing many a time. The long night 'hikes' made a man hungry and 'nibbling' on a piece of hard tack seemed to make the miles pass under foot much faster. Even the ammunition was discarded by some men. Each man was required to have his belt full, 100 rounds, and two bandoliers extra, a total of two hundred and twenty rounds. Do you blame a man for getting rid of some extra weight? Especially when he had been carrying ammuntion for weeks without once being called upon to use it. A soldier's pack is supposed to weigh about sixty-five pounds, but when marching all night it seems to weigh more like one hundred sixty-five pounds.

The original rifle issued to troops of the United States Army was the "U. S. Springfield, model 1903," a very fine weapon, accurate and easy to handle. The older men of the army had become much attached to this rifle. During training days a new type rifle, the 'Enfield,' was issued to make up the existing shortage, adopted from the British army model and chambered for our own .30 calibre ammunition, so that the two models of rifle, also the automatic rifle and the machine gun could all use the same size ammunition. The Enfield was a rather crude weapon, as compared to the Springfield. The sights on this rifle were more coarse, and accurate sniping, for which the American rifleman is noted, was not possible with the Enfield. Altogether the new issue rifle was not popular with the A.E.F. and at every opportunity they were discarded. Each time we rested in the vicinity of a 'dump' the next inspection revealed more Springfields and less Enfields in the company than at the previous inspection. When it was necessary for me to do any shooting I always used a Springfield. I never became accustomed to the clumsy Enfield.

Whenever the company was in a place for more than one day the lieutenants were certain to have a batch of letters to censor. Usually they merely glanced at the letters and then sent them on; occasionally they came across a letter that unintentionally gave indication of our position, but such cases were rare. The men generally obeyed the orders not to disclose any military information that would be of value to the enemy. At times the lieutenants would show me a letter that would have won a place in any comic sheet. The stories told usually were poking fun at 'Fritz'; very little of complaint. I recall a group of letters written by one of the N.C.O.'s. He had written to several girls at home. Each letter had promised the recipient marriage when he got home. The lieutenant who was censoring the mail wanted to know if he should stop them. I told him to let them go through; it might be that the soldier would not get back to marry anyone. It's all in the fortunes of war. The joke of those letters came after the war. That soldier did come back, although wounded, but married an entirely different girl. I won't "squeal" sergeant. Many times since the war I have been introduced to a young lady who had married one of my men since the return home, and have wondered if they knew that we read their letters from France before they did.

On this particular day, with the prospects of going 'over the top' only a matter of hours, many letters were written. A number of them referred to the general battle taking place but made light of any danger, even though they had personal feelings of how serious it might be. As I write this, in front of me is a letter I wrote to my wife from Dead Man's Hill, near *Cumieres,* dated October 10th, 1918. There is no mention of the impending attack, the letter merely telling of the balloons that were brought down, the prisoners coming in, how we were leading the simple life, carrying our homes and furniture on our backs like a wandering band of gypsies, swearing at the mud that is everywhere and of the cold nights and dreary wet days. This I believe was typical of all of us; why worry the folks at home? They could not help any. If a man's 'number was up,' well, "this is war." We were much more interested in receiving mail from home. How anxiously we looked for a letter or newspaper. How each paper was passed from one to another until every line had been read, even the advertisements.

You will understand that all our time was not spent in writing letters, reading or even saying prayers; it was possible to see small groups on their knees and when you came near them you would hear such exclamations as "Come on lady, baby needs new shoes" or "Oh! you seven come and see me" or remarks of a similar nature. You guessed it, 'Galloping Ivories,' the old army game of 'shooting craps.'

I have gone into considerable detail about our daily life at this period in order to emphasize the fact that among the troops there was no discussion of battle or possible injuries. That was a matter of routine. The only time we thought about it was when something happened to bring it forcibly to our attention, such as extra heavy shelling or 'Boche' planes overhead; then everyone would 'duck' for cover. We were not wasting any nervous energy thinking about 'Fritz.' We would attend to his case at the proper time; until then why worry about it?

As mentioned before the weaklings and unfit had been weeded out and at this time Company B, 114th U. S. Infantry was a typical infantry company, similar to others seen everywhere on the front, ready and fit for anything; when that outfit lined up it was the kind of an organization every officer hopes to command at some time. I believed that every officer and man in the company would go the limit, in spite of all the handicaps under which it had started. With all the changes in personnel, both among the enlisted men and the officers, it was now a thoroughly dependable unit of the United States army.

Shortly before dark, October 10th, the regiment was again on the move with orders to proceed to *Regneville* and to cross the pontoon bridge at this point to *Samogneux*. Lieutenant Colonel Brown designated me as guide for the 114th as I had been up there on the 8th and the information gained of the road conditions and the shelled areas would help to avoid casualties. I suggested that the wagon train be sent over the road, and that the regiment follow me by way of an old railroad bed near the river, which ran through a cut out of sight of the enemy. The plan was approved and the movement started about 7.30 P.M. Many survivors of that march have growled about the trip and rough going, but at least it was much safer and faster than the heavily shelled road, full of traffic, with all its delays while under fire and with no protection. The head of the regiment having reached the *Cumieres-Regneville* road leading to the bridge a halt was made for 15 minutes to rest. I explained to Major Taylor, whose battalion was leading the regiment, that as soon as we left the railroad and started for the bridge we would be on a flat open road. As there was still some daylight left it would be necessary to move fast, if we were to avoid being shelled. We eventually reached the bridge, crossed the river and proceeded to *Cote des Roches* on the *Samogneux-Brabant* road, arriving there about eleven o'clock the same night. Just as the rear of the regiment reached the bridge the enemy again shelled the road and First Lieutenant W. S. Bull, M.C., a doctor attached to the 3rd Battalion, who was at the rear of the column, was killed and a lieutenant wounded. They were the only casualties in the movement.

The battle we were about to enter was scheduled for October 12th, a date that seemed destined to play an important part in the history of the 114th Infantry. While on the march to *Cote des Roches,* Major Taylor and I, at the head of the column, were discussing the coming battle, where it was to take place, the date, etc.; we also talked of Camp McClellan days, of officers who had been active there and had passed out of the regiment, and of the many changes that had taken place since our arrival in Alabama. While on the subject of our early days I asked the Major if the date of the coming attack reminded him of anything of special interest, to which he replied "No." Then after a moment he said, "Oh yes, it is Columbus Day." I asked if that was all the significance it had. He could not recall any other event of interest to us that had fallen on that date. I reminded him that one year previously, October 11th, 1917, the celebrated consolidation, or reorganization or whatever you choose to call it, had taken place, when the old National Guard regiments of Virginia, Maryland, Delaware, and New Jersey had been transferred and made over into the new regiments. How at that reorganization numerous good officers had been thrown out, transferred to the Depot Brigade and, according to newspaper accounts, classified as inefficient; also that the new regiment started off with hand picked officers, selected for their social or political affiliations rather than for military ability. I had been one of the rejected, but in three months time it was necessary for someone in the 114th Infantry to recall me from the depot, and the same thing had happened to several other officers now with the regiment. I further told the major that since the reorganization I had kept my mouth shut. When recalled to the regiment I requested an assignment to any other unit in the division, as I did not want to serve in the 114th Infantry. This was not granted and I was assigned to command Company B. As a soldier I could only obey the order. How orders had been obeyed was evident from the fact that I had been retained in command of the company for more than nine months, and that the Brigade Commander had ordered me to be prepared to take command of a battalion when he directed. During that time I had seen politics and favoritism on all sides. Major Taylor replied that he had nothing to do with the original selections but he had asked for me in January. He was the second officer of the 114th Infantry who had told me that. I wonder why I was in such demand? Could it be possible there was a thought that, after all, we might get into battle some time later? I further told the major that in spite of all the handicaps I was still holding down my job and wanted him to know my feelings towards these officers who had made the first choice. I also told him: "If my number is up in the coming battles, remember that Bill Reddan goes out laughing at that bunch of peanut politicians who were responsible for the original transfers and themselves lacked the nerve to be here at the finish." Most of them had since been either relieved or transferred to dugout jobs.

Continual reference to this inefficiency and influence is the only means possible to bring home to you conditions that existed long before the beginning of the war, and in the Service had full play from the day the 29th Division was born in 1917 until it was mustered out in 1919. You are only reading of this rotten condition; we had to live in the midst of this filth, every day, for nearly two years; there was no escape from it. In the training camp, in the trenches and even in the major battles and then after the armistice—like our friends the 'cooties,' it was always with us.

I had nothing to do with the making of these conditions, but with every other officer and man of the 114th Infantry, outside of the ring, suffered an existence that was a veritable hell, over and above the ordinary hardships necessary to active military service. A book on this subject could be written showing the system and methods used and the rewards gained by political job hunters who were responsible for our miserable existence during the preceding year. The prospects of entering battle gave me a greater feeling of safety and contentment than I had at any time since going to the regiment. The coming battle would give us plenty to think about, but perhaps, for a change, we would escape the politicians for a few days. No one could tell what changes would take place when brother 'Boche' started playing with his artillery and was throwing 'scrap iron' in our front yard.

In my opinion the esteem in which the 57th Infantry Brigade was held by Major General Morton, our division commander, was very clearly shown first by the assignment of Colonel Reckord, of the 58th Brigade, to the temporary command of our brigade during the trench duty in Alsace, and now by the assignment of troops for the initial attack of the 29th Division at *Malbrouck Hill* on October 8th. The division commander assigned the 58th Brigade to the task, because, apparently, he had more confidence in them; at least they had given him less trouble. As this attack was to be made under the command of the 18th French Division, the attacking brigade would be detached from our division for a few days. General Morton probably felt that the 58th Brigade was more to be trusted than we were; he may also have expected they would set an example for us to try and equal later. An assignment of troops for an attack of this kind normally would be given to the senior brigade, other conditions being equal. In this case evidently the General did not consider the conditions as equal. We were the senior brigade, under the command of Brigadier General Leroy Upton, a man who had a distinguished record as a regimental commander and had been promoted for his work at *Chateau-Thierry*. That eliminates any criticism of the 57th Brigade commander, therefore the General's distrust must have been aimed at lower ranking officers or units within our brigade. The 58th Brigade, the juniors, were sent into this attack under the command of Colonel V. A. Caldwell. The division commander had become so accustomed to considering the Southern brigade that he probably never gave a second thought to us. Figure it out for yourself; it is far beyond my humble ability to understand how a general's mind works.

There is no intention on my part to cast any reflection on the ability or bravery of the officers or men of the 58th Brigade. I had been attached to the brigade in the fall of 1917; later saw them in action and know their value from personal observation. Many of the officers of the organization were good friends and I would have been happy to have had them alongside of me in any battle. Mention of the 58th Brigade is made merely as they appear in our picture; as a company com-

mander, and later as a battalion commander, I had many opportunities to observe the workings of the system and believe
it is my duty to state conditions as I saw them that will help to
explain why the 57th Brigade was always given the rough end
of the stick to hold, and why the casualties in our regiment
were so much higher than necessary.

General Morton had no more loyal or efficient troops in
the 29th Division than he had in the 57th Brigade, but unfortunately he seemed to place us all in the same category.
While a number of the higher officers had been relieved, there
still remained about a half dozen of the smaller 'fish' in our
brigade, and at division headquarters, whose dismissal would
have broken up the machine. More will be said later about
this machine and its effect on operations, promotions, decorations, etc. The lives of your sons, brothers and husbands were
used as stepping stones to further the ambitions of a few para-
sites who desired high rank and were keeping an eye on the
advantages of a military title when seeking electives or political appointive office after the war. Most of these individuals
had brains enough to find dugout jobs, so that their chances
of returning home as heroes were much better. These men
did not seek promotions as a reward for services in battle nor
even for the additional salary that went with an advance in
rank, but merely from a desire to pose as heroes. More of the
promotions went to officers who were close to, or attached to,
divisional units that never did a day's actual front-line duty,
than to the men who did the fighting, and I am not referring
to organizations which, through no fault of their own, failed to
reach the lines. Am I too severe in my criticism? The answer
is very easily obtained. Check the records of each of us and the
amount of time we spent on the lines.

We are now about to enter battle and you will be the judge
whether or not I am justified. As we go on I will endeavor
to show how some officers knew so little of actual combat, and
were so careful of themselves, that when they sent companies
into action they went into their dugouts and stayed there, hoping the company officers, with the help of God, would be suc-

cessful. If we succeeded then the higher commanders would be praised and perhaps receive a decoration; if we failed, then the company officers would have to stand the censure and possible degradation. I will show how these companies went into action without proper support, and once in battle received no effective assistance by additional fire power from artillery or other auxiliary weapons. Companies were simply allowed to wither and die under superior enemy fire.

## CHAPTER XI

# THE MEUSE-ARGONNE

THE *Meuse-Argonne* offensive has been described so completely that any attempt to give further details would be superfluous, so I will merely quote from various authorities in order to show conditions on the east, or right, bank of the *Meuse River* and to make only such comments as are necessary to explain our particular effort.

The sector, from the river to the east, was under command of the 17th French Army Corps. The usual plan of the French was to have an Army Corps remain in one sector, so as to be thoroughly familiar with it and the activities of the enemy on that particular front. Since the American drive commenced, September 26th, the 17th Corps had made some demonstrations, on their side, in order to keep the German Staff under the impression that the principal attack would be on the east bank of the river. As a result of these demonstrations the enemy had stiffened his lines in front of the French in the following manner. I quote from the HISTORY OF THE 29TH DIVISION:

"*First*, the infantry in the sector was reinforced. Rest battalions were brought into the main line of resistance, and selected machine gun detachments were hurried into the line, with the result that the enemy had a density on his main line of resistance of ten infantry companies and three machine gun companies per kilometer of front. *Second,* the artillery was continually reinforced. Twelve new battery emplacements were made and occupied, and sixteen old ones reoccupied. In addition, nine new long range guns were brought into action.

While at least four artillery regiments were known to be in close reserve. *Third,* the general reserves in the Corps front were reinforced. The 28th, 112th and 5th Bavarian Reserve were added to the 27th, 37th and 106th Austro-Hungarian Divisions, which had been held in reserve opposite the Corps front."

A further quotation from the division history tells of a captured German order of September 23rd containing the following:

"It is certain that the Franco-Americans are going to attack east of the *Meuse* on a great scale. We have not been able to determine whether the attack will extend to the left bank. The situation demands the greatest surveillance. Under no circumstances is the enemy to surprise us."

The German Staff was worried about an attack east of the river, such as we were about to make. It was a menace to their main line back into Germany. Even the initial attack west of the river was thought to be only a feint by the Americans to draw enemy troops away from the real point of the attack in conjunction with the French, north and east of *Verdun.*

Another quotation from the HISTORY OF THE 29TH DIVISION:

"Captured orders of the 32nd Division * (German) of October 5th show that the enemy had anticipated as many as five different eventualities, one of which was the breaking of the front by surprise, followed by Franco-American advance as far as one of the rest billets of reserve units."

Still another quotation from the Division History, a captured order of the 5th Army, German, signed by their commander, General Von Marwitz:

---

* The above-mentioned 32nd Div. was one of the units that fought against us later.

"According to the news that we possess the enemy is going to attack the 5th Army east of the Meuse and try to push towards *Longuyon-Sedan,* the most important artery of the Army of the West. Moreover, the intention of the enemy is to render impossible for us the exploitation of the *Bassin de Briey* upon which our steel production depends in a large measure.

"Thus it is come that the hardest part of the task may fall upon the 5th Army in the course of the fighting of the next few weeks; it is upon that task that the security of the Fatherland may rest.

"It is on the invincible resistance of the Verdun Front that the fate of a great part of the West Front depends, and perhaps, the fate of our people.

"The Fatherland must be able to count on every leader and every man knowing the grandeur of his mission and that he will do his duty to the end. If things come about thus, the enemy's assault, as in the past, will break against our firm will to hold.

(Signed) Von Marwitz."

The foregoing extracts from the History of the 29th Division prove conclusively that the attack east of the *Meuse River* was no surprise to the Germans and further that the French Corps commander did know, and our own Division Staff should have known, that the enemy were expecting an attack of major proportions and had made full preparations to resist our advance to the limit. It certainly was to be no surprise. After the initial attack of October 8th the enemy massed everything possible to oppose us, and if possible to get revenge for the 'beating' he had taken on the west side of the river. Every foot of ground that we were to take would have to be captured by the 'doughboy' with his bayonet.

The above describes the tactical situation. When I think of what had been prepared for us and the little that we, the men who were expected to break through this resistance, had been told, it all seems like a horrible nightmare, too unreal to understand. Even the limited information given us was always that we would have little resistance and that the enemy lines were only lightly held. How any of us were able to get through at all, even though wounded, let alone escape death, is a mystery.

Now let us take a look at the ground over which other units of the 29th Division were fighting and what we were to enter. Again I quote from other sources so there will be no opportunity to charge exaggeration. There are many books available for reference, but the best description I have read is by the celebrated war correspondent, Colonel Frederick Palmer, official observer with the A.E.F. who served with the Allied armies for several years before the United States entered the World War. Colonel Palmer was in a position to see the part played by each unit, and from personal observations, on all the battlefields, was competent to judge the various engagements. The following extracts are from Colonel Palmer's book "OUR GREATEST BATTLE" (the Meuse-Argonne). (Dodd, Mead & Co.). From the Preface:

"We had repulses, when heroism could not persist against annihilation by cross-fire; our men attacked again and again before positions were won: sometimes they fought harder to gain a little knoll or patch of woods than to gain a mile's depth on other occasions. Accomplishment must be judged by the character of the ground and of the resistance."

"Not all the heroes won the Medal or the Cross. The winners had opportunities: Their deeds were officially observed. How many men deserved them in annihilated charges in thickets and ravines, but did not receive them, we shall not know until our graves in France yield their secrets."

\*　　\*　　\*　　\*　　\*　　\*　　\*

"The 29th Division under command of Major General Charles G. Morton. . . . After nearly two months in the quiet sector at Belfort, had been marched on the night of the 8th past the ruins of the villages in the Verdun battle area for its initiation into two weeks of fighting which showed that one side of the trough of the Meuse had no preference over the other in the resistance, which the enemy had to offer."

"A system of hills extending from the Verdun forts to the Bourne de Cornouiller formed the walls of a bowl, which the French Corps in a fan shaped movement was to ascend. Their slopes were wooded and cut by ravines commanding the bottom of the bowl itself, which was irregular but everywhere in view of the heights. The 29th was to drive straight toward the Bourne de Cornouiller. Upon its success on the first day, may it be repeated, depended largely the success of the 33rd's crossing of the Meuse. The further away from the river, the stronger were the enemy's position. . . . The enemy by this time was fully awake to the plan of the 17th Corps. He unloosed that torrent of shells and gas from the heights of the rim of the bowl which was not to cease for three weeks."

"The 33rd had brought more reserves across the river. . . . On their right the 29th again and again charged for the possession of the Plat-Chene ravine, which was a corridor swept with plunging fire from right and left and in front, and saturated with gas. Casualties were enormous, in keeping with the courage of this new division inspired by the heritage of both the Blue and Gray. It was futile to persist in the slaughter of such brave and willing men; futile for the 33rd to try to hold the exposed salient of the Sivry Ridge; but every shell they received was one spared our men on the slopes of the west bank of the Meuse. Austrian troops which had been holding the line against them were replaced by Veteran Prussians and Wurtemburgers, who knew how to make the most of their positions, and who answered attacks with counter-attacks. As the left flank which must not yield the river bank, the 33rd intrenched in the Dans les Vaux valley through the Chaume Woods. We were within a mile of the Borne, but what a horrible mile to traverse. The first stage of that detached battle east of the Meuse, so important in its relation to the main battle, was over."

Commenting further on the ground conditions, the hills and the ravines, Colonel Palmer continues:

"Once the hills were taken, except for a series of detached

hills, the way was open to the plain of the Woevre and to Germany. . . . There was no ravine, it seemed, no part of the pit which was not visible to the observers from some one of the heights. . . . The approach to the bowl for our troops was along a road through a valley, which was as warranted in receiving its name as any Death Valley in the war. On the French side of the old trench line this ran through an area of villages in utter ruin from the bombardments of the Verdun Battle, then through Samogneux and more ruins, woods, and fields of shell craters into the valley of the bowl itself."

Why continue with any further description? Enough has been quoted to show the party we were about to enter. However the following paragraph from the same author will show his opinion of the part played by us on October 12th. I stated before Colonel Palmer was well qualified to know what he was writing about.

"On October 12th the Blues and the Greys of the 29th co-operating with the French, undertook in an encircling movement, which was complete in its detail, to take the woods on both sides of the roads. This aroused the spleen of the German artillery. It drew violent counter-attacks from the German Infantry, continued in two days of in and out fighting. Successive charges reached the edges of Ormont. There under a tempest of artillery fire they looked up the slope through the thickets towards the summit of 360, where the machine guns were emitting too murderous a plunging fire to permit them either to advance or to hold all the ground they had gained."

Before continuing our part in the operations may I submit the following extract from the Overseas edition of the A.E.F. newspaper, the STARS AND STRIPES. The article was written by Captain Joseph Mills Hanson and describes the fighting east of the *Meuse* during the last days of the war:

"In this region lying north and northeast of Verdun, the enemy had a maze of powerfully intrenched lines, partly surviving from the intense fighting known as the Battle of Verdun in 1916 and partly of more recent construction, but amounting in effect to a close weaving together of all defensive zones which, further westward, were spread at wider intervals across the country.

"Directly north of Verdun and east of Consenvoye these defensive zones appear to have consisted of at least six main lines within a depth of ten kilometers, the front line being called the *Brabanter* Stellung, which had behind it successively the *Hagen* Stellung, the *Volker* Stellung, the *Etzel* Stellung, the *Giselher* Stellung (unfinished), and the *Kreimhilde* Stellung.

"It was known in advance that the enemy was peculiarly prepared to offer desperate resistance in this region, because he had massed many troops in this vicinity for the specific purpose of protecting Metz against the direct American attack on that place, which he had long expected. Not only were his defensive zones powerful in themselves, moreover they were built through the exceptionally rugged hills and forests of the plateau between the Meuse and the Plain of the Woevre and they were supplied with a vast concentration of artillery and machine guns."

This then was the situation existing as the 114th Infantry crossed to the east bank of the *Meuse River*. In the contemplated drive by our regiment, we would be attacking up hill the original "jump off" positions of the German Army of February, 1916, in their mad attempt to capture *Verdun*, this attack lasting until June. During October, November and December, 1916, the French launched a counter offensive and drove the enemy back part of the way. In the summer of 1917 the French again attacked and drove the German Army back, approximately to the position we found them in. After the terrific slaughter of 1916 and 1917 the German soldiers called *Verdun* "the slaughter house of Germany." It is hoped this description will give my readers a small picture of the shambles we were about to enter.

We now come to the most difficult and trying part of our service, the duty for which we had strenuously trained for more than a year, a duty which was to demand all we had in us. For many it meant death, for others wounds and suffering for the remainder of their lives with death as the only permanent relief from their sufferings.

For the past several days it had been rumored that on the 12th the 114th Infantry was to make an attack, the exact location being a secret. About noon on the 11th, orders were received to move at 15.00 o'clock (3 P.M.). At last we were to have a real 'crack at Jerry'; no more playing, no more holding a line of trenches day in and day out with never an opportunity to 'mix things up a little.' Whatever was now in front of us would be a fight to the finish.

A rather humorous but touching episode occurred just before the company started. After giving Mess Sergeant Galanos instructions about rations for the company during the coming battle I turned to join the organization and the sergeant remarked:

"Captain, bring the men back safe and I will give them the best meal we have ever had, if I have to steal it."

I replied:

"It won't be necessary to steal anything. I am inclined to believe that you will not have as many men to feed when we again get back to the kitchen."

Little did we realize how few men would 'line up' at the 'old chow wagon' the next time the company came in for mess.

At 15.10 the 1st Battalion started for the lines, destination unknown, leaving all wagons, water carts, rolling kitchens, etc., at the bivouac at *Cote d'Roches,* with orders to be ready to follow us up when ordered.

Company B, with the rest of the 1st Battalion, 'hiked' over the *Brabant-Charny* road, east of the *Meuse River,* to the crossroad at *Samogneux* where we turned left and marched north through *Haumont-pres-Samogneux* towards *Bois de Ormont.* The march was made in rather a leisurely manner, in broad daylight, a thing we had never done heretofore in all our meanderings in a forward area.

About 18.30 o'clock (6.30 P.M.) the battalion was halted by the roadside, and all company officers assembled to receive the battle orders for the attack. The orders given by our battalion commander were verbal, with only a superficial explanation as to the enemy, terrain, supporting troops, dressing stations, ammunition dumps, etc. Particular stress, however, was laid on the necessity of keeping up communication from the companies to battalion headquarters after the battle started. It seemed as though there was more interest in what the Division or Brigade Commanders would have to find fault with, rather than any particular interest in the enemy forces in front of us. There had been no reconnaissance for the companies, although throughout our training the need for personal reconnaissance had been drilled into us at every school attended; every lecture by our own officers, as well as those from the foreign army officers who had assisted in our training, had emphasized the necessity of this. The only ones who had seen the position were the battalion commanders; in our battalion we were told that the enemy was holding the line very lightly. How this was known is a mystery to me. The lack of proper reconnaisance by the company commanders who were scheduled to make the attack was a serious error. It left us in the dark as to the enemy position. Also the fact that the orders were not written gave too much opportunity for misunderstanding, and above all prevented the company officers from giving proper thought to the plan of attack. It was a case of poor preparation at some point higher than the companies.

A copy of the written order, R.O.11, for the attack on the 12th of October, 1918, was procured from the 1st Battalion Sergeant-Major on board the ship that brought us home in May, 1919. This order was dated and timed as 8 P.M. on the 11th, about one hour after we had received our verbal orders from the battalion commander. Accordingly the battalion commanders were also operating under verbal orders at that time. The more this situation is studied the more it becomes apparent that we were going into this major battle with less real knowledge of what was confronting us than we had in our first trip into the Alsace trenches.

The verbal orders received merely gave us the few points absolutely necessary for even a start. We were informed that the attack would take place the next morning, October 12th, then told the map co-ordinates from which we were to make the "jump off."

"Companies A and B in the front line, making the direct attack—Company A on the left, Company B on the right, each company to have two platoons in line and two platoons in support.

Company C, to follow Company A in support.

Company D, the support for Company B.

2nd Battalion 114th to be on the right of the 1st Battalion.

66th French Infantry to attack on the left of the 1st Battalion.

77th French Infantry to attack on the right of the 114th.

Third Battalion, 114th, the regimental reserve.

In the attack the distance between men deployed, ten yards.

Rate of advance, 100 meters in three minutes.

Attack to be pushed to the limit, allow nothing to hold up the attack.

Disregard liaison to the right and left; if the companies on our flanks are held up or pushed back, continue the advance.

Direction of the attack, 15 degrees east of north, from the point of departure to the edge of *Bois de Ormont,* where contact would be made with the 113th Infantry, thus pinching out the 66th French Infantry who are attacking on the left of our battalion. Then the direction of attack will change for a direct brigade attack on *Crepion* by the 113th and 114th Infantry.

Zero hour, 7 o'clock.

Pack carriers and rolls to be left at point of departure under guard."

And this paragraph about the artillery, which is well worth studying as one of the reasons for so much of our suffering in the following 24 hours:

"Artillery will prepare for the attack with a 12 hour barrage, starting at 19 o'clock (7 P.M.) tonight and continuing until zero hour in the morning.  Last five minutes to be mingled with smoke shells to show that the barrage will lift and to provide a screen for the advance."

As the battle progressed we will see that whoever issued that information either failed to contact the artillery and learn just what support they intended to give us or else they were trying to 'kid' the infantry.  Unfortunately this was no place for fooling.

After the conference the officers returned to their companies, waiting until the 2nd and 3rd Battalions passed us.  Then we moved up shortly after.  Up hills and down hills, in trenches and out of them, until it seemed as if we would never reach our destination; always under fire from the enemy artillery, shrapnel and gas, in gas-masks one minute and out of them again in a short time.  In places we passed many dead, whether they were German or French I don't know.  At that time I had no special desire to investigate.  As a whole it was not a very pleasant place for a stroll; a good thing for us there was no moon shining.  When darkness came on the effect of the artillery fire became more noticeable; it seemed that the crash of exploding shells was sharper.  We would see a spark in the air, much like a lightning bug, followed a few seconds later by a terrific crash.  After watching a few of these flashes we came to expect them and could tell when the shell would burst.

This march was hard on all of us; very much like children playing the game "follow the leader."  The battalion commander may have known where we were going, with the help of the French guides, but the company officers had but little idea of our route.  While going through some old trenches, about midnight, Company B came to a halt for the very good reason that the leading unit had halted. After waiting for about fifteen minutes I went forward to ascertain the reason for the long delay.  About three hundred yards ahead the reason was found.  At a cross trench one of the connecting files had lost contact with his leading unit and not knowing which way to turn, left or right, this soldier had done the easiest thing. He simply stopped where he was until someone came up to start him again. It is needless to say that this man was wishing, most fervently, that he was back in the good old U. S. The air in the vicinity must have been blue for the next few minutes while I told that soldier what kind of an ass he was and what I would take delight in doing to him when he got out of there. It was a ticklish place to be, the leading troops getting farther away each minute we stayed there. After a rapid survey I decided to get out of the trenches and to strike across country in the general direction of the advance. To prevent surprise and to establish contact with the leading units of the battalion a platoon was sent out as an advance guard with connecting files; flanking patrols were also sent to the right and left. After advancing about 500 yards the point of the advance struck a narrow-gauge railroad, which I decided to follow to the right. In daylight the railroad proved to be a disused 'Boche' line through the *Ravine des Coassinvaux*. We were marching with our left flank to the enemy, who was entrenched about 2500 yards away, with only small detachments of the French between us. A short time later we came in contact with the rest of the battalion. We had not even been missed.

Shortly after 3 o'clock orders were received to fall out and get some rest. A few smashed dugouts were found, also sections of bashed trenches. These were used for cover for the men. The Company P. C. was established in a small dugout. About 3.30 Private William Doody was brought in, wounded in the leg. He died about an hour later. Sergeant Sampson Horrocks was brought in about the same time, badly wounded in the arm. Both men were hit with the same shell.

## CHAPTER XII

## BOIS de ORMONT

### THE BATTLE AT ORMONT FARM AND WOODS

DAYBREAK showed a cold, damp morning with good prospects of rain. The 'Boche' artillery kept up a haphazard fire, just enough to make everyone keep under cover. He was evidently suspicious that something was in the wind but did not know from just what direction to expect it.

About 5.30 'oclock I located our battalion commander and asked to be shown the ground over which we were to attack, also for such additional information as he might have received during the preceding night. The orders and instructions received up to this time had been very vague, with little information about the enemy, his strength or position. I insisted on making a personal reconnaissance, with the major, of the ground to be gone over and the position to be attacked. After seeing the terrain over which we were to fight, a ravine, the head of which was heavily wired and evidently strongly held judging from the number of French dead there, I suggested to the major that it would mean certain annihilation for the company to attempt an attack up the ravine at a scheduled rate of advance. I suggested that the company be permitted to attack in conjunction with Company A until the head of the ravine was reached, when by a side-slipping move to the right, through the trees, our original line would be gained. This would have given additional strength to overcome the resistance in front of Company A and at the same time force the enemy out of their advanced position at the head of the ravine. The battalion commander refused to change the orders, saying, "the position is lightly held by only a few troops up there who will retire when the advance begins." How he knew what the strength of the enemy was or how the position was defended is more than I know. The French, under whose command we were at the time, certainly knew exactly the strength of the enemy and their determination to hold; they had this information from captured prisoners and copies of German orders. According to the 29th Division History our own division staff knew what to expect, yet it was all kept a dark secret, at least from the troops who were to do the fighting. A little truthful information about the enemy would have made a big difference in our attack.

"Only a few troops up there, the position is lightly held." As I look back now such a remark appears to have been the most ridiculous thing that could have been said. Evidently the battalion commander was afraid that if we knew a few things about the enemy we would be better able to make plans for our part in the attack. No, we were to learn of the enemy strength after we were actually in the battle and it was too late to make changes. It is my opinion that all information concerning the enemy was obtained from the French and they gave only such information as absolutely necessary, and even that was in a manner tending to minimize the difficulties facing us. The French 17th Corps knew that heavy resistance would be met. They had been on this sector for several years, with repeated attacks by both French and German troops, over the same ground we were about to attack. In fact most of the German-Austrian and French troops now in this area had been facing each other for almost a year. The French had pushed this same enemy back as far as *Samogneux*.

There was only one thing left for us to do—"obey Orders," no matter what the price. Of course I was merely an officer of the line the same as the other company officers and supposed to know but little of strategy, only to lead soldiers into battle to be killed as the result of carelessness, stupidity or inanity of higher authority.

About 6.25 all the officers and non-commissioned officers of Company B were assembled at the entrance to a small dugout.

I gave them their final instructions and the following verbal orders:

"The 114th Infantry, having been assigned to the 18th Division, French Army, will attack the enemy positions in *Bois de Moirey,* on the right, and the *Bois de Ormont* on our left, and the ground in between both woods.

The 77th French Infantry will be on the right of our regiment and the 66th French Infantry on our left, between us and our 113th Infantry. The 66th Infantry will continue to advance with us until we join up with the 113th Infantry, when the French will be pinched out.

Zero hour 7 o'clock. This company will attack up that ravine on my right. (Pointing out the ravine.)

Company A is attacking on our left, Company E, 2nd Battalion, on our right.

Company D, Lieutenant Kilpatrick commanding, will be in support of this company.

From point of departure, the advance will be by compass direction, 15 degrees east of north, until the intermediate objective, the edge of *Bois de Ormont,* is cleared. The direction will then change toward the east for a direct attack on our ultimate objective, *Crepion.*

This company will attack in two waves, two platoons in attacking wave, second platoon on the left, Lieutenant Mitchell in command; 3rd platoon on the right, Lieutenant Elms in command; 1st platoon in support of 2nd platoon, Sergeant Wittenweiler in command; 4th platoon in support of 3rd platoon in command of Lieutenant Heinzmann.

Distance between men deployed 10 yards.

Distance between first and second waves 60 yards.

Distance between attacking and support platoons 150 yards.

Platoon commanders take such formations as will be suitable for the attack in its varied stages.

Ammunition to be used sparingly, firing only when a target is visible.

Attack will be pushed vigorously; make every effort to engage the enemy with the bayonet. Do not stop for prisoners. "Mopping up" will be attended to by Company D.

Rate of advance will be 100 meters in three minutes.

Smoke bombs will fall on enemy lines five minutes before attack starts, also for five minutes preceding the lifting of each standing barrage.

Liaison to be established by all platoons to right, left and rear.

Each platoon send two runners to me here.

The company will be under cover of the hill on the left of the ravine, ready for the attack, at 6.45.

Messages will reach me at the junction of the second and third platoon in advance of the 2nd wave."

A few minutes were spent in clearing up some minor points and then each of us went to his particular work. How many of that group of fine young men, as they stood there wishing each other "the best of luck," ever thought that within a short time many of them would be dead or badly wounded. It is a good thing we cannot see into the future. If we could have seen what was to happen within the next twelve hours, how would we have felt?

At 6.45 the First Sergeant reported that the company was ready. Giving the company a brief outline of the plan of attack, cautioning against wasting ammunition, I directed them to push the attack and to get at the enemy with the bayonet. Then I allowed the men the few remaining minutes before zero hour to themselves.

Of those who have waited in positions for the signal to attack, who can explain the feelings or thoughts of a soldier during the last few minutes before a battle? He fixes his bayonet, sees that his rifle is working properly, loads it, turns the safety lock, doing a dozen things, automatically from force of training. Just a faint trace of nervousness. Still there is a great deal of 'kidding' among the men. One young soldier drew the edge of his bayonet back and forth across the sole of his shoe just as a man would strop a razor. His 'Buddy' asked, "What are you going to do, shave the Kaiser?" The reply was, "Just preparing for a painless operation on my friend 'Fritz'." Another pair of habitual gamblers were trying to make bets on each other as to who would get wounded first. Never a thought of themselves, or of what might be their individual fate; no patriotic 'ballyhoo' as to why they were in France or the enemy in front of them. A few of us were thinking of a wife and children, hoping if it was our turn to 'GO WEST,' that the folks back home would not feel too badly.

During this short interval the hands of my watch moved to 6.50, to 6.55, then to 6.56. When the smoke bombs fell on the enemy line at 6.59 the platoon commanders were signalled to get ready. Watching the second-hand make the last trip around, as the minute-hand reached the hour I gave the signal to attack. Company B 'Goes over the top.' We are in it at last and hell breaks loose. Since that day as a commander of other companies, battalions and various units never have I seen a finer body of men. They went at the task as calmly, and under perfect control, as if they had been on a drill field.

While waiting for the attack, the company was under cover of a rise of ground on the west edge of the ravine. When the signal was given the company executed a side-slipping movement to the right front, extending at double time as they came out from under cover. This movement was made without the loss of a single man. After the battle the company officers were complimented by the officers of the 3rd Battalion who were on the hills in rear of us, in reserve, and in position to observe the movement. Entering the ravine we were greeted with a burst of fire from machine guns and rifles that was like the heat from a blast-furnace door. About five minutes after the enemy saw us his artillery came down and we caught everything he threw. As one 'wag' said, "They even threw the rolling kitchen, but they took the 'chow' out before throwing it."

In order that my readers will understand exactly what we were up against and the very evident lack of intelligent preparation for such an attack as this, let us leave the actual battle for a moment and call your attention to a few things that were very apparent the minute we stepped into the ravine.

The distance from the entrance of the ravine to the enemy barbed wire was about 900 or 1000 meters from where we started the attack. Now, the verbal orders of the battalion commander stated that a twelve-hour preparation fire would be laid

on the enemy lines, starting at 19 o'clock (7 P.M.) the previous
night, and during the attack would precede us in the nature of
standing barrages on the enemy wire and trenches. Our artillery fire during that night was hardly noticeable. About 6.45
on the morning of the battle there was some slight increase of
fire from our supporting artillery, a very thin curtain, having
no effect on the enemy position or wire. Friend 'Fritz' must
have thought we were afraid of getting the guns dirty. Altogether the artillery was of no use to us; without it we might,
by moving rapidly, have surprised him. With it he had a warning and 'Jerry' never missed a warning; he was too suspicious.

Another point; our artillery falling on the enemy position,
at the head of the ravine, was lifted, and placed on their rear
area at the same moment that we entered the ravine, approximately 1000 meters away. Advancing according to the prescribed schedule, 100 meters in three minutes, it would have
taken us approximately one-half hour to reach the enemy wire,
even if we could have advanced without interference. A barrage, such as we were told we would get on this occasion, is laid
on a position preceding and during the early stages of an attack
to keep the enemy down and to prevent him from effectually
firing on the advancing infantry; also to break down his defenses and to blast openings through his wire for the attacking
infantry. Our troops in a well planned attack would be close
enough behind this friendly barrage so that when the artillery
fire lifted the attacking infantry could rush the enemy line before they recovered their firing positions. When properly timed,
and with co-operation between the artillery and infantry, this
type of attack has proven very successful. Whoever prepared
the schedule for this attack by the 114th Infantry left Company
B about 1000 meters away from the enemy line when the barrage lifted. It allowed the enemy time to complete his breakfast, smoke his pipe, and still be in the firing trenches in ample
time to receive us, and to mow us down at his own sweet
pleasure from the top of a hill. He surely did a most thorough
job.

The advance continued according to schedule until about

three hundred yards in a hill on our right came into our line of advance. I ordered Lieutenant Elms with the third platoon to take it. The platoon advanced up the hill taking advantage of such cover as was available, the 4th platoon following in support. The 2nd platoon was halted in shell holes in the low ground on the left and assisted the 3rd platoon advance by fire on the enemy position. The platoons, meeting small resistance, swept up the hill and over it with a rush. About 75 yards over the top of the hill the two attacking platoons halted until the 1st and 2nd platoons reached the same general line, when the whole company resumed their attack formation and continued the advance. The enemy fire across the top of the captured hill was terrific, mostly from machine guns in *Bois de Moirey* on our right in front of the Second Battalion position. The infantry, German, in our front dropped back as we advanced. The capture of this hill was important, assisting as it did our Second Battalion, also bringing part of Company B on nearly a level with the enemy. I accompanied the 3rd platoon in this attack, allowing the action to be handled by the platoon commander, Lieutenant Elms, until he had gained the top of the hill. The Second Battalion was suffering heavily from *Bois de Moirey,* and were advancing more slowly than Company B. It was necessary for me to keep close check on the compass direction, as ordered by the battalion commander, so that the company would not get over too far to the right, and thus lose contact with Company A on my left, or mask the fire of Company E on the right.

By this time the company was about half way up the ravine and our casualties were becoming heavy. Still we were unable to see but very little of the enemy. What we saw were merely a few individual soldiers usually running from one position to another. The fire was mostly machine guns into our right, with some sniping from high ground in rear of the enemy trenches. This rifle fire was deadly accurate and from positions so well hidden that we were unable to locate them. A number of the best shots in the company had been detailed to watch especially for enemy snipers and attend to them alone, but the enemy was so well camouflaged, usually in trees, that my snipers on low ground were unable to have much effect on them. Most of the casualties in the ravine were from shrapnel fired by German artillery directly in front of us, evidently located near *Bois de Ormont.* You will note from this description that Company B was being cut to pieces by artillery from the front, machine guns from the right and snipers in front and on the right. The only weapons we had to fight this slaughter with was pistols, rifles and automatic rifles (Chauchat) in the hands of my own men. We received absolutely no additional fire power from our supporting artillery, machine guns, 37 m.m. guns, trench mortars or other auxiliary weapons. WHY? WHO WAS RESPONSIBLE? In emphasizing what Company B was going through, remember that another outfit, Company D, following us in support was getting the same medicine and losing men about as rapidly as we were in that damned ravine. The 1st platoon was ordered from local support to the left, up the hillside to extend the line which was thinning out from casualties.

Written messages were being sent by runner to the battalion commander, but the runners were not getting back. After the battle it was learned that most of the runners delivered the messages but were killed or wounded trying to rejoin their company. Verbal messages were being carried back by the wounded non-commissioned officers who were able to walk. They were instructed to stop at battalion headquarters and to explain conditions. Several days after the battle I was informed that my messages had not reached the battalion P.C., yet a couple of months after the ending of hostilities these messages were found among the records of the 1st Battalion.

Some time about 9.30 a message was received from the battalion P.C., stating that two machine guns and their crews were on their way up to our assistance. Whoever sent those men out either failed to understand the proper use of machine guns or else did not know the ground we were fighting over. Sending machine guns out into that ravine to assist advancing infantry was madness. All credit to these gunners, they did their very best to reach us. I saw them coming up the ravine in the face of certain death trying to reach their comrades in the infantry. It was a useless sacrifice; they were wiped out before even reaching our position. They might have been some good to us if placed on the high ground in our rear or on the flanks. What we needed there was well-placed artillery fire or better still a couple of one-pounders to blow out the enemy machine-gun nests. The manner in which this attack was being handled must have made the enemy think he was fighting a 'bunch' of imbeciles. A French officer, a few days after the fight, placed a finger on his forehead and remarked "Votre malade ici," indicating that we were sick in the head—crazy making such an attack.

Undoubtedly I shall be censured for criticizing. The question will probably be asked, "Did he consider himself better qualified or that he knew more about the battle than his superior officers?" For the sake of argument let us grant that the higher officer probably knew more about what we were supposed to do, up to the time we entered the ravine. Once in there and the attack begun, there was no one for me to look to for advice. It was necessary to depend on my own judgment. From personal contact with conditions as they developed during the fight, I was more familiar with actual facts and was not applying theoretical strategy as developed from a map. At no time during this operation did any officer senior to me, or any staff officer, come into the ravine to inquire about the actual conditions. There was not a soul of higher rank than I who knew what was happening or how the situation was being handled. The responsibility was mine and there was no desire to shirk it. No attention was being paid to messages, written or verbal, that were being sent back; requests for assistance were being ignored. How the various headquarters were making decisions is beyond my humble ability to understand, even at this late date.

Company A, on our left, was delayed for a time at the enemy trenches, finally breaking through and continuing the advance. Our efforts to maintain liaison with them failed; the ground between us was across an open, fire-swept field and runners were unable to get to them. Private Alston Miller, one of my runners, was severely wounded in the neck and shoulder by machine-gun fire while making an attempt to get a message to Captain Rohrbach. Miller reported back unable to get through. He was then ordered to the dressing station and instructed to stop at battalion P.C. and report our position and conditions to the commanding officer; also to request that our supporting artillery blast the wire entanglements in front of us; and to ask that our one-pounders be sent up to knock out the machine-gun nests that were tearing the right flank to pieces. This was but another effort to have the battalion commander do something to support the company. It was being annihilated piecemeal, but as usual nothing was done about it.

By this time the casualties had become so heavy that every man of Company B was on one thin line and the advance became one of infiltration, each man getting forward from shell hole to shell hole, or from bush to tree stump, or any other cover available. All attempt to maintain a scheduled advance had passed. Nothing but pure unadulterated grit kept the men going.

It is to the credit of every soldier in Company B that they kept going forward under such punishment until the enemy barbed wire was reached.

The non-commissioned officers were being hit hard. In efforts to lead their men into striking distance of the enemy they were being killed or wounded very fast. After the lieutenants and sergeants became casualties it was not unusual for some young corporal to find himself in command of his platoon, or what was left of it, and all credit to them, they did a good job in carrying on the attack. Citing acts of bravery among the men of the company it is a difficult task and rather than slight even one man it is better not to mention any special deeds.

Lieutenant Chester Elms was wounded in the jaw and shoulder shortly before reaching the enemy wire. Even when directed to the rear by Lieutenant Heinzmann, Elms kept on fighting until ordered back the second time. Then gathering up a number of the wounded who were able to walk, he had them assist other men who were unable to get back alone to the dressing stations.

Lieutenant Robert L. Mitchell was shot by a sniper and died about 100 yards in front of the German position. Mitchell was a good officer, leading his men up that ravine, never thinking of himself, always of his men. When shot he was directly in front of me cautioning his platoon to take cover, his arm extended giving a signal to move to the left, out of machine-gun fire. A sniper got him before he could save himself. The death of Lieutenant Mitchell was regretted by every man in the company. Although it had been our privilege to know him only a few days, he having joined the company the previous Sunday night, in that short time he had shown himself to be a very capable officer.

The fighting over the last 100 meters in the ravine was something those who were in it will never forget. And those who were not in there cannot imagine the conditions. I realized that the only way to save the few survivors left in that hole was to get them up forward a short distance under the protection of a slight bluff directly in front of the enemy wire, which would afford us some cover from direct rifle or machine-gun fire, and then hold on.

During the morning we saw the enemy was preparing to counter-attack from their position on our right. Immediately a runner was sent back to the battalion with this information and a request for a barrage to be placed in front of us. A message was received from Heinzmann, in command of the survivors of the 3rd and 4th Platoons, also reporting the anticipated counter-attack. He was making preparations to break it up. Whether this attack would be directed at us or at the Second Battalion was, for the moment, a question. Company B was the most advanced unit; Company E was slowly fighting its way up. The attack was not launched at us but at our Second Battalion, possibly with the intention of driving Company E back and then sweeping in behind us. Lieutenant Heinzmann and his men did mighty good work with their rifles and caused the enemy severe losses during the attack. It was one occasion my company had to get in some effective rifle fire on the enemy. The request for a protective barrage in front of our lines was again ignored.

This counter attack succeeded in driving back the Second Battalion, making matters even worse for Company B, leaving my right flank completely up in the air, with no protection. So far as was known at the time only Company E had been driven back. Again the liaison system failed. At no time during the remainder of the day did our battalion or any other source inform me that the troops on my right had dropped back. This was a serious position for us, which the enemy was quick to recognize. He lashed us from the woods on the right with all the fire power he had. Up to this time we had been losing most of the men down in the ravine, among the first and second platoons; now we were getting it from the flank into the third and fourth platoons. Troops will stand considerable fire from the front but when caught in a flanking fire, they generally run. It was a tough spot to hold, nothing to fight back with but rifles. We were unable to charge the enemy position. It was out of my sector in front of a neighboring battalion. To get over there would have meant blanketing their fire. It was simply cold-blooded annihilation and we were left out there to take it and like it all the rest of the day.

While on this point would it be improper to ask a few questions?

1st. When the Second Battalion fell back, why was Company B not notified so that our right flank could be protected?

2nd. When the First Battalion Commander knew that the troops on our right had fallen back, why did he not put in a combat liaison group between Company E and Company B?

3rd. Why were the one-pounders, trench mortars, or machine guns not put on the right flank, to at least keep 'Jerry's' machine guns from so effectively using Company B for a target?

Asking questions does not bring back our dead. The answer is plain enough. Higher authority did not know what to do and furthermore, were too busy keeping their own hides out of danger to pay any attention to what was happening to B Company.

Now it was simply a case of hang on.  It was impossible to get through the thick entangling mass of enemy barbed wire; our supporting artillery had failed to make any breaches in it. Time and again efforts were made to cut an opening in the wire, the men using their small hand wire-cutters.  Each attempt resulted in exactly the same thing, nothing but the loss of more men.  Several times men were trying to make an opening, every rifle and automatic rifle in their platoons was firing at the enemy position, in an effort to keep his fire down until these men could cut through the wire.  Again the same results, a burst of machine-gun fire, followed by a few artillery shells, and it was all over—more casualties as a result of these efforts. After that I decided any attempt to get through the wire in daylight was out of the question.  The only thing left was to hold the ground we had gained until darkness fell and then endeavor to continue the advance by moving to the right and possibly around the wire; or we might find an opening.

Another message was sent back to the battalion commander stating that every time we showed a head we were losing, of my intention to hold the position until darkness, or else for him to have our artillery break up this wire and make an opening for us to continue the advance.  And also to shell the machine-gun nests in *Bois de Moirey* which were tearing the company to pieces from that point.  I requested some word from him as to plans for our assistance.  I never received any answer to this message.

This was but another of the many instances of lack of cooperation between higher command and the units on the line. The whole attack, as far as Company B was concerned, was very severely lacking in proper artillery and auxiliary weapons support.  The German artillery and machine-gun support to their troops was perfect.  Every time we made a move, no matter how small, we were on the receiving end of a "hail of scrap iron."  During the late afternoon the action developed into a sniper's battle, both sides merely holding their own positions and keeping the enemy in theirs, causing each other as many casualties as possible.

As our casualties increased, so also increased the difficulties of getting the wounded to the rear. Many of the litter-bearers had been wounded or killed in their efforts to get the wounded to the dressing stations. The wounded who had not been moved were calling for water and screaming with pain. Additional men could not be spared to help them. Every man able to fire a rifle was needed on the line. During the afternoon, in all messages sent back aid for the wounded was requested. Even these were ignored. It was impossible to get out the wounded at the head of the ravine. The only thing we could do was to move them out of direct fire. Even then we were unable to move all of them. The battalion stretcher-bearers were having a hard time getting to our position.

About 4 o'clock in the afternoon, in a conversation with Lieutenant Heinzmann, I explained to him the seriousness of the situation, also of the efforts that had been made to get in touch with the battalion commander by runners and walking wounded, but that battalion headquarters was paying no attention to my messages. Furthermore our losses were very heavy and if the casualties continued at the present rate we would have but a few men left by nightfall.

After discussing the situation for a few minutes Heinzmann offered to make an effort to get back to the battalion P.C. and put the situation squarely up to the major, in an effort to get assistance for us so that we could advance out of the trap we were now in, and be able to do something under cover of darkness. I said to the lieutenant: "It is my place, as the company commander, to stay with the outfit as long as there are men on the line, so I cannot leave here. I will not order you to make the attempt. You understand that you are taking your life in your hands. The snipers are covering the ravine, but you may be able to make the battalion commander understand conditions up here and possibly get the support that is badly needed." After a little further conversation we shook hands and parted. We have spoken about this occasion many times after the war, and it was often said that neither one of us at the parting ever expected to see the other alive again. Death was very close. The lieutenant got through all right, although he had a bullet-hole through his gas-mask. Probably he was not intended to be shot; perhaps he will be hung.

The battle continued, with 'beaucoup' artillery, one-pounders and minnewerfers from 'Fritz.' The damned 'whiz-bangs' would sail over and break in back of us. After that we would get a dose of gas shells; then into the bushes with his one-pounders. 'Jerry' sure made life a misery for us that day. About half an hour after Heinzmann left me a runner arrived from the battalion P.C. with a message stating: "The Brigade Commander insists that the position be held. A company is being sent up to your assistance."

For a short time that made me feel better. I was almost ready to forgive them for the apparent neglect during the earlier part of the battle. This was only the second message that had reached me all day; the first one stating that machine guns were coming up, they never reached the line; however, we had seen them trying to get through. In this case we were again due for disappointment; if a supporting company was ordered to report it never reached our position. At no time during the entire day did any unit, large or small, report to me or get near us. Company D that had followed us into the attack as a support company, on their own responsibility, had moved over to the left of our line in an effort to close the gap between Company A and Company B, but had been almost wiped out in the attempt.

About 18.30 o'clock (6.30 P.M.) with evening coming on and nothing done to help us through this muddle, it became very evident that we were not to receive any assistance from the battalion P.C. No word had been received about Lieutenant Heinzmann. The only conclusion was that he was a casualty somewhere behind, or if he had reached battalion headquarters he was unable to get any assistance for us. I decided to take things into my own hands and fight this 'little bit of war' in our own way, with the limited number of men still able to fight; as near as I could estimate, there were about 40 all told. The plan was to move to the right under cover of darkness on the possibility of making our way through the wire or around it. As for leaving a gap in the line, it could not be any worse than it was at the moment. There already existed a gap between us and Company A on our left, they were in the western edge of *Bois de Ormont*. Company E on our right about three hundred meters in rear of us and somewhat to the right, causing another gap. Company B was stuck out there like a sore thumb.

If successful in this attempt we might be able to join up with the rest of our battalion before morning. If unsuccessful? Well! Who cared? It was also possible that during the night some one in authority back at headquarters might wake up to the fact that there should be another company in the 114th Infantry and would make some effort to find out what had become of B Company—if we were all dead or captured. During the day orders of the battalion commander had been obeyed implicity; now, however, I felt that something must be done, and done quickly, as the darkness that would cover any movement we might make would also make matters worse for us in the position we were now holding with a limited number of men stretched out over about 300 meters. The enemy, knowing exactly where we were, would undoubtedly attack in an effort to wipe us out or capture us.

At this time the company post of command was in a 'fox hole' on the high ground on our right, and about where the center of the line should have been. I had taken the men out of the ravine, and under command of the surviving sergeants and corporals, had established small combat groups across the sector, making a thin line of resistance that could not have stopped even a local counter-attack by the enemy. There were no supporting troops between us and our battalion headquarters, and any determined enemy attack would have compelled these few men of Company B to fall back, thereby splitting our line wide open.

Serious as the situation was then, I have 'chuckled' many times since at the thought of our being driven back and the enemy suddenly appearing at the battalion dugout. Many a 'stout heart' would have stopped beating right then and there.

Does this prove the contention that the seriousness of the situation was not realized? Charity compels me to believe that failure to understand conditions was responsible for this lack of support. It would be too horrible to think we were being deliberately used as sacrifice troops.

Since the ending of the war statements have appeared that units from the 66th French Infantry were sent in to fill the gap between Company B and the Second Battalion. Such a statement is positively without foundation. There were no troops on our right, except Company E, 114th Infantry, which as previously stated was about 300 meters to our rear. As for any French soldiers being there, the only ones seen then or later were dead ones, who evidently had been killed several days before this attack. From personal experience the closest any men of the 66th French Infantry ever came to us was back in the *Ravin de Coassinvaux,* where our battalion P.C. was located. Their companies were somewhere in the vicinity of *Ormont Farm,* to our left front.

Shortly before dark I ordered the First Sergeant and the gas sergeant to get the organization together near the company P.C. While they were gone another survey of the enemy position in front of us was made and I could see no evidence of their trenches being occupied. This led to the belief that the position opposite had been evacuated, the enemy having fallen back and holding us principally with machine-gun fire from *Bois de Ormont* and *Bois de Moirey,* and the unbroken wire in front of us. This further convinced me that if it were possible to get around this wire our advance could be continued.

About twenty minutes later the first sergeant reported the company assembled. I looked them over and counted *thirteen men.* Were my eyes deceiving me—thirteen men and myself? All that was left of 153 men and five officers who had gone into action twelve hours earlier, with the exception of a few runners and Lieutenant Heinzmann back at battalion headquarters.

To explain my feelings at the moment is impossible. I have

never felt more alone at any time in my life; what happened to me from then on was of no consequence, death or wounds could not have been worse. In fact death would have been a relief. Picture if you can that terrible ravine, full of our own 'buddies,' wounded, dying and dead. Your boys. All that was left of that fine organization, Company B, was 14 of us. Many long, weary months had been spent in training these men so that when they went into battle they would at least have an even chance for their lives. Now all to be seen was death and desolation, and to hear the awful cries of the wounded, for whom we could do nothing. All of this was the result of what? A few distasteful words will answer the question — COWARDICE — INCOMPETENCY — and SOCIAL-POLITICAL INTERFERENCE. All of which had played its part and was responsible for placing and retaining in command officers who lacked the knowledge, intelligence and experience necessary to properly command combat troops. All of this flashed across my mind as though stricken with a club. I must have gone mad. Ordering the men to follow me I started for the rear, with some insane idea of finding the responsible officers and showing them the results of their blundering. I was in a good frame of mind to commit murder. Simply went 'loco.'

After starting for the rear I recall nothing, until the following morning, except the cries of the wounded. Even now, oftentimes in my sleep, those cries are still heard. Shortly after daybreak I awoke and found myself lying in a dugout with Heinzmann and the survivors of the company nearby. These men have often told me since that coming out of the ravine I acted like a maniac, raving about this utterly useless waste of life, the men partly carrying and dragging me out. Apparently they were afraid I would do damage to some people or to myself and to prevent this removed my trench-knife and revolver. When the party reached the point from which we had made the jump-off in the morning they met Heinzmann on his way back to the lines, alone. He took charge of the men and had me put into a dugout under the care of the medical officer, who kept me 'doped' all night. Every time I woke up they gave me more sedatives. They tell me that all through the night I raved about the slaughter, and on several occasions tried to leave the dugout and to get to the battalion P.C.

Permit me to again quote from Colonel Palmer's work, OUR GREATEST BATTLE (Dodd, Mead & Co.):

"For mistakes the infantry must suffer. It is the infantry which always pays the price, in blood, for all mistakes; the transfer of an officer to Blois or the demotion of a general officer would not bring back their dead."

Another quotation, read some years ago, by an author unknown to me is appropriate as fitting into my experience on this occasion:

"For always on the leader's heart must fall
The sharpest lash, the wounds that cannot heal,
To them is given the wormwood and the gall
Of hurling life against unhuman steel."

To me had been given the "wormwood and the gall" of hurling my company against "unhuman steel" in the form of artillery and machine-gun fire. If every ranking officer of the 114th Infantry had been relieved, or demoted, it could not correct the horrible mistake of this attack. Colonel Brown had come into command of the regiment too late to make the changes necessary to give us competent leadership.

In the early morning, on the 13th, I managed to get some degree of self-control, except for the memory of the previous day. No matter how I tried to drive the picture from my mind it was always there. My head felt as though a riveting machine was pounding on it all the time. Yet I realized the necessity of getting control of myself, if only for the sake of the few men of the company who were still alive. It was peculiar, but at the moment I was in exactly the same situation as one year before, October 13, 1917, at the Depot Brigade in Camp McClellan—a captain of the United States Army without a company. But how differently the company had been taken from me. In Alabama it was easy to forget, that was only injured pride, but out here something deeper had been hurt, something that never again would allow me to forget, something that for the remainder of my life was to be a horrible nightmare, ever present, waking or sleeping. Citations for efficiency, decorations for gallantry in action came to me later, but I would gladly have foregone these honors to have saved the men under my command from this unwarranted annihilation. No matter what my feelings were there still was a job to be done, above all else was the task of 'carrying on,' the war had to be won at any cost. To quit now would be quitting on our comrades who had 'gone west.'

Lieutenant Heinzmann was almost as wild as I. He was continually cursing battalion headquarters and raving about the incompetency he had found there. Heinzmann told me then, and has repeated the same thing many times since, that when he arrived at the battalion P.C. the previous afternoon, he was unable to get any intelligent action or support. When he explained conditions facing Company B the only satisfaction he could get was, "the Brigade insists that the line be held." When he asked for a supporting company to take up and help us hold the line, he was told to go and get a company from our reserves, 3rd Battalion, 114th. This Heinzmann endeavored to do, but the company he was ordered to take up was so badly disorganized, casualties among its men and their officers having been evacuated, he was unable to get any support there. Reporting these conditions back to the battalion P.C. he was then told to take some machine gunners up, but he could not find these men. Many times since the war we have talked over this situation and from his continued repetition of the same story it is quite evident there was a severe lack of organization at the P.C. Heinzmann has often remarked that it appeared to be a madhouse with no directing head. We could whip the German and Austrian armies in front of us, but we could not lick the enemy in front and American inefficiency in our rear. The enemy in front we could reasonably expect to follow certain general rules; from the rear we never knew what to expect, it was far more dangerous than the front.

About six o'clock I told Heinzmann that I was going to the battalion P.C. and for him to remain with the men, to keep them under cover until I returned, or until he received other orders. What the results would be when I met the battalion commander was hard to foretell. In my present state of mind anything might happen. The only thing for me to do was try and keep cool and await developments. One thing fully determined on was that, no matter what the consequences to me personally, I would not sacrifice any more lives in that ravine under the existing leadership; before making any further attack I intended to carry this matter to the regimental commander, explaining what we were up against and my lack of confidence in the commanding officer of the battalion. If the colonel would then assume the responsibility for results there would be but one course left—walk out in front, in the open, and let the enemy gunners finish what they had started the day before.

The meeting with the battalion commander would have been laughable if the conditions had not been so pathetic. Heinzmann's description of his visit the previous day was more than verified. In the intervening space of time there had been no improvement. As I entered the dugout the first salutation was: "Captain Reddan, you will have to go back to the line, headquarters insists that the position be held." Never any question as to the number of men left in the company to hold the line with; no thought of the lives already wasted, not even a suggestion of the impossibility of holding that particular spot or even attacking from a different position with proper support. No, according to his asinine orders I was to take the few men left and go right back again, under the same conditions and to the same position. What in the name of common sense, did he suppose I withdrew the men from the line for. A rest? Go back—for what? Complete annihilation? Not if I had anything to do with it. The only thing on his mind at the moment was fear that the general would be displeased because we were unable to do the impossible—whip artillery and machine guns, bare-handed and alone, coupled with his inefficiency. At the moment, with all I knew of the ravine, nothing would have pleased me more than to have been the guide for some higher officers on a trip up to that line. I would have been perfectly willing to take my chances, but unfortunately you cannot get some officers into those sorts of places.

When informed that we would have to go back in again I just 'blew up,' all the suffering and bitterness in me surely came out as I expressed my opinion: "I obeyed your orders yesterday, in opposition to my own judgment. You sent us into the attack and then left us without support, even neglecting to answer the messages sent down to you by runners and walking wounded. You did not know what was in front of us, or if you did, then the information was not given to me. You made no effort to find out how we were progressing and you made no attempt to see conditions for yourself. If any further attack is to be made by Company B give me another company to fill our ranks and I will make the attack in my own way but you must keep your hands off. You made a mess of things yesterday and I will take no more orders from you until the regimental commander is acquainted with the conditions. I am going down to the regimental P.C." To say it was hot in that dugout would be putting it mildly, there were fireworks in there; the only intelligent thing to be gotten from him was: "You must go back and hold the line, the general insists that we hold." I repeat, the Battalion Commander was afraid of the General and lacked the back-bone to protect the troops under his command. Later, as a battalion commander and even as a company commander there were occasions on which I took exception to orders of Brigadier General Upton, and always found that if the objections were reasonable or the orders not workable, as in this case, the General would listen and give us co-operation. The Major then ordered me not to go to the regimental P.C. I insisted that despite his objections I was going so that the Colonel would understand exactly the situation we had been facing. I had no intention of being made the 'goat' in any inquiry that might be made at a later date.

Turning to leave the dugout I found Lieutenant Heinzmann standing at the foot of the steps. When I asked what he was doing there instead of with the company as ordered he replied: "I thought I had better follow you in case you needed any help." Loyalty of the highest order. I was always sure of the whole-hearted support of this officer, under any and all circumstances. Again directing him to take charge of the company, and picking a couple of runners as guides we started for the regimental headquarters.

After a short distance one of the guides disappeared; whether he was killed or simply 'ducked' I never knew. The enemy artillery was covering the area pretty thoroughly and it required considerable dodging to keep out of the shelled area. Still in a somewhat dazed condition I failed at the time to appreciate the danger. Trying to think straight was a hard task; the only thing I could visualize was the slaughter of the previous day; a pain in my head was driving me almost crazy. My eyes, having been burnt with gas, were giving considerable trouble, making it hard to see where I was going.

Near the *Ravin d' Haumont,* shortly before reaching regimental headquarters, I saw smoke and in a subconscious way knew that smoke meant fire and fire meant food. Suddenly I realized that I was hungry. The only food tasted in the preceding 40 hours was a couple of pieces of hard-tack and a few sips of water. Keeping the smoke in sight I entered the ravine. It was a shambles. A number of rolling kitchens, water carts and escort wagons, with all their animals had been caught in a barrage the previous day, only a very few having escaped destruction. The rolling stock was demolished, dead animals and dead men lying all around. An effort had been made to get the kitchens and supplies closer to the line so that hot food could be sent to the troops. Spotted by enemy artillery observers a blanket of fire was promptly put down on the wagon train. It is easy to imagine conditions among those animals when the fire dropped on them.

Fortunately all of the kitchens had not been destroyed. Spotting one drawn close up to the side of the ravine that had escaped destruction, I had the pleasure of finding a soldier friend there, a mess-sergeant of the 111 M.G. Battalion, who immediately handed me a cup of coffee, then fried some steak and soon I was enjoying a steak sandwich that, undoubtedly, was the best I ever ate. It may have been that the sergeant sliced a piece off one of the horses lying there, but no matter it tasted like chicken and I am still grateful to the sergeant for his generosity.

While eating there was an opportunity to note conditions in the ravine; the sergeant told me it was 'hell' in there when the 'Jerrys' opened up. The only reason he escaped was that being near the side closest to the enemy guns, he missed the first blast and had an opportunity to get his kitchen under cover at the side in a small dead spot. The meal finished, which seemed to put new life in me, we continued the trip to headquarters.

This whole area was certainly getting their share of the fire-works. Since the end of the war I have read the German sched-ule of artillery fire, for the 12th and 13th of October and it shows their fire was exceptionally heavy on this sector. Many regiments of artillery were brought up from reserve and two artillery regiments transferred from the west of the *Meuse River* to the east side to assist in breaking up the attack of the 29th Division.

Arriving at the 114th P.C., at *Haumont-pres-Samogneux,* I went to the dressing station to have my eyes attended to. The doctors wanted to send me back to the base hospital but I informed them that I would not go back and they finally treated my eyes after which I felt better.

Conditions in the vicinity of the headquarters were not good, too many men loitering about. The stairs leading down to the P.C. were lined with men seeking shelter from the artillery; the regimental band and details of all kinds were without leader-ship, with apparently nothing to do but keep out of the fire. Evidently they were left out there to take care of themselves the best way possible; there did not appear to be anyone worry-ing about their being killed. Major McGuire, the regimental surgeon, was endeavoring to have a detail of men from one of the division ambulance companies go up front and help to evacuate their wounded comrades. The major asked me to talk to the sanitary men. I did explain the conditions to them, told them about the wounded waiting to be removed to the hospitals and the necessity of getting them out of the shell-fire. I had been talking to one of the sergeants, but was unable to make any impression on him. The only answer from him was, "My orders are not to go farther forward than the regimental dressing station." There was no use talking to that fellow, he was taking advantage of orders to cover up his own fear. I walked away from there; my frame of mind would not permit any arguments, too liable to explode at any moment to the disadvantage of the sergeant.

Headquarters of the 114th Infantry was in a dug-out well under ground, occupied also by some French headquarters, probably the 66th Infantry. There were a number of French officers and men in and around the place. Finally locating Colonel Brown I reported to him. The conversation with the regimental commander was very interesting, his attitude being exactly the opposite of my battalion commander. The colonel's first question was; "In heaven's name, Captain, what happened yesterday?" I explained the situation to him, how the company had been annihilated and in my opinion the fault lay at battalion headquarters, that most decidedly something was lacking at that point. Continuing I explained that prior to the 'jump off' my information was that "The enemy was holding the line very lightly," when as a matter of fact the enemy had orders to hold the position at all cost; also that apparently the battalion commander was lacking in knowledge of the conditions facing us, that once the attack started we had been left to our own resources, no attention being paid to the messages sent back explaining conditions and information of the enemy; that our artillery and auxiliary weapon support was of no value; my requests for support from these weapons failed to bring results, also that requests for infantry support, to help hold the ground gained, were ignored. I added that only two messages had been received during the day. I informed the Colonel that the survivors of Company B were ready to make another attempt if the regimental commander would assign replacements to fill up the losses in the company. If this plan was acceptable to him, permission was requested to make the attack in my own way, without interference from the battalion in whom confidence was lacking. Under such conditions I felt success was reasonably sure.

Colonel Brown's information from the 1st Battalion appeared very meagre, particularly in reference to what had transpired and the position held by the troops on the line. I went over the maps with him and showed the location of Company A, the position we had been trapped in, the points from which we had been getting the heaviest fire and the reason we had been unable to reach *Bois de Ormont*. I showed him the line reached by Company E at the time the enemy launched the counter-attack and the position they now held. The Colonel asked a number of questions, among them, what I had done, what the battalion had done to support me, etc. He indicated that he was satisfied with the effort made by Company B. At no time did Colonel Brown appear to be dissatisfied with my work or the work of the men under my command. After some further discussion of conditions he directed me to go back to the company and await orders that I would receive from him during the day, as to his desires. He sympathized with Company B for having taken terrific punishment but was satisfied they had done everything possible to accomplish the mission assigned to them.

\*　　\*　　\*　　\*　　\*　　\*　　\*

Before continuing the narration let us stop and analyze what had transpired during the operations, even some points that should have been known as much as a year before this attack, if proper attention had been given to lectures and pamphlets provided for our information.

There are quotations from letters of officers, who were in the operations, sent home shortly after the affair and published in daily newspapers at home. Quotations from official reports of United States and German organizations as well as the "His-

1. "Kitchen Mechanics." Mess Sergeant and Cooks of Company B, near Samogneux.

2. SAMOGNEUX-BRABANT Road at Chalk Cliff Dressing Station. MEUSE RIVER and Canal at right.

3. After an Artillery Barrage.

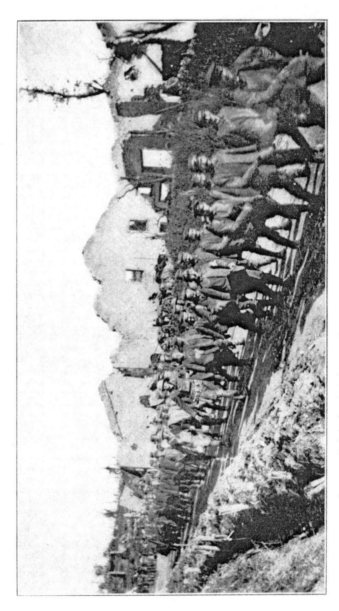

Company B Bringing in Prisoners of War Captured at Bois BELLEU, 26 Oct. 1918

tory of the 29th Division." Also opinions expressed by company officers of the 114th Infantry within a few days after the battle.

In describing this attack it has been given as we developed conditions during the action. These conditions were very much different from those we had been led to expect or look for, as explained in verbal instructions and orders from the commanding officer of the 1st Battalion. Many times since the war ended I have studied the written order of the commanding officer of the 114th Infantry, for this attack, "Field Order No. 11, P. C. Mood, 11 Oct. 18—20 o'clock (8 P.M.), Map: Verdun B. 1/20,000," which apparently was typed an hour or more *after* the 1st battalion officers had received their verbal orders for the attack. There are some discrepancies between the verbal orders we received and the written order. The orders of our battalion commander stated that the 66th French Infantry *would attack* on our left, until such time as the 114th Infantry was in position to connect with the 113th U. S. Infantry, when the French would be pinched out of the line. The written order of the regiment states that "the 114th Infantry will be *assisted by fire* from the 66th French Infantry." There is considerable difference between support by fire and a direct attack, as we were given to expect.

Artillery support was of no practical value. The curtain of fire was too thin, and what little there was of it was placed entirely too far in front of our infantry to be of any value. Brigadier General Upton in his report of the engagement states,

"The artillery preparation for this attack was not as expected and placed too far back on the enemy lines." Our regimental and battalion orders stated

"Artillery preparation will commence at 19 o'clock, (7 P.M.) 11 Oct. 18 and continue throughout the night. During the attack fire will be in the nature of standing barrages on various objectives, the last five minutes of which will be executed by smoke shells in order to show clearly that the barrage will lift and to provide a screen for the advance."

As one of those present at the event my observation is that there was no preparatory fire, or rather it was so weak as to be unnoticeable among the usual desultory firing in a forward area. The only smoke shells that I saw fall were about 1000 yards in front of my company at 6.56 A.M., and continued for five minutes, just as we 'went over the top.' As explained at the beginning of the attack there was no artillery screen for us at any time. The firing throughout the battle was of no use to us, the barbed-wire that eventually stopped Company B's advance did not have any openings made by artillery fire, as it should have had if our supporting artillery had been firing for twelve hours; our artillery fire on the enemy machine gun nests registered absolutely zero.

In every message sent back to the battalion P.C. the location of the company was given, also a request for our artillery to place their fire on the enemy machine gun nests that were tearing our right flank to pieces; in addition a continual request for the artillery to smash the barbed wire that was holding us. In spite of all these messages we were allowed to continue merrily on our way, unaided. The answer to the artillery problem is very simple—shortage of ammunition. Operations Reports of the 29th Division state that Staff Officers of our division were trying to make arrangements with the 33rd U. S. Division and the 18th French Division for additional ammunition, also they were trying to get counter-battery work on the enemy artillery positions. These same officers suggested that all trench mortars, with their ammunition, be sent up to the line to fill out the artillery shortage. All methods brought the same results—NOTHING.

The machine guns assigned to our battalion for this attack were used to support the attack of Company A operating on my left. At no time were any machine guns assigned to Company B so that I could use them as necessary during the engagements. The only guns ever near my position were those wiped out in trying to get to us in the ravine several hours after the attack commenced.

The regimental auxiliary weapons were unable to perform

their usual tasks for various reasons. According to the report of Headquarters Company: No reconnaissance could be made prior to the attack. The Trench Mortar Platoon was unable to support the infantry as an ample supply of ammunition could not be brought forward and the terrain at this point of attack was not suited to the use of this weapon. The 37 m.m. guns were unable to get into action as reconnaissance had not been made, in one case the guns could not fire from the position to which they had been sent, as the low trajectory of the weapons made it dangerous to our own infantry.

In order to have you understand that the men were anxious to get into the battle permit me to recite an incident that took place about 6.30 o'clock, just before we made the attack. While standing in front of the company P.C. Corporal Alfred Greene, of Headquarters Company, came along with a one-pounder gun on his shoulder and asked me to allow him to accompany us during the battle. Knowing that this gun had not been assigned to me I directed the corporal to obey his orders. He pleaded to be allowed to go with Company B. Even though this gun would have been a great help to us in keeping down enemy machine gun fire, and would have saved us considerably, I was compelled to resist Greene's pleadings. Why did this corporal want to go with us? Was it possible that he realized conditions?

Should anyone raise the question, where was the aerial observation? In justice to the one plane that did get over our lines it is only fair to say that he tried to keep in touch with the troops on the ground, but unfortunately every time he came over us he was chased back, while the enemy aeroplanes were continually signaling their batteries our exact position. The enemy had three planes in the air at all times to our one lone machine that was trying to do a little something for us.

Many times I have tried to analyze this battle and find a reason for the heavy loss of life in view of the little material gain made. Each time the same conclusion is reached. The companies, both enlisted men and officers, certainly went at the task with all the vim and vigor they had; how those men kept going in the face of such murderous fire is beyond my understanding. Company B, under the conditions they faced and lack of support, would have been justified in simply 'bolting' to the rear. In spite of the terrific punishment they were receiving they continued the advance, never letting go of a foot of ground once gained until they were stopped by the wire. Then they attempted to do what the artillery should have done —make openings in the wire with small hand wire-cutters. They hung on until almost annihilated; even then they were 'game' to stick it out if so ordered, but I could not give that order. It was too much to ask of them.

Should anyone feel that I am simply expressing my own opinion, permit me to quote from an official report of the German troops opposed to us on this occasion. A Group Order dated October 12th, 1918 states:

"1. An attempt of the enemy to break through at *Moirey,* well prepared by a united artillery action and *carried on with a reckless exposure of the infantry* was, thanks to the unsurpassable stand of the Saxon, Prussian, Wurtemberger and Austro-Hungarian troops, broken down *with severe loss to the enemy.*"

(The enemy above referred to is the 114th U. S. Infantry.)

The same Group Order then continues with instructions for a continuation of the battle on the following day, making additional preparations for defense and ordering additional infantry supports up to their line. It orders up one battalion of the 84th Regiment, Light Infantry; The Landstrum Battalion, Ingolstadt, and the 48th Infantry Regiment. All to cooperate with the 228th Infantry Division and the 32nd Infantry Division of the German army to break up our attack.

There is also entered in the War Diary of the 228th Infantry Division, German, an official supplement from the 32nd Infantry Division, German, received by radio at 11.52 P.M., October 12th, 1918. This supplement gives a very accurate account of our operations, as viewed from the German lines, in this battle:

"The 29th American Division, Infantry, attacked, in dense masses, the narrow strip of the *Volker Position,* between *Moirey Wood* and *Ormont Wood.* In spite of our severe infantry and machine gun fire, the dense masses succeeded in driving through the *Volker Position* and breaking into the *Bois de Moirey.* The enemy, at the same time, attacked the *Ormont Wood* from the north, west and south. One half 2nd Battalion, 177th, pushed forward to the *Volker Position* and forced the enemy back over that. American nests that had held themselves in the *Volker Position* were cleaned out in stubborn hand to hand fights. The enemy suffered extremely heavy losses there. Three hundred dead Americans are lying here and in front of the *Volker Position.*"

The foregoing references to "dense masses attacking the *Volker Position*" and that "one half 2nd Battalion, 177th, pushed through and forced the enemy out" probably refers to the counter-attack against our 2nd Battalion, mentioned during the early stages of the battle. The supplement continues with a further description of the action and the repeated attacks of the 1st Battalion, 114th Infantry, continually being made against their position in *Bois de Ormont,* held by the 3rd Battalion, 177th Infantry. The supplement also states that we "were bringing up numerous reserves from the direction of *Ormont Ferme.*" This probably refers to Companies C and L of our regiment, advancing to reinforce Company A, also to the companies of our 113th who attacked *Bois de Ormont* from the west, when the 66th French Infantry failed to advance according to the schedule of battle, leaving our battalion exposed on the left. This supplement continues with the statement:

"The last reserves (German) of the division, two Pioneer companies, were put into position. . . . The ravines which had principally fed the attack were placed and held under destructive fire throughout the entire day, the *Haumont Ravine* with yellow gas."

The above quotations are but a few extracts from the report of the 32nd German Division. Merely enough to show what the men of the 114th Infantry were 'up against' and to emphasize that they did more than their simple duty. I have quoted from the opinions and reports of American officers, as well as from enemy official reports; now let us see the opinion of an enlisted man of Company B, in a letter to me several years after the end of the war.

"The Heights of the Meuse. They were all of that and more. The powers that be ordered the 114th Infantry to take the *Bois de Ormont* on Hill 360, one of the highest of all and probably the strongest German position in the sector, if not on the whole Western Front. Ordered them to take it in fact, if not in words 'With their bare hands' and they tried and died like the soldiers they were, unafraid. The attack was worthy of the heaviest kind of a twelve hour barrage. With such preparation the regiment would have taken all of their objectives under competent battalion command, is my belief."

There you have the opinion of one of the sergeants of the company, a man whose duties placed him in a position to see many things.

It is hoped that you are not becoming tired of these references. They are submitted as evidence that the criticisms made prior to our entry into the major operations were justified. It was evident what would happen with the type of command, under which we were serving. Other officers knew the conditions but 'kept their mouths shut' at the time, expressing their opinions in letters to the 'folks back home' at the first opportunity. If you have any old copies of local newspapers around the house, read over some of these letters sent home during November and December, 1918. The NEWARK EVENING NEWS and the NEWARK SUNDAY CALL published quotations from many of the letters I sent to my family. The PASSAIC DAILY NEWS quoted from letters of Lieutenant Heinzmann to his wife. On November 25th, 1918, Heinzmann stated "Company B had only 14 men left, and *Ormont* was worse than *Chateau-Thierry* and *St. Mihiel* together." On another occasion one of his letters came near getting him into serious trouble. He criticised the battalion commander for his handling of the attack at *Bois de Ormont.*

On November 27th, 1918, Mayor G. N. Segar of Passaic sent a telegram to U. S. Senator Joseph Frelinghuysen stating:

"From letters received from officers of 114th Infantry. . . . Great loss in killed and wounded due to something miscarried. . . . Please make complete investigation."

The New York and New Jersey papers stated:

"Something went wrong leaving the division without artillery support at *Ormont Woods.*"

This same article carried the pleasant news that I had been killed in this battle. On February 13th, 1919, Captain Fred. Rohrbach, commander of Company A in this battle, made a statement that "Company B was held up by enemy wire at *Ormont Woods.*"

From the time the United States entered the war reports of operations on the various fronts, giving in detail the methods of attack and defense used by the French, British and German armies, were issued to all officers for study and as a guide for future operations. About November 1917 I received a copy of "War Department Document No. 641," issued from Washington, D. C., August 1st, 1917. It was one of those pamphlets marked "Confidential, not to be taken into front line trenches." "Notes on recent operations No. 2." This was a captured German document, issued to their troops explaining the methods to be used in attack and defense. It was reprinted for our information.

Page 33 of the above pamphlet tells of the German operations around *Verdun* from February 21st to April 15th, 1917. There we find names that the 114th Infantry was to become well acquainted with, from personal contact, such names as *Bois de Haumont, Meuse River, Bois de Caures, Forges, Cumieres,* etc. Page 35. "III. Disposition and method of Battalion Attack" Paragraph 2. "Method of Assault Waves" states "The

Assault is not launched until the artillery has completely over-thrown the trenches, destroyed the obstacles, and prevented the defenders from using their arms." Our supporting artillery and auxiliary weapons did none of these things; as a result the 114th Infantry "paid in blood" for the mistake.

It cannot be claimed that the conditions were new. This pamphlet had been in our possession for about a year prior to our entry into this same zone. All instruction by lecture, in addition to study of this and similar pamphlets, had emphasized the impossibility of infantry penetrating unbroken, barbed-wire entanglements while under fire. Certainly the company officers, whose job it would be to lead their men in any attempt to get through such entanglements, knew the useless-ness of the effort. Had the conditions been reversed and the Germans ordered to attack our position, under the same conditions as we attacked theirs, it is not unreasonable to suppose, according to this War Department Document No. 641, that the attack would not have taken place until their artillery had completely "destroyed the obstacles and prevented the defenders from using their arms." Yet the very things that the German Staff forbid their troops to do, the 114th U. S. Infantry, in its superior intelligence, attempted to do. Is it any wonder the Germans called our attack "a reckless exposure of infantry"?

Another point is to be remembered, one that still remains a mystery. Company A was on our left in this attack. As the battle progressed and the resistance in front of them became more determined, two companies of the 113th Infantry were sent into the attack and materially aided them; also Company C of our battalion went in to reinforce Company A. Later Company L, 3rd Battalion, regimental reserve, was ordered to the help of the other two companies. Why did not our bat-talion commander call on the reserve battalion to send at least one company to the assistance of Company B? Could it be possible that the impossibility of penetrating through this wire was realized and he decided not to sacrifice any more troops in a useless effort? If such was the case, why was I not ordered to withdraw or ordered to make the attack from a different angle? No, we were left alone out there until annihilated, as was the company in support of us, Company D, trying their very best to help by protecting gaps in the line, until they too were 'wiped out.' The answer is simple enough; someone higher up did not know what to do.

Company A, with the assistance of these additional troops, by pure grit and under the able leadership of Captain Rohr-bach did get into *Bois de Ormont* and they held their position, under heavy shelling, against repeated counter-attacks by the enemy. Captain Rohrbach would have made a battalion commander in whom we had confidence. Unfortunately ability did not count and as he was not in the "ring," like many others he was "S.O.L."

Here is another fact for consideration. The 114th Infantry was attached to and operating under orders of the 18th French Division and not under control of our own 29th Division commander. Two French regiments, one on the right and another on the left, were to attack with us, and failed. It appears very much as though the 114th U. S. Infantry was left 'holding the bag.' Who was interested in us? To whom could we look for help? Our regiment was the last regiment of the 29th Division to be assigned to action. Major General Morton's lack of confidence in us was again manifest. We were paying the price of political interference. Do you wonder that I object to having my life used as a political football or stepping stone to higher ambitions?

Before closing the account of our small part in the attack on *Ormont*, there is one point in the "History of the 29th Division" page 175, to which objection is taken. The History states:

"The right of the First Battalion likewise was driven back by direct machine gun fire from nests established in the trees, and in concealed emplacements, to a position in line with the Second Battalion."

The right of the First Battalion was Company B and as its

commanding officer I most strenuously deny that the company was ever driven back. As previously stated, after overcoming all resistance and until held up by a mass of intact barbed-wire entanglements, unable to advance, without any intelligent direction, unable to establish contact with battalion headquarters, without support from the artillery, auxiliary weapons or infantry, we were as much alone as if in the middle of the Sahara Desert, with nothing but death facing the few of us who still lived. On my own responsibility, without suggestion or orders from anyone, fully realizing the situation and for which there are no regrets, even now, I finally and reluctantly gave orders to the THIRTEEN survivors of the company to "get out of here."

> COMPANY B, 114th United States Infantry, was NOT driven back at *Bois de Ormont*. It was wiped out on the front line. Annihilated by German fire, yes, but actually sacrificed by American incompetency, cowardice and petty political interference.

While these were the experiences of my own command, the same or similar conditions were experienced by the remainder of the regiment. Many times since the war I have talked with other officers of the outfit, as well as former enlisted men, who were in this little fracas, and they have expressed the same opinions.

Consider these casualties of the 114th Infantry, at *Bois de Ormont:*

|  | Enlisted Men | Officers |
|---|---|---|
| Killed in action | 135 | 6 |
| Wounded | 733 | 23 |
| Missing in action | 105 | — |
| Total | 973 | 29 |

Why continue these quotations? Mention has been made of but a few that are available if anyone cares to search the records. In trying to show conditions, in addition to my own opinion quotations from various sources have been used, so that there will be no thought of bias. I lay no claim to being infallible; I possibly made mistakes. If so they were faults of judgment rather than of the heart; at least I did not uselessly sacrifice the lives of the men under my command. I faced the same hardships and dangers as they. I did not order them into battle and then seek shelter in a dug-out until it was over. I took my chances with the men for better or worse as the case might be. After a battle such as this had been, officers are apt to be criticised and undoubtedly some of the criticism will fall my way; but criticism has more weight coming from someone who was there and knew the conditions. Not as one former officer of the regiment who never went overseas remarked when he heard of the losses: "This would never have happened if I had been in command." These militia soldiers were wonderful tacticians and strategists when fighting a battle at home.

CHAPTER XIII

## "CARRYING ON"

AFTER BOIS DE ORMONT

AFTER my conversation with Colonel Brown I felt better. At least he appeared to realize that Company B had received a severe manhandling, also that we had done our full duty, perhaps even a little more than was reasonable to expect. He also understood my lack of confidence in the battalion commander. What action the Colonel would take in the matter I had no means of knowing. Withdrawing the survivors of the company from the battle lines without authority was a mighty serious matter; under ordinary circumstances it could mean trial by a military court, and conviction would result in severe penalty for me. If an officer under my command had done such a thing I certainly would have preferred charges against him and then pushed the case to the limit. In this case, however, I was convinced that any court of competent military authority would sustain my action. We had obeyed orders until such time as it became painfully plain that our position was untenable without support from the battalion commander who as far as I could see had lost control of the situation.

Leaving the regimental P.C. I met one of our chaplains, Rev. A. N. Smith. Many times since the war the chaplain has recalled that morning and my appearance; he has told me that I was the most disreputable, filthy-looking, wild-eyed man he ever laid eyes upon, spotted with blood as I was from helping the wounded during the fight. My uniform was ripped and torn from trying to get through the barbed wire, I was plastered with mud from dropping into shell-holes, and had not shaved in more than three days. The only part of my equipment in place was my gas-mask and the service pistol at my side where it could be reached in a hurry if necessary. I have often thought of those days and wondered what our friends at home would have thought of us if they could have seen that dirty, filthy, even half-crazy outfit that had so often been complimented on its smart, soldierly appearance on parade, in happier and more peaceful days. We were ragged and dirty, yes, even hungry, and almost dead on our feet from the need of sleep. These men were fighting for you and what they believed to be the just cause of the United States, and they never 'let you down,' not even when almost annihilated. When you feel that taxes are high and are disposed to criticise the veteran, please remember our *Ormont Woods,* and all those other woods of France, where so many thousands of our comrades gave their lives or their health, that you might enjoy the benefits denied to them.

The trip back to Company B was another gruelling trip. The area between the regimental P.C. and the forward lines were thoroughly covered with shrapnel and gas. The enemy shelled all roads and paths or any spot that might be used as a shelter for troops; it became a game between the enemy shells and myself as I tried to figure to be away from the place where the next shell was likely to land. Somebody's prayer must have been with me in reaching the company P.C. without a scratch. On the way up I had gathered together some runners who were also endeavoring to get to the front with a whole skin. With their help a small quantity of food was collected, our old friend 'canned willie,' 'gold fish,' beans and hard tack being the principal items. We also managed to get a water cart through with us. Shortly after the water was taken from the cart it was blown to pieces. The food we brought up with us was carried on two stretchers that had been discarded.

Shortly before rejoining my company in the *Ravine de Coassinvaux,* I met my old companion in misery, Father Michael J. Corr; as usual he was very busy attending to the wounded. The meeting was more in the nature of a re-union, we had not seen each other for several days and the usual rumors had reached both of us that the other had been killed.

We were happy that the rumors were greatly exaggerated and each had escaped without injury. If we had been Frenchmen, instead of Americans, we undoubtedly would have been kissing each other. From the stories told me by the men of the Second Battalion, with whom he had been in the fighting, Chaplain Corr had proved himself to be a real soldier as well as a priest. On one occasion, while giving consolation to a wounded man and holding the soldier in his arms, an enemy sniper again shot the wounded man and killed him. Our Reverend Chaplain had a mighty close call that time.

Upon rejoining the company I found the men in fairly good condition considering what they had gone through, although somewhat bitter against the useless waste of life. They were rested, and after eating some of the food we brought back, were willing to 'tackle' whatever might be assigned to them. The first thing necessary was a complete check of the organization to find out how many of the company were actually fit for duty and what our total casualties had been.

The following is the result of the check and shows the strength of Company B, 114th U. S. Infantry on the morning of October 13th, 1918.

| | | | | |
|---|---|---|---|---|
| Killed in action | 1 officer and | 27 enlisted men—28 | | |
| Wounded in action | 1 " " | 51 " " | | 52 |
| Gassed | | 21 " " | | 21 |
| Shell Shocked | | 2 " " | | 2 |
| * Missing in action | | 6 " " | | 6 |
| Captured | | 1 " " | | 1 |
| Total Casualties | 2 officers and | 108 enlisted men—110 | | |

In addition to the above the morning report showed:

| | Officer | Enlisted Men |
|---|---|---|
| In hospital, previously wounded and sick | | 22 |
| On duty, in kitchen and as guards | | 11 |
| At school or on special duty, etc. | 1 | 10 |
| Total | 1 | 43 |
| Plus Casualties | 2 | 108 |
| Total Ineffectives | 3 | 151 |

* 'Missing in action' undoubtedly killed and later buried by other units.

There were left, available for duty of all kinds, including scouts, runners, etc., 3 officers and 45 enlisted men—all that remained of a company of 6 officers and 196 enlisted men. Deducting the men on duty with the battalion scouts, at the company kitchen, wagon and water cart drivers and details for guard at headquarters, it left the company with exactly 2 officers and 12 enlisted men available for battle duty. It would take some one with greater military ability than I possess to show me how to win battles with a company of that strength.

The regiment was endeavoring to hold the positions gained, although suffering from the German machine gun fire which continued to be very heavy; in fact the enemy placed entire dependency on holding positions upon their machine guns; artillery was smashing the area around the battalion headquarters positions. Our artillery was not very active, being short of ammunition. In no way was it comparable to that of the enemy. The trench mortars and 37 m.m. guns were unable to function, and our machine guns were not getting results. As stated on several previous occasions the men and junior officers were giving their best, taking terrific punishment and still fighting, but somewhere above us there was a lack of understanding. I have thought that the battle of *Bois de Ormont* was handled in much the same manner as a peacetime maneuver in the camps at home; only if an error was made in these maneuvers it was not serious and could be corrected, but in battle errors cost human lives. There is no critique held after a battle; you simply count the dead and wounded and balance them against the gains. If the operation has been handled intelligently there could be no criticism. In my humble opinion our attack at *Ormont* lacked intelligent leadership and coordinated effort. Who was to blame? Are you able to figure it out?

Several hours after rejoining the company an order was received from Colonel Brown directing me to take a detachment consisting of the 12 survivors of Company B in addition to 9 men and one lieutenant from the 1st Battalion scouts, giving me a patrol of one lieutenant and twenty-one men, and make a reconnaissance of our lines from the vicinity of Company A, in the edge of *Bois de Ormont,* then east to our Second Battalion, for the purpose of observing enemy activities that might endanger our weakened position, also to break up any enemy patrols working along the front. The patrol was directed to leave the 1st Battalion P.C. at 22 o'clock (10 P.M) and to remain in 'No man's land' until 3 o'clock the following morning.

At this time I was still under command of the same battalion commander. When the order to take out this patrol was received it was necessary for me to report the fact to him and make arrangements for the additional men from the scouts. Up to this time I had not seen the major since early in the morning, before I went to regimental headquarters. What my reception would be was problematical, but that did not worry me.

Reporting at the battalion P.C. I was received like a long lost brother, as though nothing had happened and with no indication of any disagreement. In fact I was questioned about the position occupied by Company A, there being some dispute as to its exact location. The French had them in one place and reports from Captain Rohrbach gave a different location. After going over the maps as well as the messages received and from my own knowledge of the position of the previous day, I gave my opinion and suggested that I verify the position when out with the patrol later. If the information was required at once I suggested sending Lieutenant William Pickard of the battalion scouts to verify the location. The lieutenant was very capable in this type of work having proved his ability on several previous occasions. This was done and the position of the company established.

During the evening the necessary preparations were made and the patrol ordered to report to me at the battalion P.C., at 9.45 P.M. Then gave the non-commissioned officers their instructions and directed that the patrol get as much rest as possible before the time to leave. As for myself, I could not rest. Every time I closed my eyes that horrible nightmare of the ravine was present, so I spent the time getting my personal effects together and writing a letter home. A soldier never knows what will happen, especially out where we were going.

At the designated hour with the patrol ready to start, I turned to leave the dugout. The major called me back, wrote a message on a slip of paper and handed it to me with the remark, "Good luck to you 'Bill,' this will give you something pleasant to think about while out there." On the slip he handed me was this: "Colonel Brown is assigning you to take command of our 3rd Battalion, tomorrow morning. Success and good luck to 'Major Reddan.' " He informed me that the matter was to be treated as confidential until I received orders from the regimental commander. Peculiar, but the prospects of promotion had no effect at the moment. I was not interested and never gave the subject a second thought at the time.

The detachment worked its way out, over barbed wire, through trenches, in and out of shell holes, through enemy artillery and machine gun fire. Passing many of our comrades who had been killed in the fighting of the two previous days, we finally reached a point opposite the enemy position near the eastern end of *Bois de Ormont;* smaller patrols were sent to the right and left of this point, at which I established a command post for the time being, and from which I could control the sector assigned for the patrol to cover. Nothing of consequence developed other than several brushes with small enemy patrols which were quickly driven off by our men.

In describing the battle of October 12th mention was made of several authorities, stating that French troops filled in the gap between the First and Second Battalions. Again I repeat there were no French troops at this point, except dead ones. This patrol covered the area between the two battalions and we were the only troops in the vicinity.

Little of importance occurred while out there until about 4.30 o'clock, when our supporting artillery commenced shelling the edge of *Bois de Ormont,* the line of fire falling about 250 yards in front of our position, towards the north, working into the woods, then back towards us, then forward again.

This barrage gave a feeling of security until shortly before 3 o'clock, when, just as we were about ready to start back to the battalion P.C., 'Jerry' opened up about three hundred yards in back of us on the area we had to cross to reach 'home.' He was splattering 'scrap-iron' all over the sector. Rather a ticklish spot to be in, between those two fire zones. Gathering the small detachments together we finally weaved our way through the German barrage in single file. Shortly before 4 o'clock we arrived at the P.C., our mission completed, tired, but satisfied that we had been able once more to keep the 'Dutchman' in his hole.

Arriving at Battalion Headquarters I found Lieutenant Heinzmann, who had remained at the P.C. when the patrol started out, had been caught in a shell burst and was in a bad nervous state, delirious and raving about us being out in 'No-man's-land.' I learned that he had been quite anxious about us. When the barrages opened up he became fearful that we would be unable to get back so he decided to go out and look for us. About seventy-five yards from the dugout a shell exploded directly in front of him, throwing him to the ground; in his frame of mind, the exploding shell was the 'last straw.' He had been through too much in the preceding three days and his system collapsed.

Heinzmann, in his delirium, raved about our experiences on the 12th, constantly crying out that I had been killed and wanting to go out to find me. The medical detachment had their hands full keeping him in the dugout. When I returned he was lying on an old bunk, raving and calling for me. It hurt to see him in that condition, a case of nervous exhaustion. Our battalion surgeon suggested that I remain with the lieutenant and try to make him understand that we had all returned safely. After a couple of hours he regained some control of himself and when he realized that I was alongside of him and safe he continued to improve. I hope you will pardon me for going into details in this instance, but I am merely reciting incidents as they occurred. This was no new condition; men were breaking under this terrific strain and shell fire; one of the corporals in the company was paralyzed from a shell explosion and for several months did not know his own name.

Can you appreciate my feelings when I saw the lieutenant in that condition? It was the first time that he had ever shown any signs of consideration for me, other than in a strictly military sense. As for nerves, I never knew that he had any; he was one of the coolest men under fire I have ever known. With all the trials of the past few days such a manifestation of loyalty was deeply appreciated. It was evidence that the one man who had been closest to me in this mess still had confidence and a personal regard extending beyond our military relationship. Since the war the paths of Lieutenant Heinzmann and myself have naturally separated, but many times I think of that occasion and congratulate myself on having had at least one officer in the company who thought enough of me to risk his life for me.

On the morning of October 14th, Lieutenant Colonel Brown, commanding officer of our regiment, directed that I take command of the 3rd Battalion, 114th Infantry, the major of that battalion having been gassed and evacuated on the 12th. In directing me to take over this command Colonel Brown took occasion to compliment Company B for its work at *Bois de Ormont* and assured me that the company had done more than its duty. He also expressed his appreciation of the leadership of the company officers, and was assigning me to command the battalion, as he expressed it:

"The 3rd Battalion suffered heavy casualties in the last attack. It is short of officers and needs considerable re-organization in preparation for continued action. You are assigned to this command and recommendation is being made for your promotion to the rank of major. Make whatever changes you think necessary among your officers and advise me as soon as possible when your battalion is ready for battle."

In October 1917 I was transferred from the company as a result of politics. January 23rd, 1918, I was ordered back to the old outfit against my wishes, believing that I was being brought back to the regiment only because others had failed. Again I was transferred from the company, but what a difference. This transfer was due to the fighting spirit and efficiency of the same company that I had been stamped as incompetent to command one year previously. Now, as a result of that same company's record under my command, I was given command of a combat battalion and recommended for promotion by the regimental commander. I present my compliments to those officers responsible for the attempted degradation; they really, though unwittingly, did me a favor by the original transfer at Camp McClellan. They put some combativeness into me that Company B eventually turned loose on the armed enemies of the United States. Where were those officers through the past three months of combat service?

The prospect of a higher command was no compensation to me for leaving the few survivors of Company B; I felt rather blue at parting with them. No captain ever had a more loyal or better company under his command. If I had to enter battle again, no greater favor could be granted than to have my comrades of Company B, 114th U. S. Infantry alongside of me as they were at the attack on *Bois de Ormont,* October 12th, 1918. I knew that the company, or rather what remained of it, would be in good hands under the command of Lieutenant Heinzmann. I would miss the company that I had often 'cussed out,' sworn at, trained and finally led into battle. No officer could ask for or expect greater loyalty and faithful service than I had received from the members of the company. We had been 'through the jaws of death' together. What else could have brought us closer?

Complying with the Commanding Officer's orders I proceeded to the headquarters of the 3rd Battalion, in the *Ravine de Coassinvaux,* and found my old friend, Captain Albert A. Rickert of Company K, in temporary command of the battalion. He had automatically assumed command when his major went to the hospital. Like the rest of us Captain Rickert was about 'all in' from the effect of the fighting; he was very much plastered with mud and filth, with one hand bandaged for a slight wound, and very busy caring for his own company as well as taking charge of the routine of the battalion.

Captain Rickert was a very efficient and dependable officer who would have made a good battalion commander.

Conditions in the battalion were very much upset. Company L, under the command of Captain Harry Harsin, was on the front line with the 1st Battalion, supporting Companies A and C; Companies I, K and M had suffered heavily on the 12th. The battalion was very short of officers, Company I, especially, having no officers for duty with the company. All of them had been either killed or wounded or on other duty, Company M had only one officer left with the organization. Company K had but two. The first thing necessary was a re-assignment so that each company would have at least two officers for duty. In order to accomplish this it became necessary to assign some of the battalion staff officers to duty with the companies and then to re-assign the staff duties. This was accomplished during the day, without loss of efficiency, and continued until the regiment was relieved some time later.

One noticeable thing in the battalion was its aggressive spirit, in spite of the punishment they had received. There is nothing harder on troops than to be in a support position, where they suffer casualties without the satisfaction of being able to inflict punishment in return. There is none of the satisfaction of a hand-to-hand fight for them. Their present willingness to attack was indicative of a real combat unit. When inspecting the companies I explained that we would be one of the attacking battalions in the next attack and directed the company officers to keep that point continually before their men. I found some complaint of the heavy losses due to being exposed to artillery fire, which were considered as unnecessary.

For the next few days the battalion was busy carrying out wounded and escorting prisoners to the rear; on the return trip these men would bring up rations, ammunitions and supplies. All of these had to be carried by hand, it being impossible to get any animal or motor transport near the battalions. The road being across open country, in plain view of the enemy, activity there was sure to bring artillery fire down on us. One of the fortunes of war was rather ironically demonstrated on this same road; a small detachment of German prisoners was being escorted to the rear by one of our men. The soldier was hustling the prisoners down the open road at a fast walk, when without warning the enemy artillery opened up and killed the prisoners. The guard escaped without a scratch. On another occasion while standing on a small knoll, watching a few carrying parties coming up the road, I saw one of our men carrying a box on his shoulder. All at once that soldier seemed to be enveloped in a blue flame. When the flame and smoke had cleared away a few seconds later the soldier had disappeared. There was no trace of him, merely a hole in the road where he had been. The probable explanation is that the soldier had been carrying a box of grenades and one of the enemy shells made a direct hit on the box. Who that soldier was, where he came from, what company he belonged to, I do not know. On the casualty list he would be carried as 'Missing in Action.' Somewhere in this great country of ours a father, a mother or perhaps a wife bid that soldier good-bye and anxiously looked forward to his return; but it was not to be. I wish we knew who he was, where he came from, so that his family would know he was not 'Missing in Action' but was 'Killed in Action.'

Another task falling to the lot of my battalion was burying our dead comrades; this was most disagreeable work from several angles. It was a tough job having to bury men that we had soldiered alongside of, shared our 'grub' with, and slept with only a few days before. Now they were gone. More than one husky soldier broke down when he came across the dead body of his 'buddy.' The clothing of each dead soldier had to be searched for personal effects, which were turned in to the Quartermaster Depot for transmittal to the next of kin. Many times, since the war, I have received complaints from members of the bereaved families, who claimed they never received the personal effects of their deceased soldier kin. That is quite possible. On numerous occasions I have stood alongside of a dead soldier while his clothing was searched and nothing was found. The burial details were very conscientious in this matter and extremely careful to turn in all property found. Then again, many times we found bodies without identification tags or other means of identifying the soldier; in these cases all we could do was make a package of the articles found, attach a description of the body and the location in which we found him. It was a tough job, but after all they were our 'buddies' and it was only by 'the will of the Almighty' that we were burying them instead of conditions being reversed.

In addition to the duties described, we were required to supply patrols for various purposes. At all times the battalion had to be prepared to go into action should 'our friend the enemy' try to make a break through or push our other companies back. Several times it was necessary to order the battalion to 'stand to,' when the enemy showed signs of unusual activity. On one occasion, about one o'clock in the morning, a runner, all out of breath, dashed into my P.C. with a verbal order from my old battalion commander, directing me to move my battalion up to his support immediately, as the enemy was endeavoring to break through his position. In view of the fact that there was very little rifle or machine gun fire at the time, and there would have been considerable firing if an attack was in progress, I merely ordered the battalion to 'stand by' for a possible attack.

There were two reasons I did not comply with this order. First, the 3rd Battalion was not under command of the 1st Battalion, but, as the regimental support, was under the direct command of the regimental commander and orders for me would come direct from the regimental P.C. So that there would be no delay I had the companies assembled and ready to move, at the same time sending a runner back to Colonel Brown, explaining the message I had received, my course of action and requesting that the 3rd Battalion be permitted to move up to the line.

The second reason for not complying with the major's order was recognition of an old trick of his, worked on us several times in the *Alsace* sector, when he ordered the battalion into the reserve trenches, telling us that "the enemy has broken through our front line," when as a matter of fact it was simply a training maneuver. When his message reached me on this occasion it required no great study to recognize our old friend and to understand that this was merely a case of nerves. Excepting for artillery shelling the night was fairly quiet.

While on the subject of artillery fire, it might be well to explain that troops in support position were under continuous fire, both shrapnel and gas, as well as machine guns. Every day men were either killed, wounded or gassed while performing their various duties. Machine gun fire from *Bois de Moirey,* the position that had raked through the flank of Company B in the attack on *Bois de Ormont* was still very active. Up until the 114th Infantry was relieved in this sector on October 30th the enemy serenely sat on the edge of *Bois de Moirey* and plowed into us whenever he felt disposed, and nothing was ever done to shell him out of there. Why the French Command, under whom we were serving, failed to smother this position has always been a mystery to me. It is certain that had their infantry been in our position they would have dropped back out of that line of fire until the French artillery had blown every machine gun out of the woods. Incidentally this was the point which the 77th French Infantry was to take care of during the attack of the 12th, but they did not like the machine guns and the 114th suffered that pain in the side during the entire time on the line. Poor old 114th Infantry, you were being mauled from the front, flank and rear.

The P.C. of the 3rd Battalion was in a dugout, occupied also by a detachment of the 66th French Infantry consisting of an Adjutant and 6 or 8 bewhiskered French soldiers. As may be imagined there were many embarrassing as well as ludicrous incidents occurring at times. Usually the American soldiers left the Frenchmen to themselves, but there were occasions when our men tried to show our allies just how much they loved them. This generally occurred in the evening when the French ration detail returned from the rear with numerous canteens of wine and rations for the next day. We were not especially interested in their food, but a drink of wine was a lifesaver in that cold, wet mud. Space will not permit me to tell of the ingenious methods employed in an endeavor to separate the Frenchmen from his wine. It was a tough job, but I think we at least got our share.

In the dugouts we were continually finding evidence of recent enemy occupation, this area having been captured from the enemy only a few days previously. Whenever anything of apparent German origin was discovered we were careful how we handled it. It might be as the soldiers called it "a booby trap." An innocent-looking shovel sticking in the ground or an enemy helmet laying on a bunk and other such innocent-looking paraphernalia if picked up might be the means of blowing dugout and everyone in the vicinity into "Kingdom Come." On one occasion somebody found several tins of beef, Austrian rations. Having in mind the "booby-traps" it was thought risky to eat it; after considerable debate the suggestion was made that a can of beef be opened, placed on a mess tin and given to one of the French soldiers. If he ate it and lived all would be well. If he died? The only thing we could do for him then would be to see that he was given a military funeral. For the next few hours a close watch was kept on the 'Frog.' When there seemed to be no ill effects we started a small fire and for the first time in four days enjoyed a warm feed. We might have been eating horse meat but it tasted good and we were hungry. What is the saying about "A hungry stomach having no conscience"?

Gas in the ravine was a source of many casualties. In the dugouts it was especially dangerous; men off duty were apt to be sleeping at any time. For that reason gas sentries were posted at all times to spread the alarm at the first indication of gas. In the 3rd Battalion P.C., having both French and American soldiers, there was a gas sentry from each unit, doing the same duty at the same time. When the gas alarm was sounded all American troops were required to get into their masks and stay there until the order "all clear" was given. No matter whether the gas was light or heavy the same rule applied and was rigidly enforced. The French had a somewhat different method of handling gas protection; when their sentry gave the alarm the French soldiers in the dugout would politely inquire if the gas was little or much. If heavy they donned their masks and remained perfectly still, absolutely no unnecessary movement; if the answer came back that it was only light gas, every Frenchman started up his vile smelling pipe and smoked like 'blazes,' all hands at the same time fanning, with newspapers, etc., towards the dugout door. I don't know which was worse, the enemy gas or a Frenchman's pipe; too much of either would be sure death. Personally I think the gas was more to be desired; it would be less painful and not so lingering.

In the course of a conversation with an officer of the 66th French Infantry, talking about the action that still continued around Hill 360, also the strength and position of the enemy and his tenacity in holding on in spite of all our attacks, the conversation turned to the operations of the 114th Infantry and the attack at *Ormont Farm* and *Bois de Ormont*. This officer remarked that our attack on the 12th was magnificent, that he never expected to see troops attack so recklessly and with such little consideration for their losses and still keep on attacking. He did, however, qualify the statement by placing his forefinger to his forehead and exclaiming "114th Regiment, American, beaucoup de malade ici." Meaning, generally, that we were sick in the head—in other words, crazy. He did not need to tell me that; by this time I was thoroughly convinced we were all lunatics. Continuing the conversation I asked why their regiment had failed to advance with us and protect our left during the attack? He very frankly answered, "There was too much artillery and machine-gun fire to advance through."

After four years of actual contact with the enemy and having made numerous attacks on trench positions, they were undoubtedly qualified to know what kind of fire it was possible to advance through with a minimum of losses. We, in our enthusiastic ignorance, had attempted to do what the French and the Germans, with their experience, knew to be impossible.

The Germans had said that we attacked with "a reckless exposure of infantry," and the French had politely intimated that we were crazy in even attempting to take *Bois de Ormont.* Both the enemy and our allies must have considered that the 114th Infantry was, to use a slang expression, "a plain bunch of nuts," without any sense. What their opinion of our higher command was I hesitate to suggest. From opinions expressed by captured Germans I gathered that they had considerable respect for our fighting ability, but felt it lacked intelligent coordination.

A few days after taking command of the battalion Brigadier General Leroy Upton, commander of the 57th Brigade, made an inspection of our position, stopping at each of the battalion P.C.s, noting conditions, etc. When the general arrived at my headquarters he inquired if the battalion was in condition to attack, what information we had of the enemy and other routine questions. Apparently he was satisfied. The general referred to the attack at *Ormont,* stating that the resistance in front of the brigade was worse than his division had met at *Chateau-Thierry.* As he had been a regimental commander in that battle, decorated and promoted for his work there, he was undoubtedly qualified to make a comparison. He commended Company B for holding their position when the left of our second batalion was driven back. The general then informed me that when the 114th Infantry came out of the lines I would be entitled to wear gold leaves, instead of bars, on my shoulders. A recommendation for promotion to the rank of major had been made for me and he had approved the recommendation. This commendation from General Upton was unexpected and appreciated.

Let us wait and see what happens. Don't forget, colonels

and general were not the only power in the 29th Division. The real, effective power was not in France, but in the United States, working through a group of political officers in the Division.

October 13th, 1918, brought a couple of changes in the regiment that were interesting. Lieutenant Colonel Fitzhugh Lee Minnigerode, of the regular army, was assigned to the 114th. About the same time Lieutenant Colonel H. B. Brown, the regimental commander, was promoted to the rank of colonel and transferred to *Tours* as Deputy Provost Marshal, assistant to Brigadier General H. H. Bandholtz, Provost Marshal General of the A.E.F. Colonel Brown was the only commander of the 114th Infantry who was promoted and assigned to higher duties while in command of our organization. The transfer of Colonel Brown placed the regiment under Lieutenant Colonel Minnigerode.

In the rear areas and supply 'dumps' rumors of all sorts were circulating as to the casualties in the infantry. Our friends at the depots heard varying reports of us lying wounded out front, or that we had been killed, captured or missing. One of my former lieutenants heard so many rumors that he decided to make his own investigation and find out whether I was dead, or if still alive, where, and in what condition. He made the trip but had some difficulty in locating me. The lieutenant stayed in my dugout for the night, returning to his own outfit the following morning. Being from the same 'home town,' each acquainted with the other's family, we kept busy comparing the latest news from home and inquiring for men we had known, many of whom had been wounded and evacuated to the base; also others who had passed on to the Valley of Eternal Peace. As a result of the lieutenant's visit it was possible to send a cablegram from *Verdun* to my family and let them know I was still in the land of the living, although it was uncertain how long that pleasant state of affairs would continue.

About the middle of October rumors began to float around that the 26th U. S. Division was coming in alongside of us, also to relieve some of our units. This was good news. We would feel much more comfortable with American troops alongside;

our experience with the French regiments had been too costly; their vaunted dash and bravery were not demonstrated while we were looking to them to protect our flanks. Personally, I came to regard them as very careful of themselves and eager to avoid, as much as possible, any unnecessary exposure to enemy fire. Perhaps we would have felt the same way had we been fighting for four years. As they were supposed to be fighting for their homes and with all the sentiment attached to the city of *Verdun,* I had looked for much more activity on their part. After our experience with them I came to the conclusion that on the defensive, fighting from entrenched positions, with powerful artillery support, the French soldier was in his element; when it became necessary to leave the cover of the trenches and actually charge into enemy machine-gun fire, with its certain losses, there was something missing. It may have been they were worn out. Whatever the reason, it was mighty costly to the 114th Infantry.

Aside from a rather lengthy account of the battle of *Bois de Ormont* I have purposely refrained from going into the details of life on the front lines to spare you the story of hardship, suffering and death. It is not a pleasant story or dream that the participants are anxious to remember. It is a story of constant attack and counter-attack, the everlasting sniping of both sides when it was risky to expose ourselves even for a second; the incessant patrolling night after night; machine guns that sounded like riveting machines, tearing into us every time the enemy became suspicious or saw us move; enemy artillery, both light and heavy calibre, throwing shrapnel over the entire sector, and finally the gas-shells that kept every low spot continually saturated, until everything we touched seemed to be gas soaked; our blankets, uniforms, all we owned covered with gas-soaked mud and filth. I have refrained from telling of the little sleep we could snatch, just a cat-nap in a wet shell-hole or smashed-in dugout, with only one wet, gas-saturated blanket for a cover. Our food consisted principally of canned beans, salmon, corned beef, hardtack, etc. In order to get even this limited supply the ration details had to make their way through heavy fire. Drinking water was at a premium, a canteen full often lasting several days. Hot coffee and bread were simply something to dream about. I recall seeing a small truckload of bread up near the front line. With mouths all set for a taste of soft bread we discovered it could not be eaten as it had been exposed to gas.

To record the individual acts of bravery performed would merely be a repetition of names of the men who had taken part in the fighting, there had been so many cases of men endangering and even sacrificing their lives in isolated attacks on enemy positions or in an attempt to aid a wounded comrade or trying to reach a 'pal' who was in a tight spot.

Several days after taking command of the 3rd Battalion, the commanding officer of the First Battalion came to me and said: "The French general has awarded fifty Croix de Guerres to the 114th Infantry for their part in the action last week. It has been decided to award three medals to each company and five to the battalion and regimental staffs. I want you to submit the names of three men from Company B for these medals." Answering the request required no special mental effort. "Thank you for the offer," I said, "but I would not think of trying to select three men out of the company for decoration, holding them as examples of bravery above the other men. If decorations are to be awarded I will recommend the survivors of the company in addition to those of the dead and wounded who I believe earned decorations."

This suggestion was rejected as expected. One very easy way to have settled the matter would have been for me to submit the names of Lieutenant Heinzmann, First Sergeant Fachet and to have my own name included. They would have been acceptable as each of us had played a more or less important part in the battle. There could have been little, if any, criticism. It is much more satisfactory to look back and know that Company B, 114th Infantry, accepted no favors for the part they played at *Bois de Ormont*.

Medals issued like rations, by the basketful. Not for any specific act of bravery, but rather as a gesture of goodwill, just as one might give a dog a bone for performing some trick for a friend's entertainment. While I had anything to say about it Company B was not providing any entertainment for the satisfaction or glorification of anyone. What became of all these medals is a mystery to me. The History of the 29th Division shows the names of only nine officers and men who received the Croix de Guerre. Where are the other forty? Years after the war ended I saw, and heard of, medals being worn by men and officers who did not receive them while the regiment was in existence. "There are more ways than one of killing a cat." It may be that there is more than one way to get a medal pinned 'on a manly breast.' We will hear more of this matter of decorations later.

Early on the morning of the 17th the 1st Battalion was relieved by a battalion of the 104th Infantry, 26th U. S. Division. The 1st Battalion marched back to its old bivouac in *Cote des Roches* for rest. During the day orders were issued for my battalion to be relieved between midnight and three o'clock the following morning, the 18th, the battalion to be clear of the regimental P.C., at *Haumont pres Samogneux,* at that hour.

The particular task assigned to the battalion of the 104th that had relieved our 1st Battalion was to clean out *Bois de Ormont.* Being junior to this new commander, he a major and I only a captain, and he having established his P.C. but a short distance from mine, it was the proper thing according to military usage for me to call on him, to offer the facilities of my staff and such information of the enemy position and strength as well as maps, etc., as we possessed. Early in the morning I proceeded to the major's dugout, introduced myself and made the offer; the major thanked me but thought he would not need any assistance as the task assigned to him appeared to be quite simple. He informed me that he had instructed one of his captains on the line to send a platoon through *Ormont Woods* and clean it out.

One platoon to clear out *Bois de Ormont!*

The remark knocked me speechless for a moment. When finally my speech returned I tried to explain that two battalions of our regiment, in addition to units of the 113th Infantry, had made an attempt to clear out those woods, had been at it for almost a week, and all we had accomplished was a mere toe-hold on the edge of it. The major was very determined to proceed with the attack, nothing I said would alter his plans. I was unable to convince him of the enemy's determination to hold that woods at all costs. He ended the conversation by saying: "We will take the woods, it will be very simple. Don't forget, captain, we were at *Chateau-Thierry*, we know how to handle 'Jerry'; we will have him out of there in short order." I certainly disliked to see such a useless sacrifice, but there was nothing for me to do about the matter. It was none of my official business and the only way was to let him learn, from bitter experience, the same lesson we had learned the week before.

About four o'clock the same afternoon a sergeant, of the battalion above referred to, came into my P.C. and "presented the major's compliments and would Captain Reddan step over to the P.C. as the major wanted some information." Arriving at battalion headquarters I found the major very much excited; the platoon he had sent in to clean out the woods had, instead of doing the cleaning out, been wiped out itself. Unfortunately for the men who made the attack 'Jerry' must have had a lease on that 'neck of the woods' and declined all invitations to vacate, no matter how insistent the efforts of even the 26th Division.

There was nothing additional to tell him, I merely repeated my warning of earlier in the day and told him that in my opinion it would take more than a regiment to 'oust' the enemy out of *Ormont Woods*, also that *Bois de Moirey,* on the right, would have to be taken at the same time. I explained that if he was lucky and gained possession of *Ormont* he would be unable to hold it, as the interlocking system of enemy artillery and machine-gun fire, from the flanks and front, would make the position untenable. Making this statement required no exceptional military ability; I was but repeating the experiences of our 57th Brigade during the past ten days. Units of the brigade had succeeded in pushing the enemy out of Ormont but each time we gained possession we had, in turn, been driven out again by German troops.

No matter what was said the major continued to insist that he was going to take the position. Our conference ended when he told me he was going to make a battalion attack during the night, that he would have an accompanying gun, 75 m.m., on his front line to knock out the enemy machine-gun nests. There was no use of my talking, he was determined to capture the woods. I did suggest, however, that as my battalion was going out he withhold his attack until we were out of his sector; there was no sense in our men being uselessly sacrificed. He agreed to make his zero hour 3 A.M. by which time my battalion would be well on its way out, and then the party would be up to the 104th Infantry.

I regret my inability to recall that major's name, he was a real commander and a battler. He knew what he wanted and how to go about getting results; from conversations with him I understood that he had been promoted from a captain to the rank of major a short time previously. His mistake was in "sending a boy on a man's errand"; he failed to appreciate the strength of the enemy position, in addition to their determination to hold the woods. The major had intimated that the reason our brigade had been unable to capture and hold *Bois de Ormont* was that as we were in our first major operation in this battle we had allowed the enemy "to get away with something." When his battalion made the attack, even with the accompanying gun, they made some progress for a time, until the enemy turned on the heat and simply smothered the attack with everything the Germans had in the form of scrap iron, or as the 'doughboys' used to say, "They threw everything they had at us, including the morning reports and rolling kitchens."

In compliance with orders the 3rd Battalion was relieved by a battalion of the 104th Infantry during the night. Company L, still attached to our 1st Battalion, was already out; Companies I, K, and M, moved out one company at a time, starting at midnight, at one hour intervals, with orders to proceed to *Cote des Roches*. The relief was completed without incident. The battalion reported all clear at the regimental P.C. at 3 o'clock and then proceeded to the assembly point at our old bivouac.

The prospects of a few days' rest were very comforting; the thought of a hot meal was even more enticing. The trip from *Haumont* to *Cote des Roches* was made to appear as a mere stroll by the thought of getting my lips into a cup of hot coffee and the possibility of a mess-pan full of "army slum." Captain Rickert had even promised me some doughnuts made by his company cooks. The prospects for all of us were quite rosy. Arriving at the bivouac I found that orders to have a hot meal ready for the men of each company as they came out had been obeyed. Everybody was busy, if I am permitted to quote slang, "filling his face," and what a job they were doing; officers and men alike, rank meant nothing here, eating and sleep came first.

## Chapter XIV

## "STILL AT IT"

### REST TO ETRAYE RIDGE

BEFORE continuing with our further experiences, let me try to have our civilian friends form a mental picture of the men as they looked to me at daybreak that morning. It was the first time I had seen the men together since taking command of the battalion. While on the lines I had seen them only in small groups, never more than fifteen or twenty together at any one time. Now was an opportunity to "size them up" and to form some opinion of what I had to work with. I found a group of youngsters all worn out, tired and ragged; nearly every man in the battalion was sneezing, coughing and bleary-eyed from loss of sleep and the effects of gas. Many of them were so completely exhausted they curled up and went to sleep wherever they happened to be the moment they had taken a cup of coffee; they were so dead tired that even the 'cooties' failed to keep them awake. This was our battalion, a fair example of every battalion in the A.E.F. as it returned from the front. They were dirty, filthy, lousy, clothing in rags, ripped and torn by barbed wire and enemy bayonets; just walking skeletons, but with it all they were still soldiers of the United States, your sons, brothers or husbands. These men had faced the supreme test and it was only by the will of the Almighty, and their own skill, that they were not lying up at *Ormont Farm, Bois de Ormont* or *Death Valley* with their 'Buddies' who had gone into action with them.

Yes, they were worn out, they had good reason to be tired; from the end of September to this time they had continually been under fire or in action. With very little rest the 114th Infantry had been in range of the enemy guns, in the lines, or moving from one position to another since about the 1st of August. There was more work to be done, and after good food and so far as possible a chance to clean up, they would be ready for another fight or frolic with our friend the enemy. We were a disreputable looking crew, but knew that under fair leadership we could whip 'Jerry.' While he had given us a good fight, we knew we were just a little better than he was; after our experience we would be more than a match for him at our next meeting.

After completing the meal orders were issued to prepare another hot meal to be ready at noon; the men would sleep for possibly four or five hours and then wake up hungry. After their experiences, with "jumpy" nerves and the artillery firing, prolonged sleep at this time would be impossible. While inspecting the company kitchens during the morning I found that no preparation was being made for the noon meal of one company. When questioned the mess sergeant informed me that meat had not been issued and he was having beans for dinner. Beans again! After all of them we had eaten in all forms while on the line. Further inquiry developed the fact that rations were not being issued to the companies. Instead they were being piled in 'dumps' close to the regimental supply. All a mess sergeant had to do was go to the dumps and take all he wanted. In this case the mess sergeant was too lazy to go after supplies. Needless to say that man did not remain as a mess sergeant.

During the morning some idea of what the 29th Division had accomplished was obtained. I learned that our 58th Brigade, Maryland and Virginia National Guard Troops, had made good progress through the enemy lines in the direction of *Molleville Farm*. Our own 'Jersey' troops of the 113th Infantry working on the right of the 58th Brigade, were having hard work in their advance, due to heavy concentration of fire from our old acquaintance, *Bois de Ormont*. At this time the 115th and 116th Infantry regiments were clearing out the *Grande Montagne*. My old outfit, 1st Battalion 114th Infantry, had been sent up as a reserve for the 58th Brigade. With the battalion, of course, were the remnants of Company B. Poor fellows, they were out of the line only about 24 hours, when they were ordered back in again. Therefore on the morning of October 19th all troops of the 29th Division were in action, except the 114th Infantry, which was the division reserve; the 1st Battalion near *Brabant-sur-Meuse,* 2nd and 3rd Battalions at *Cote des Roches.*

From conversations with the troops on the front at the time I failed to note any idea as to when the war would end. We were all hoping it would end quickly in order to stop the terrible hardship and suffering. There was little indication on the part of the enemy that he was ready to quit. The Austrian troops had all been withdrawn from in front of us and replaced with veteran German division shock troops, who stubbornly contested every foot of our advance; men who met each of our attacks with extremely heavy artillery and machine-gun fire and then counter-attacked repeatedly against every position we captured. No matter how many times ground was gained in *Ormont Woods,* the enemy attacked those positions until he bore us down by sheer losses from artillery and then charged into us, again and again, until we were actually smothered out.

From the manner in which American divisions on other parts of the Western Front were smashing through, it was apparent that 'Jerry' was having his hands full, but he was on the best side of the argument, his reinforcements and supplies were close in rear; when forced to retire he fell back on his reserves and artillery support; on the other hand every mile we gained took us farther away from our supporting troops and artillery. As the enemy fell back he received a greater concentration of artillery fire, as we advanced we got farther and farther away from our artillery and in consequence received less protective fire, until at times we were without support of any kind and had to depend entirely on the weapons in each infantry company. As our troops advanced into positions from which the enemy had been ousted we moved forward into positions on which the enemy had complete firing data; he knew the exact range to every trail, road, woods, dugout, trench, etc., and in addition had developed an interlocking system of fire that covered every inch of ground.

In writing this record of experiences in the World War I have, on several occasions, referred to political interference in the former New Jersey National Guard. Should you feel that this originated in my own mind as a result of disappointment, or from any source other than facts, permit me to quote a conversation held in regimental P.C. 114th Infantry at *Cote des Roches* on the morning of October 19th, 1918, only a few hours after I had brought my battalion down from the front lines. While talking with Lieutenant Colonel Minnigerode, commanding officer 114th Infantry, the regimental adjutant handed a paper to the Colonel and remarked, "Does the Colonel wish Captain Reddan to see this memorandum?" Colonel Minnigerode read the memo, looked at me and blurted out: "This is a damn shame. I dislike to show you this, Captain, but you will understand my position." Taking the sheet and reading it I certainly did appreciate his position. There was only one thing for him to do, obey the order. As a Regular Army Officer with many years of service to his credit, and the prospects of further years of army service after the war, he could not afford to antagonize his superior officers at that time. The memorandum, from 29th Division Headquarters, directed the Commanding Officer of the 114th Infantry to recommend for promotion, to the rank of major, two captains of our regiment, mentioned by name. If Major General Morton had gone to every extreme to find someone closely allied with the New Jersey political machine he could not have found, in the entire division, a man more closely allied with the State House at Trenton, N. J., and its filthy political machine than one of the men this memorandum directed Colonel Minnigerode to recommend for promotion.

What was there for me to say? Handing back the sheet I remarked: "The fortunes of war, Colonel. I presume this relieves me as commander of the 3rd Battalion. Shall I return to command Company B?" To which Colonel Minnigerode replied: "You are not relieved. Another recommendation will be sent forward for your promotion. Continue on with your battalion."

At the risk of becoming boring I repeat that recommendations of Colonels and Generals, in the 29th Division, were merely routine. In the background, never seen, but always active and alert, with connections beyond the division, extending to a powerful political ring in Trenton and even to Washington, was a power that controlled, not alone this promotion but many others in the division among the officers from New Jersey. This ring was powerful enough to promote its friends and to block the advancement of any officer who showed a tendency to remain aloof from the machine. That memorandum never originated in the mind of Major General Morton, it was merely a typewritten notation, on a small sheet of paper; even the Division Commander's signature was typed.

It would be a simple matter to continue with examples of political interference continually appearing in the 114th Infantry. Why keep on repeating the same story? Major General Morton was fighting this ring from the time the division was organized. Brigadier General Upton knew of this condition and was at all times on the watch for it. Unfortunately these Generals were not familiar with conditions existing in the "Jersey Guard" for years prior to the World War; nor were they acquainted with the political standing of this same ring and the advantages they hoped to gain upon returning home from the war with additional rank and if possible a medal hanging on their 'manly' breasts. Such a thing as going out to win the war, that could not be avoided other than in a routine way, never entered their minds. The biggest thing of all to this crowd was the advantage to be gained, politically, by appearing before the voters back home as a 'War Hero,' even if it was gained by sacrificing "other men's lives," suffering and misery.

"War heroes!" How can any man call himself an officer and a gentleman, as he is supposed to be, and at the same time use the lives of the men under his command as stepping stones to advance his own political ambitions? As often heard in the A.E.F., "bars may make an officer, but it requires more than an

Act of Congress to make a gentleman." I might add that apparently Almighty God could not make these individuals see their obligations or stop their selfishness. The interesting part of this whole mess was the fact that the majority of the ring referred to were in the higher ranks or staff positions, and were so 'slick' that little suspicion was cast their way. Only a very few were in companies doing the actual fighting on the front lines.

Facing artillery and machine-gun fire, barrages, gas and enemy bayonets were horrible. It was hard to see our comrades torn to bits alongside of us. All of this we expected, this was war, the enemy was receiving as good as he gave, at least we were facing each other and it was a case of the best man winning; but this eternal stabbing in the back was so unexpected, we were defenseless against it; it was worse than any battle, cutting down the morale of both officers and men and did us more harm than the entire German army.

For the next few days we remained in the ravine, keeping under cover from the enemy's shrapnel. *Cote des Roches* had been shelled so much during the war, by both German and French artillery, that the only thing in it were shell-holes of all sizes. These shell-holes had been converted into living quarters by many of the men, by the simple method of stretching a shelter tent, flat, across the hole. When a shell was heard coming over it was laughable to see everyone diving for the nearest cover, especially those men who lived under the shelter tents. I often wondered if they expected a piece of canvas to protect them from flying shrapnel. Merely a case of nerves and safety first.

There were other instances of a laughable as well as a serious turn all the time, even during battle all was not serious. We had our little jokes and enjoyed them; these laughs were probably the only thing that helped us to retain some small degree of sanity, and to offset the horror around us.

An incident occurred in this ravine which I am very loath to tell of, yet it is part of the story and demonstrates one of the points to which I have previously referred.

Colonel Minnigerode, in a conference with some of the battalion and company commanders one morning, gave us the commendations of the French generals, as well as Major Gen-

"Our Death Valley." Company B advanced into this ravine at 7 A.M., 12 Oct., 1918. In twelve hours the company had been almost annihilated by enemy machine gun and artillery fire. "A reckless exposure of infantry."

1. "Cold Steel." A regiment, with fixed bayonets, on parade.
2. "Crosses row on row." The ladder of political greed.
3. "Sunny France." Company B standing inspection in the snow.

"The old swimming hole," also fishing hole. Junction of the Apance and Saone Rivers. Billets of Company B in the building at the left.

"Grande Rue et Chateau" (The Main Street), Chatillon-sur-Saone. As usual the Cafe du Commerce is seen at the left.

eral Morton and Brigadier General Upton, also expressing his own appreciation of the work done by the 114th while on the lines. He then asked our opinion as to future activity of the regiment. The natural answer was that we needed clothing and equipment for the troops, and replacements to fill the ranks. That was all right, everyone there realized the need of these things, but unfortunately some of those present began to whine and complain and very strongly urged that the regiment be sent into a rear area for a time. Even though the Colonel explained there was no hope of the regiment going out, that as a matter of fact the Division Commander was expecting the 114th Infantry to make another attack, this group still continued to whine. True the complaining came from only a very few of the officers, but unfortunately they were of the ring mentioned, men well known for their affiliations, who certainly were putting the regiment in a bad light. No matter how much the Colonel emphasized the necessity of making another attack, after which we could expect to be relieved, they still continued to plead to be sent back. It became tiresome listening to this whimpering and whining, and was plainly evident that the Colonel was thoroughly disgusted. In order to save the situation the offer was made to have the 3rd Battalion make the attack. This ended the discussion; the Colonel apparently was satisfied.

When the conference was called, orders had already been issued, although we did not know it at the time, for an attack within the next few days in which the 114th Infantry was scheduled to take part. Colonel Minnigerode knew this and was merely trying to break the news to us gently, appreciating that we were tired out and needed rest. He also realized that orders have to be obeyed, no matter how unpleasant; most certainly he never anticipated any such whimpering.

Prior to the description of entering the *Meuse-Argonne* offensive, I made this statement: "The 114th Infantry was 'licked' before entering battle due to lack of confidence in the battalion commanders," and this conference, in addition to conditions during the active battle operations, certainly proved that my opinion of 'excellent soldiers and junior officers, but poor battalion leadership' still held good. Again I repeat—

all due to a rotten, cowardly, political system that made it possible for inefficient officers to retain their commands, thereby cluttering up the higher ranks. Watch for a repetition of this statement the next time the 114th Infantry goes into the lines.

On October 20th I again came in contact with my old Company B. They had returned to the regiment after being up front for the second time. Naturally I was very glad to see the few survivors who were still able to perform a soldier's duty; more than one cup of coffee I drank with them at the company kitchen. It seemed to me that every time I was in the vicinity of 'B' Company's kitchen either the mess sergeant or cooks were offering me coffee or something to eat. Whether it was so or not, the men of the company always appeared glad to see me. In fact one of my most cherished recollections of that 'Hell Hole' is the expression of respect and comradeship I received from the company; they appeared to accept me as a comrade as well as their former company commander. No matter what duty I was on, or where duty carried me, I always felt at home when back with Company B.

I can imagine the former members of the outfit reading the above and exclaiming—"Poor old 'Skipper Bill,' he must be expecting to die soon when he shows any sentiment." You rarely find sentiment in an army officer, but, nevertheless, any man who had gone through what these men had been through and had been in it with them, would have to take his hat off to them if he had any heart or any spark of feeling in his make up. To say that these men were 'game fighters' would be but a weak expression. They were more than that. Even though practically dead on their feet, from what they had already done, yet they were still game to go in again. Poor 'devils'; if they had only known the enemy in their rear; yes, even in the lines with them. Perhaps it was better that they did not know. Accidents *do* happen in a battle.

The reader is probably thinking too much attention was being paid to this subject of injustice and selfishness, and that the criticism is too severe. What has already been told has not been a pleasant task; neither were the conditions under which

we were serving pleasant. How many made the excuse of illness or that they had been gassed in order to be evacuated to a
Base Hospital and in that way escape some arduous or hazard-
ous duty? Others were relieved from duty, and sent to the
rear, when the regimental commander was unable to get them
out of dugouts to take command of their organizations that
were fighting to hold some precarious position. Place yourself
in the position of one of our enlisted men facing an active,
fighting enemy, taking advantage of every opportunity to kill
you, and your own ability and swiftness the only means of
preventing such a catastrophe; add to this the knowledge that
some of your superior officers were too cowardly to get out of
their dugouts and face the same dangers that you were facing.

Many, many times since the war ended, former enlisted
men have recounted incidents that occurred on the front, and
to say the least these remarks are not complimentary to some
people. On numerous occasions, especially when a group of
the former officers get together, I have been surprised to hear
them recount things that happened, to hear their experiences,
and to note the bitterness still existing against the system we
had been 'up against.'

The question undoubtedly rises in the reader's mind, what
is expected or what is to be gained by recounting such a tale?
The answer is very simple: "I expect nothing, no reward, no
more consideration than received during the service." This
recital of my experiences is just another unpleasant task, the
same as duties assigned during the war when others failed or
found some excuse to evade. On the morning after the battle
at *Bois de Ormont* I vowed to tell the true story of that battle
if I survived the war, as a memorial to my men who were uselessly sacrificed there. Also to bring credit, as far as possible,
to those enlisted men and officers of the 'Jersey Troops' who
placed duty above personal considerations or ambitions, even
to the extent of facing death or a life of suffering. If this is
accomplished, then I am well repaid for the effort. To use a
military expression: "The mission is accomplished."

However, let us continue with the story. For the few days

the regiment was in rest the men were getting considerable sleep and making up for their lost meals, and in a small way cleaned up. While the regiment was not in the actual front line, still it was necessary to be ready at any moment for a sudden call to go up front again, in the event 'Jerry' showed a desire to push us back. With the exception of a few patrols that were sent up front, there was little duty being performed.

On the afternoon of October 21st, while talking with one of our regimental staff captains, he remarked that an attack on the enemy position was to be made the following morning, the 22nd, in which the 113th Infantry was to play a prominent part, and after they had reached their objective our regiment would relieve the 113th. He also informed me that he and a lieutenant from the 2nd Battalion, 114th, had been detailed to observe the coming fight, and particularly to locate the position reached by the attacking regiment, in order that the 114th could relieve the 113th Infantry. In the course of the conversation I expressed a desire to be a member of the patrol as I would like to see our neighbors from home, many of whom were personal friends, in action. The Captain remarked, "You are a battalion commander and it is hardly likely that you will be sent on patrol duty." I replied, "In command of a battalion that's true, but after all I am still a captain although on special duty. Also the information gained by me will be valuable when it becomes time for me to put the 3rd Battalion on the line up there." I suggested that the Captain refer the matter to Colonel Minnigerode and, if agreeable to the Colonel, to let me know. Within an hour orders reached me to accompany the patrol. In the light of what transpired later I have often wondered if I was being 'put on the spot.' And I am still wondering.

Late in the afternoon, the staff captain, lieutenant and I started for the front, hiking by way of *Brabant-sur-Meuse* and then following the road to the northeast in the direction of *Molleville Farm*. Eventually reaching the P.C. of the 1st Battalion, 115th Infantry, we obtained a runner who led us to the dugout and P.C. of Captain H. Grymes commanding Company D, 115th Infantry. After talking with Captain Grymes and getting first-hand information from him about front line conditions, it now being about 2 o'clock in the morning, we decided to remain at this point and get a couple of hours' rest before daylight, at which time we would start to locate the 113th Infantry. We were saved the trip however, orders being received during the night postponing the attack 24 hours. I might add that we were entirely too far to the left, as the 116th Infantry was south of the 115th Infantry, and 113th to the south or right of the 116th. At daylight, in view of the changed orders, we decided to return to our own regiment.

While the trip up front had not produced the expected results, we had gained some information about the impending attack and the position held by the 29th Division. Our division center, near *Molleville Farm,* was held by our 116th Infantry, with the 115th Infantry on their left to protect the left flank of the attack, the 113th Infantry on the right of 116th, facing *Etraye Ridge* and *Hill 361,* the 26th U. S. Division on the right of 113th Infantry. The general plan was to capture *Etraye Ridge* and force the enemy back off this high ground, from which he could see about 5 miles into our rear area. The capture of *Etraye* would also materially assist in the capture of our old friends *Bois de Ormont* and *Bois de Moirey,* both positions still holding out in spite of determined attacks by the 29th and 26th Divisions.

The capture of *Bois de Etraye* was not going to be an easy task. As previously stated the enemy forces opposed to us were veteran German Storm Troops, who held every position until dead. Prisoners were captured, especially deserters, who told of detachments being put into the lines with orders to hold out at all costs. On many occasions positions were captured only to find the defenders dead or so badly wounded they were unable to continue the fight. The capture of the ridge was going to be a man-sized task that would take everything the 29th Division had in its trick bag to win. The German officers realized that if they lost *Etraye,* the positions of the past three weeks would be reversed; we would then be on the high ground looking down on them as they moved back across the plains. In that case the next stop for 'Jerry' would be the 'Fatherland.'

Other divisions of U. S. Army and our Allies were romping forward 10 or 15 kilometers each day, sort of playing hide and seek; the enemy would hide and the Allies would chase after them until they were located. The 29th Division never met that kind of warfare; we had to battle every foot of the way, with the enemy waiting for us at each turn of the road, behind each rock or tree, every trench massed with infantry and machine guns, and over all a blanket of artillery fire and gas. It will be understood that the more enemy troops we engaged on our front, which was the crucial point in the German defense, the less resistance other American divisions were finding west of the *Meuse River*. If the 29th Division could make a break in the enemy line it would mean a complete withdrawal of all enemy troops in northern France. It was vital for the Germans to hold up this attack, east of the *Meuse,* for the next week or so, in order for their troops further north to be able to withdraw and avoid capture.

Perhaps you think I have given too much detail about this pending battle. My only excuse is that the New Jersey troops, engaged in the operations northwest of *Verdun* have never been given the credit they deserve for the work they did there.

Reaching *Cote des Roches* about 11 o'clock I went back to my battalion, attending the usual routine affairs, and then to mess, after which a little rest and sleep, in preparation for another 24 hours on the front. We had about one and a half hours' rest during the preceding night, after about 15 miles hiking up to the front and back again. The same was to be repeated the coming night with a battle at daylight thrown in for good measure.

My dreams of rest were rudely shattered by the usual interference from runners, orderlies, etc., from headquarters with messages of the most unimportant and trifling nature. Such things as 2nd Lieutenant Sniffle of the U. S. Quartermaster Corps wants to know what Company B, 114th Infantry, did with four extra potatoes they received on Christmas Day, 1917. Were these potatoes properly used and accounted for, and a warning to the company commander to personally supervise the future drawing of rations for that company. Or perhaps a letter stating that Private Jones, who had been killed on September the 39th, had been overpaid three cents on the April pay roll and Captain Hawkshaw of the Pay Department desired an immediate refund from Private Jones. These are of course fictitious examples but they serve to give an idea of the ridiculous things continually annoying the various commanding officers, when their attention and whole effort was required on more serious matters.

One of the communications received was about an unpaid bill of Company B, contracted by a former officer of the company before I was assigned to that command. The bill, owed to Armour & Co. at Anniston, Alabama, was for beef purchased in the late fall of 1917. The letter had been through the office of the Adjutant General of the Army at Washington, D. C., then sent to headquarters of the A.E.F. at Chaumont, in France, and then to me, with indorsements by every officer into whose hands it came. By the time it reached me there were something like twenty endorsements on it, and the nearer it came the more insistent became the demand that the bill be paid "immediately, if not sooner." A concrete example of army "buck passing."

My indorsement on that letter was short and to the point. At last I was in a position where I could take a chance on expressing my opinion and not have to worry about any staff officer attempting to place me under arrest for insubordination. They would not follow me where I was going, and life up there was too uncertain to worry about the future.

Delinquent accounts are collected under varying conditions and circumstances, but it was the only time I ever heard of an attempt being made to collect a bill on a battlefield. You have visions of an organization commander leading his troops into battle, waving a sword, urging his gallant men on to death and glory. You may even picture him as wounded or dying but still struggling on toward the enemy; at least that is as it appears in the motion pictures. That was not the way in the A.E.F. All we had to worry about was paying a bill.

Here I was in the middle of real man-sized war, trying to get a little rest before taking part in another battle, yet, according to the 'buck passing' indorsements on that bill, winning the war was a secondary consideration to a demand for payment of a bill that Armour & Co. had allowed carelessly to be contracted by someone else. War has its laughable sides as well as its horrors. This situation was ridiculous.

A few other such interruptions and all desire for sleep was gone, so was the afternoon. About dusk other events caused me to sit up and wonder. A messenger from regimental headquarters arrived with information that the staff captain, who had originally been commander of the patrol, would be unable to make the trip and for me to take command. The captain had gone into *Verdun,* earlier in the afternoon to try and get a bath, and while there he became ill. I forwarded the information and directed the lieutenant to report to me at 114th P.C., ready to start at midnight as previously arranged. I then invited another lieutenant to accompany the patrol. He complained of not feeling well but would try and make it. I advised the regimental commander of my plans, then proceeded to make the necessary preparations for the trip. About 11 o'clock P.M. I received word that the lieutenant, who had been with us the previous night, would be unable to accompany me as he was very ill and felt that he would be unable to stand the trip to the front again. Things were commencing to look serious; two officers had reported sick and only a half-hearted acquiescence from another lieutenant, who was not feeling well. If he should be unable to go matters would be seriously complicated; the regiment was short of officers and all officers are not fitted for the special task before this patrol, so my choice was limited. All I could do was wait and hope that the lieutenant who had been invited to go with me would be able to make the trip. Waiting brought the usual results. At 11.45 P.M. I sent a runner to inquire if the lieutenant would make the trip. The answer came back "SICK."

Sick! So was I. Here was a battle about to start in 5½ hours, a hike to the jump-off position that would take at least three hours to reach; information of vital importance to future operations of the 114th Infantry to be obtained, and three of the four officers picked for their supposed ability to obtain this information reporting sick and unable to perform this duty. I am not a doctor, but I'll bet that hot-water bottles applied to the soles of the feet of these sick men would have helped a whole lot to start their blood into circulation again.

For me to go out on the patrol alone would not be good sense. If I should gain all the information possible and be unable to get back to the regimental commander with it, due to being killed or wounded, the trip would be wasted. Information gained by a patrol is of no value when it fails to get back to higher commanders. I was in a quandary, again left alone and holding the bag. What a fool I had been to volunteer for this tour of duty; from past experiences I should have known better.

While standing at the entrance to the 114th Infantry P.C. trying to figure out a solution to the problem Colonel Minnigerode came out of his dugout. Explaining conditions to the Colonel, he asked what I intended to do. I replied that in my opinion the only solution was for me to go to Company B and have one of their sergeants accompany me. The Colonel laughingly replied, "Still thinking of your old company. Give my compliments to Lieutenant Heinzmann and tell him you are to have any man in Company B that you want with you." I answered, "I know the men in Company B, they have been with me on similar patrols and never let me down yet, they will not fail me now." The Colonel wished me good luck, again stressing the importance of obtaining the information and getting it to him.

I explained the situation to Lieutenant Heinzmann and told him that I wanted First Sergeant Joseph Fachet to go with me. Heinzmann naturally objected; I was asking for his second in command, and taking a sergeant away was leaving him very short-handed. After some further discussion the matter was settled to my satisfaction. In making a selection from Company B I knew exactly what to expect; there was not a non-commissioned officer in the company but was familiar with the type of work required. In asking for Sergeant Fachet I knew that should anything happen to me he would carry on and complete the mission. This confidence was the result of previous demonstrations under trying circumstances as a result of their training.

Perhaps I am handling this recital in a rough-shod manner. Undoubtedly this tale will not be to the liking of some individuals; but what of those officers who were performing their duty? Many of them sick with heavy colds, on the verge of pneumonia, or suffering from gas. I had a very annoying cold at this time, but still we kept going until actually mere skeletons. What of the enlisted men? They could not evade duty by saying they were sick or had a cold. They had to keep going until a temperature of 101 degrees was shown. When an order was issued to an enlisted man he had no option but to obey.

"His not to reason why. His but to do or die."

Although some officers, apparently, were unable to realize it this was real war, where men were killed and wounded, not a summer encampment of the militia. Soldiers were needed here, not political half-wits. The only military sense some people had was to keep themselves out of danger without being found out. Do you suppose, for one moment, that I get any satisfaction telling a story as rotten as these conditions were? I do not. But if the men and officers, who were doing their duty, are to receive the credit due them, and to have our people realize the unnecessary hardships under which this duty was being performed, then the other side of the picture must be shown.

The old cry of the A.E.F., "Carry On," was applicable in this instance, as in all other cases. No matter how much suffering it entailed the war had to be won. Failure or neglect on the part of others must not be allowed to interfere with the task assigned. Nice, pleasant memories to take into a battle. However, I had a good man with me and felt confident we would successfully complete the mission.

Shortly after midnight Sergeant Fachet and I started up. Near *Brabant* we got a ride on one of our trucks as far as the dressing station at the southwest end of *Bois de Consenvoye,* then hiking through the woods toward the right of *Molleville Farm.* On the road, in the woods, we met a major of the 26th Division waiting for his battalion that was coming in to take part in the battle. From him I obtained information of their plans and their position on the right of the 113th Infantry. We then continued on until in the vicinity of *Molleville Farm,* and, as far as it was possible to judge at night, to a position on the right of the 116th Infantry and slightly behind the junction of that regiment and our 113th Infantry. It was now about four o'clock in the morning and as the 113th would be drawn back from their original front line position to allow our artillery to put down a barrage on the enemy positions in the sector about to be attacked, I decided to remain in a small dugout nearby until daylight. The sergeant and myself proceeded to make ourselves comfortable and to get a smoke, which we badly needed, also to lay our plans of procedure and how best to obtain the information we had been sent for. The task itself was not particularly complicated, the biggest difficulty would be to get to a position from which we could keep in contact with the battle as it developed and be able to get the information of how the 113th was progressing. Our greatest danger would be from enemy artillery fire, which would be falling heavily on our support positions, about where we would be most of the time, at least until the 113th had established their new position. This attempt to capture *Hill 361* would arouse all the venom of a wounded lion. We could expect a terrific mauling and 'Jersey' troops had again been given a tough nut to crack.

At 5.30 A.M. our artillery opened on the enemy. Oh Boy! That barrage was a 'honey.' It was music to our ears; at last we were getting real artillery support, the 'Jersey doughboy' was getting the support that heretofore seemed to have been denied us. Of course 'Heinie' had to butt into the fracas. It was only a matter of a few minutes before his artillery let down on us and, believe it or not, his fire was annihilating roads, trees, dugouts;

everything was being blown to pieces. At the position we now were in there were ten fairly large dugouts and several smaller ones, the entrances to which faced the enemy lines. The Germans knew the exact position of each and turned their artillery on the dugouts, blowing the entrances to bits. Had there been any troops in them they would all have been killed. Sergeant Fachet and I were standing in the doorway of one of the smaller dugouts when a shell landed in the earth over the entrance; right there and then I started to say my prayers and bid farewell to everybody. Luckily the shell was a 'dud' and did not explode, its nose was stuck in the earth about four inches. The morning was rather damp and chilly but after the experience with the 'dud' I was perspiring and the sergeant did not need an overcoat. The spot was getting too hot to be comfortable so we moved up a little closer to the front line.

At 6 o'clock our machine guns joined in the party and at 6.15 the 'doughboys' went "over the top." As we were working our way up we met a detachment of the 112th Machine Gun Battalion coming out on the run after putting down their barrage, trying to get away before enemy artillery could locate them. In command of the detachment I met an old friend of Camp McClellan days, Captain Lyons. We had but a few seconds to exchange greetings. It was good to meet a friend up there, sort of made you feel that, after all, the real men of the 29th Division were game and doing their bit. We also commenced to meet some of the walking wounded. From them I was able to obtain information about the 'jump off' and how the attack was progressing along other parts of the front.

From time to time we changed position, so as to advance with the attack. These changes were always under artillery fire and as we came closer to the front we also ran into machine-gun fire. Going through this heavy woods was rather difficult; we had to be careful not to get lost. Then again the shells were cutting down limbs of trees and they were as dangerous as the shells; as usual the enemy mixed his artillery fire with considerable gas. It became more difficult to keep going, trying to follow our course. In gas-masks for a short time and then out of them, at the same time dodging machine-gun bullets and trying to keep out of artillery fire, with it all knowing where the 113th Infantry was and how the advance was progressing. Some time when you feel that your nerves are a little ruffled try a trip similar to this; it is a great soother for unruly nerves. It is guaranteed to either kill or cure.

For several hours the attack seemed to be progressing favorably in spite of the stiff resistance of the enemy. Batches of prisoners were being sent to the rear. Altogether it seemed as if the Newark City Hall was about to be placed on *Hill 361*, as the 113th Infantry stubbornly fought its way up the hill. While making a dash to change our position I suddenly heard about four shells coming and by their sound they were low. Yelling to the sergeant to drop, I slid for the cover of a fallen tree, just made it when those shells burst; then I thought someone had stuck a red-hot poker in my left leg below the knee.

Of course, I realized what had happened; the question was how serious was the wound? For a moment I was afraid to look, but eventually discovered a splinter of shrapnel had entered the leg, between the top of my field boots and the leg-strap; also several other pieces of shrapnel had cut the leather of the boot but had not penetrated. I was probably just on the edge of the burst. The sergeant, luckily, had escaped. Calling back to him that I had been hit he came over and applied my field dressing packet. The wound was not serious but was painful when standing on the leg or trying to walk. Taking advantage of available cover we remained close to the action until it became evident that the 113th was progressing through *Bois de Etraye*. Then began the journey back to *Cote des Roches*.

The trip back to the Regimental P.C. was something I shall never forget. Making our way through a shell-torn woods, dodging shells, half blind and gagging from the effects of gas, in addition to a wounded leg, made walking a misery; altogether I was in agony. We eventually reached the road through *Bois de Consenvoye*, from *Molleville Farm* to *Brabant*. This road, a main traffic artery for our troops, naturally was being shelled heavily by German artillery. On the road were soldiers of all descriptions, runners carrying messages between front line troops and various headquarters at the rear. German prisoners of war were being taken back. Wounded men from the 29th and 26th Divisions were being carried on litters as well as any number of men gassed and wounded who were walking. The sights along the road were pitiful, the wounded dodging shells and the shell-shocked men screaming each time a shell landed near them. To make things more interesting a 'Boche' plane, flying low, followed the road playing his machine gun on us. Each time he came over us we would drop until he passed, then go on again until he made a return trip. He flew over us three times, but as far as I could see he failed to get any of our men although he certainly gave us a horrible scare.

At the southern edge of the woods, where the road came into the open, I witnessed the most inhuman act that it was my misfortune to see during my time on the front—German artillery, shelling one of the advance dressing stations, killed some of our men, already wounded, and added more injuries to others, also blowing the rear end out of an ambulance loaded with wounded. On the ambulance at the time was a friend of mine, a lieutenant of the 113th Infantry, who had been wounded at *Etraye* early in the morning. The lieutenant had reached the dressing station and was ready to start for the rear on the ambulance when that damned 'Heinie' battery fired on them. There was positively no excuse for it; both the ambulance and the dressing station were displaying the Red Cross emblem. The enemy plane probably gave the signal which brought down the shelling; as he made the third trip over he shot up to higher altitude and fired a signal rocket that was promptly answered by this artillery shelling. Needless to say all of us who were able got away from that spot, as fast as possible, when the shelling slackened.

So far I had avoided all our dressing stations, in order to get back and report to Colonel Minnigerode, personally, after which I would have to conform to the orders of the medical officers. I hoped to avoid evacuation to a base hospital. If pos-

sible I would have liked to remain in command of my battalion
when they went up to the lines again. It was my belief that in
the next fight by the 114th Infantry the 3rd Battalion would be
assigned to attack, as per my request of a few days previously.

Passing through *Brabant* we commenced to meet the more
advanced kitchens of the various regiments, most of them hidden behind piles of debris or broken stonewalls. The kitchen
detachments were busy keeping hot food ready for such men as
could get back for it or to send it up to the front line whenever
an opportunity presented itself. While walking down the road
I was hailed by a member of the 104th Engineers. This soldier
knew me and when he saw me limping along he came running
over and insisted that I go to his kitchen and have some hot
coffee and food. I did take the coffee but was unable to eat
anything. Sorry I cannot recall that soldier's name; if he is
still alive he will realize the incident is not forgotten and that I
appreciate his kindness and that of the men with him. These
little kindnesses, extended under the most trying conditions,
made it possible to 'carry on' in spite of the hardships.

Just as we reached *Brabant* I was stopped by Major Jean
Wolf, Medical Officer, 113th Infantry, who asked me where I
was going, and why I was not in a dressing station? Explaining to the Major that my leg wound was only a scratch and the
Medical Officers with the 114th Infantry would give me the
necessary attention, I also told him of the necessity for reporting to Colonel Minnigerode. Listening to my story the Major
led me back to a dressing station, examined the wound, then
turned me over to one of his assistants with instructions that I
be sent to the rear. To make matters worse, another Medical
Officer, Captain Williamson, came into the station, made an
examination and had me tagged for gas, in addition to the leg
wound. This brought on quite an argument as I refused to be
evacuated until I had reported to my regimental commander;
while the argument was at its height two captains of the 114th
Infantry came in. I appealed to them to help to help me convince the doctors of the necessity of my getting back to the regiment where our own doctors would care for me. It was all to

no avail; instead of assisting my argument, these captains started in to tell me that I ought to be in the hospital. After some further treatment, and a whole lot more argument, it was agreed that I be allowed to report back to the regiment, which was only a short distance down the road, and then to be evacuated. That was all I wanted; to get away from the doctors and if possible to keep out of the hospitals.

About two o'clock in the afternoon, we reached the 114th Infantry P.C. and reported to Colonel Minnigerode, who expressed his appreciation for the information we brought back, also his regret that I had been wounded and directed I be given the necessary medical attention at our first-aid station. Captains John J. Halnan and Leslie T. Bolton, our medical officers, examined me and ordered that I be transferred to the Base Hospital. All the arguments in the world failed to convince those two hard-boiled doctors that I would be all right and fit for duty again if given a day or two of rest. Nothing I said could change the order. As Captain Bolton told me, "You are in a weakened condition from the effects of gas and the wound in your leg, you will need attention that we cannot give you up here. You will not be fit for duty again for some time; the proper place for you is the Base Hospital."

Before continuing with the story permit me to take this opportunity to offer a small tribute to a group of men, seldom heard of, but whose untiring labors and self-sacrificing spirit contributed, in a large measure, to the comfort of our wounded men. The Medical Detachment of the 114th Infantry. The men and officers of this unit at all times placed the care of the sick and wounded above all personal considerations. Captains Leslie T. Bolton and John J. Halnan of the 1st Battalion and Lieutenant 'Jimmy' Strickland of the 2nd Battalion were always up front, most of the time under heavy shell fire, dressing wounds and sending the wounded back. I have seen these men out in the open with an utter disregard for their personal safety, as long as they were able to ease the suffering of some doughboy and get him back. These officers received no rewards for their work, but we of the regiment appreciated them and I am simply expressing the sincere thanks of the wounded and sick men of the 114th Infantry. Then there were the litter-bearers, who had to carry the wounded for several miles back to the ambulances, then make the long trip back again to the front line stations, continuing this, always under fire, day and night for weeks. Both officers and enlisted men of the detachment were a credit to the Medical Corps and always upheld its highest traditions, "Never forsake the wounded."

So ended my participation in the active battle operations. In a short time I was placed in an ambulance and started for the Base, arriving at Base Hospital No. 43, *Blois,* France, October 26th. Before reaching the hospital the gas was beginning to show its effects and for more than a week I was unable to take any food. My experience in the Base was uneventful and has no bearing on this story so I will pass briefly over the time spent in hospital.

## CHAPTER XV

## AFTER ETRAYE RIDGE

\*　　　\*　　　\*　　　\*　　　\*　　　\*　　　\*

SHOULD it appear that continual reference is made to lost promotions causing disappointment and discontent, please remember, this is but an example of how the ring worked, it was the key-note of the whole situation; they are but a few extracts from personal experiences. As stated many times, this mad scramble for promotion was responsible for much of our misfortune. These are facts, not rumors. They were the experience of most of the combat officers in the regiment. If there is any question about this, a glance at the records of the 114th Infantry will show that of the officers of the regiment, commanding companies in battle through the *Verdun* operations, only one capain was promoted. If inefficient, why were they retained in command?

There was no question of ability. As a matter of fact the battalion commanders were wholly dependent on the company commanders, leaving the entire conduct of operations in their hands, knowing the companies would obey orders no matter how heavy the losses. Again I repeat, the battalion commanders were useless. They may have been considered efficient in the old militia days at Sea Girt or other State camps, but in battle they simply failed to function; the position was too big for them. In the regiment we had men who were capable and had the nerve to carry on. Men such as Captains Fred. Rohrbach, Albert A. Rickert, Harry Harsin, Chester A. Williams, Harry Doremus and others. Why continue, the answer is always the same—the unseen power?

In the army two methods are usually applied as an award for merit: Decorations, in the form of medals and citations for efficiency and bravery in action; promotion to higher grade for those who demonstrate ability. These awards have a tendency to urge military men on to exceptional bravery and performance of duty above the ordinary routine. When these rewards for merit are properly distributed by higher command an 'esprit de corps' is built up that is unbeatable. Let these awards be given out indiscriminately or without consideration for merit and we have a condition of dissatisfaction and unrest that will break down the morale of an organization faster than will enemy bullets.

So that you may know how some promotions were obtained and how hungry the individuals were for higher rank, even though in their heart they knew they were not qualified to hold higher command, let me cite an incident which took place a couple of nights after I was evacuated to the Base. The incident was related after my return from the hospital. It will give you another 'peep' into the system.

Lieutenant Colonel Minnigerode and several of his staff officers were in the regimental P.C., in *Cote des Roches,* when the telephone rang and was answered by one of the staff. The following transpired, as told to me by one of the officers present at the time and whose veracity I have no reason to doubt:

After some conversation, the officer who had answered the 'phone turned to Colonel Minnigerode and said: "Brigade is calling and want a recommendation for a major."

Colonel Minnigerode replied: "I have already recommended Captain Reddan for promotion."

The Staff Officer: "I have told them that but the brigade replies that Captain Reddan having been wounded and sent to the Base cannot be promoted while in the hospital; they want another name in place of Reddan right away."

The Colonel hesitated for a moment and replied: "I am afraid I will have to let the recommendation pass, I cannot think of another officer to name at the moment."

While the Colonel was talking the staff officer was writing on a slip of paper, then handed the slip to the Colonel with the remark, "How will that name do?"

Colonel Minnigerode looked at the slip in a rather surprised manner, hesitated, and then said, "All right."

The staff officer went back to the telephone and sent in his own name for promotion to be a major.

Rather a 'slick' way of going up the ladder, don't you think? Much more opportunity to gain advanced rank when you had a dugout job, far less chance of injury and lost promotion than if out on the front line in a fight. The fact that an officer was wounded, in line of duty, made no difference; once separated from our organizations, even though in hospital recovering from wounds, under A.E.F. orders there could be no promotion until such officer rejoined his outfit.

For a change let us see what others thought of conditions in the 114th Infantry. You will recall that the command of Company B passed to Lieutenant Heinzmann at the time of my assignment to the 3rd Battalion on October 14th. The lieutenant remained in command during the remainder of active operations and until my return from the hospital. If, by the recital up to this point, you have gained the impression that the story is too one-sided or that conditions are being exaggerated, there is submitted for your consideration the official report of Lieutenant Heinzmann covering the operations of Company B from October 24th to the 30th. This report was made out by the lieutenant while I was still in the hospital. I knew nothing of the report until after my return to the company, when the lieutenant told of his having incurred the displeasure of the Brigade Commander and of the possibility of his being tried by a military court if he persisted in having the report go into the records. Heinzmann was very much disturbed about the matter and asked my advice. After listening to his recital of conditions, with the few remaining N.C.Os. of the company verifying his statements, I advised him to let the report stand. If there were going to be any trials we would have something to say about

*Bois de Ormont.* The only change he made was to eliminate the names of officers whom he had criticized in the first
report. The original should be on file with the records of the
29th Division in the War Department at Washington, D. C.
I say "should be on file" because one can never be sure of what
is in the files, so many records have been 'lost' or at least disappeared, especially those reports attempting to tell the true
story, or recommendations for decorations or promotions, particularly when the beneficiary was not in the good graces of the
reviewing board or someone connected with it.

\*          \*          \*          \*          \*          \*          \*

## OPERATIONS REPORT, CO. B 114th INFANTRY.

"1. On October 24th, this company left *Cote des Roches*
at 18 o'clock to take up, what we understood at the time, a support position in conjunction with the remainder of 1st Bn., for
a period of forty eight (48) hours. After considerable delay of
some unknown reason, this company arrived at *Ravine de
Molleville* at 3 o'clock on the morning of the 25th October and took up a support position in rear of our front line.

2. When making relief of the former organization in support, no data could be obtained from any member of the company as to the direction of the enemy, nor the distance from the
front line. The main thought which prevailed among both
officers and men of the relieved organizations was a hasty exit
from the vicinity. Consequently, the men of this company were
scattered over a large area in the confusion, and without any
knowledge of where our other units were.

3. At about 16 o'clock on the 25th of October, Orders were
received to relieve companies G and H, 116th Inf., who were in
the line at *Bois d'Etrayes,* but relief could not be made
until 23 o'clock due to the heavy bombardment of the enemy
artillery in the valley and in the neighborhood of P.C. It was
difficult to obtain runners, the guides from the 116th failed utterly and no strenuous efforts were made at our P.C. to obtain
guides, with the result that considerable time was lost, and in
case of attack, would have proved rather disastrous; all due to

indifference at P.C. Companies A and B were consolidated on making the relief, with the members of Co. B, on the right of the line, in liaison with Co. F, 114th Inf.

4. On the 26th one man was killed and another wounded in an endeavor to locate the lines, which were difficult to find as no runners were available who were familiar with the sector. The result being, party was hit by machine-gun bullets, which gun should have been located, as position was known to members of the 116th Infantry.

5. On the evening of the 26th Companies A and B were moved to the left of the line, relieving Co. C, 116th Inf., and causing us to cover a three company sector, which was accomplished by Co. F, 114th Inf., increasing the front of their sector, and relieving some of our G.C.'s., and also by increasing distance between G.C.'s.

6. On the 27th, one man of Company C was killed by one of our own 77's falling short. Repeatedly our shots from allied artillery were hitting our lines and the difficulty arose of sending information to rear. One runner was started immediately, but on the trip consumed the greater part of an hour. A VB. rocket was fired with no results; as only one other was available it was held in reserve until probably an hour later when a French aeroplane came over the sector, flying very low and our last rocket was fired and was seen by the aviator, who circled around the sector several times and then went to the rear, and firing stopped shortly.

7. Our location was shown to aeroplane by means of handkerchief as no marking panels were available and supply of rockets had been exhausted.

8. On the 28th, orders were received for relief of companies A and C, 116th Inf., who had established line on left of our units after having been relieved the day before. An effort was made at dusk to make this relief but Commanding Officer of Co. C refused to have his company relieved until morning. About 22 o'clock an order was received stating that relief must be completed, but in the meantime the members of Company A and B had been placed wherever shelter could be obtained due to the dense forest and impossibility to relocate G.C.'s., as the company sector was very irregular. The relief was completed at dawn.

9. The morning of the 30th October this company was re-lieved by a company of the 315th Infantry (79th Div.)

10. This company had twenty-six (26) men holding the line, who were relieved by approximately sixty (60) men.

11. During the time this company was on the line not a par-ticle of hot food or liquids was received, although the kitchen daily forwarded food and coffee. The men existed on corned beef, bread and water during the entire stay and even then it was necessary to withdraw men from the line to obtain rations.

12. Repeated requests were made for ammunition, grenades and rockets, but the only grenades obtained were by ration party, who were greatly handicapped, and had to carry some for a distance of three kilometers. Ammunition was not re-ceived, and the only rockets received were three and six star, calling for barrage, and from aero to ground for marking lines. Flares were an unknown quantity and could not be procured, whereas the enemy had flares in the air every twenty minutes. At night it was simply a hit and miss proposition, as nothing could be seen, although sounds of digging and wiring parties could be heard.

13. No support was received on the line from machine guns of any description as after the withdrawal of the 58th Brigade the machine guns were also withdrawn, which left the valley on left of line held by riflemen whereas the enemy controlled it by machine guns.

14. Aviation was of no assistance in the protection of the line, as the enemy repeatedly had his planes marking our lines and using machine guns in an endeavor to cause casualties.

15. None of the unit commanders, other than the companies on the line, visited the sector, and at no time was a personal reconnaissance made by officer in charge, either personally or by intelligence section. The result of which was that orders were received which were formulated on paper and not by any knowledge of the sector, and which made it almost impossible to execute properly.

16. The morale of the men was greatly weakened due to the casualties caused by our own artillery, also by the repeated false statements as to length of time we would be in support and re-

serve, and that our enemy was weak, whereas it was found entirely different, by actual contact, and not theory.

"GROVER P. HEINZMANN,

"1st Lt., 114th Infantry, Comdg. Co. B."

\*     \*     \*     \*     \*     \*     \*

There you have the opinion of the man who had taken over my position, commander of Company B. Had this report been dictated by me I could not have composed one that would have substantiated better the statements previously made that incompetency and, although distasteful to say it, self-preservation, or any other name you want to call it among some officers was the worst enemy we had to fight. Is this a strong statement? Well! think this one over. The commanding officer of the 114th Infantry was so disgusted with conditions on the line during the period covered by Heinzmann's report that he personally made a trip to the front, visiting the Battalion P.C.'s., and ordered the commanders to get out of their dugouts and take personal command of their line. In one case the colonel relieved a major of his command because he was found in his dugout after being ordered to get out with his battalion.

Lieutenant Heinzmann's report contains little comment on the activities of the enemy or his own company, no comment on the fighting of his men, nothing about the men patroling 'No-man's land,' nor about the everlasting sniping that was kept on 'Jerry' to keep him in his own back-yard. Nothing of the usual activities of an infantry company when holding the line; nothing but a severe criticism of his commanding officer, couched in language that will pass without reaction on the lieutenant. Knowing Mr. Heinzmann as well as I do, and reading his report which is substantiated by stories from the men of our own company as well as those of officers and men of other companies in the regiment, repeated time after time, then and through the years after the war, the conditions existing at the time covered by the report must have been rotten. As stated in the résumé of the battle of *Bois de Ormont*, companies were put on the line and left there to be annihilated, or to exist the best way they could without any assistance from higher command. Again the companies were giving their last ounce of strength and taking severe punishment while those to whom they had every right to look for leadership were safe in a dugout.

Before closing the story of our part in the operations northwest of *Verdun*, when the 29th Division was relieved by the 79th Division, October 30th, let us again look into Colonel Palmer's excellent book "OUR GREATEST BATTLE," (Dodd, Mead & Co.). In it we find a story of accomplishment in spite of handicaps and discouraging command, an unbiased account of our little contribution to the success of this battle, the greatest battle in all United States history.

"The 29th's three weeks' service in the hell's torment of the bowl was now over. In its place came the 79th, National Army, which also was from both sides of the Mason and Dixon line, north and south mixing in its ranks. . . . The isolation of units in slippery ravines and woods, and the depth of shelled area, required two nights for relief. The 29th's 5636 casualties were balanced on the bloody ledger of its record by 2300 prisoners. This was a remarkable showing; testimony of harvest won by bold reactions against counter-attacks, of charges which made a combing sweep in their sturdy rushes, even when they had to yield some of the ground won. Man to man the Blue and Greys had given the enemy better than he had sent; but not in other respects. They could not answer his artillery shell for shell, or even one shell to three.

"My glimpses of the battle east of the *Meuse* among the *Verdun* hills recalled the days of the *Verdun* battle, while the French were stalling, with powerful artillery support, on the muddy crests and slopes and in slippery ravines. When they retook *Douaumont* and *Vaux* they had a cloud of shell-bursts rolling in front of the charge. We were going relatively naked to the charge. This had been our fortune in most of our attacks in the *Meuse-Argonne,* as our part in driving our man-power to hasten the end of the war. There was something pitiful about our artillery in the bowl, trying to answer the smashing fire of the outnumbering guns with their long-range fire from the heights. The artillery of the 29th for three weeks kept its shifts going day and night, while the veteran artillerists of the 26th had problems in arranging patterns of barrages to cover the in-filtering attack which put new wrinkles in their experience.

"Of the 29th's wounded, thirty-five per cent were gassed. The whole area of the bowl was continually gassed. Sickness was inevitable from lack of drinking water, warm food and proper care. While the Germans could slip back to billets on the reverse slopes, and to shell-proof shelters, let it be repeated that our men had to remain all the time under nerve-racking shell-fire in the open, and under soaking rains that had made every hole they dug on the lower levels a well. Some of the woods they occupied were shelled until they could see from end to end through the limbless poles of the trunks. The desolation of *Delville* and *Trones* woods in the *Somme* battle were repro-duced; but the 26th and 29th were there to attack, and they kept on attacking. The fire they drew was a mighty factor in the success of our thrusts against the whale-back. It should be enough for any soldier to say that he served east of the *Meuse.*"

In my opinion there is no one more capable of describing battle or expressing an opinion on our activities than the writer of the above quotation. Colonel Palmer, as a war correspon-dent, covered the fighting long before the United States entered the war; he was with the French and British forces at various times. After we entered the war he saw all our divisions in ac-tion. He knew war with all its horror and hardships. Colonel Palmer's description of the *Meuse-Argonne* battle is worth reading in its entirety, especially by the infantrymen of the 29th Division.

After the ending of hostilities, the Overseas Edition of "The Stars and Stripes," the official newspaper of the A.E.F., pub-lished an account of the activities of the various divisions. In the edition of April 25th, 1919, a résumé of the operations of the 26th Division, in the vicinity of *Bois de Ormont,* was published; showing that even this excellent division was unable to dislodge 'Jerry' from his observation point on *Hill 360,* or to get him out of our old friend *Ormont.* A comparison of our experiences at *Ormont Farm* with this article will make clearer the extremely hard task assigned to the 114th Infantry. It may convince you that the 'Jersey' troops were given 'the dirty end of the stick' in this battle.

"The 26th Division, coming into line on October 16-17, attacked on the 23rd in a generally northeastern direction through *Le Houppy* and the *Bois de la Reine* against the *Belleu Bois,* on the left; the *Bois de Chenes* in the center, and the *Bois d'Ormont* on the right, the attack being made by the 57th Brigade on the left and the 51st Brigade on the right, supported by fire of the 51st Field Artillery Brigade.

As had been indicated, the country was rugged by nature and well fortified. Immediately before attacking the 26th Division took over a part of the right of the 29th Division sector and, through a protecting mist, the 101st Infantry at 6.15 (A.M. advanced in liaison with the troops of the 29th Division up the *Etraye Ridge* and seized the observatory at the top. The 102nd Infantry pushed forward on the right and by mid-afternoon the front had occupied the whole of the *Belleu Bois* and the *Bois de Chenes* and the west edge of the *Bois d'Ormont.* Under very heavy artillery and machine gun fire, however, *Belleu Bois* was relinquished, and it was necessary the next afternoon to attack again, at the same moment that the 102nd Infantry advanced into the *Bois d'Ormont,* fighting all the rest of the day and most of the night following, against most bitter resistance. The 101st Infantry penetrated 500 meters into the *Bois Belleu,* only to be forced back finally by a fourth counterattack after it had repulsed three of them.

In the *Bois d'Ormont* the 102nd Infantry had a similar struggle and, although it got through the greater part of the woods to the base of Hill 360, in the eastern end, the enemy clung to this valuable observation point, from which he could see as far as the Meuse, and it could not be taken before dark. The attack was renewed the next morning but the attacking forces were so depleted that they were not merely unable to make gains but were gradually forced back by evening to the western edge of the woods.

After a very heavy artillery preparation a renewed attack on both flanks was delivered at 11 A.M., October 27th. The 3rd Battalion of the 104th Infantry by 4 o'clock in the afternoon occupied all of the *Bois Belleu* definitely. The troops on the right again penetrated the *Bois d'Ormont,* but were met by the most devastating bombardment which had yet been experienced, though they clung to their gains through the night and a part of the next day, they eventually had to give them up and on October 28th the enemy still retained the *Bois d'Ormont.*

The 26th Division lay without further aggressive action, being relieved on its left by the 79th Division, and, in turn, relieving the 26th French Division on its right, until November 7th, when it resumed offensive operations on the front between *Beaumont* and *Bois d'Ormont,* near which latter point it came in liaison with the 79th Division."

(The article then indicates that neither the 26th or 79th Divisions took *Bois d'Ormont* until a general withdrawal was ordered by the German High Command, about November 8th.)

It was not my privilege to command Company B as it came out of the lines, but it is simple enough to visualize their appearance. I had taken Company B into action with nearly 200 men and 5 officers. They were now coming out with about 25 men and 1 officer, Lieutenant Heinzmann. They had paid a high price but what a record they and the entire division had made. In spite of all obstacles they had made good. Until relieved by the 26th and 79th Divisions, the 29th had carried the heavy load of being on the extreme right of the entire Allied swing and the 114th Infantry, our regiment, had been the pivot of the *Argonne* drive. Failure on our part would have meant a serious check to the Allied forces, and undoubtedly would have prolonged active operations.

The regiment after leaving the lines on October 30th was assembled at *Cote des Roches.* Company B remained there until about 4.30, when they marched to *Jardin Fontaine.* The march was uneventful. The men have often told me it was good to be going out with the prospects of rest and hot food. They felt rather sorry for the troops they met on the road that were going up front.

On October 31st Company B left *Jardin Fontaine,* at 12.10 P.M., and were taken by trucks to *Bussey la Cote,* remaining at this point until the armistice put an end to hostilities.

During the stay at *Bussey la Cote* the regiment received the much needed replacements, Company B being filled up with about 150 men mostly from the 38th Division, men from Indiana and Iowa. There were so few non-commissioned officers left in the company, after the operations that practically all the survivors were advanced to higher rank.

CHAPTER XVI

## "FINIS LA GUERRE"

### ALL OVER, 'OVER THERE'

IT seems to me that some place or time I have heard that "the Almighty Father is the special protector of infants." From what transpired in the next few days it would appear as though "Our Heavenly Commander" took the 114th Infantry under His wing. On November 10th orders were received directing the regiment to move, in preparation for an attack on *Metz.* Without knowing the war was about to end, in compliance with orders the 114th Infantry, at 7 o'clock on the morning of the 11th started the change of station, expecting to be in action again within the next few days. After traveling several miles Lieutenant Heinzmann received an order directing him to return with Company B to *Bussey la Cote,* as an armistice had been signed and hostilities would cease at eleven o'clock.

You may ask what the feelings were of the soldiers when told the war was over, knowing that they would not be required to again enter battle. No man can explain just what the individual feelings were; those who had been in the 'big push' certainly were glad it was over, but each individual had a feeling distinctly his own. All were rather stunned by the sudden cessation of hostilities, even though we had heard rumors that the enemy were asking for terms on which the war could end. Most of those with whom I talked thought the war would continue until the Spring of 1919, at least. When we heard the fighting was to end officially at 11 o'clock we could scarcely believe the report. The change from war to peace was too sudden to understand. One minute looking forward to entering the lines again, with all its horrors and hard-ships, and the next minute trying to realize it was all over. No more night marches, no more raids, no more trips into 'No-man's land,' no more waiting under artillery and machine gun fire, no more barrages, no more 'going over the top.' All Over! After all there were good prospects of returning to "God's Country."

The 114th Infantry was assembled at *Chardogne* to cele-brate the ending of the war. The regimental band, under the direction of 'Chief' McNeice, was kept busy playing, some speeches were made. Then to wind up the celebration the flares and rockets intended for use against our late enemy were set off, thus ending our part in the World War in a blaze. Back of all this celebration however was the remembrance of our 'old gang' who would never again go home. As a token of remembrance and respect the regiment stood at attention, in silent salute, to those soldiers of the 114th U. S. Infantry who had made the supreme sacrifice.

Those of us in the hospitals also thought of our 'buddies' and in silent reverie remembered them. In my mind I could see again the men of Company B who had been killed or wounded, "In the service of the United States"—our honored dead, who had

"Laid down their lives for their country."

\*     \*     \*     \*     \*     \*     \*

You will recall that I had been evacuated to the Base on October 23rd, and, of course, was not present with the regiment after that date. What is written of the last days of service on the front is taken from reports and from conversations with members of the organization after my return from the hos-pital. There was one incident, however, which occurred in the regiment toward the end of October that had considerable bearing upon my leaving the hospital. You will recall that Colonel Minnigerode had found it necessary to relieve a bat-talion commander for failing to properly command his organi-zation while on the front.

Base Hospital 43, to which I had been evacuated, was located at *Blois,* in the central part of France. In addition to being a hospital town it was also the re-classification depot for officers relieved of command of their units for various reasons. These officers were examined by a Board of Officers who reviewed the charges against them. After trial these men were then assigned to other organizations, or if the examining board felt that an officer was unfit for his rank they sometimes gave the defendant the option of accepting a lower grade. When the Board decided that a man was temperamentally or professionally unfit they ordered his return to the United States for discharge from the army.

Several days before the armistice was signed, while still in bed, Chaplain Smith, 114th Infantry, who was also at the Base Hospital, having been gassed, came into my room and informed me that the major whom Colonel Minnigerode had relieved from command was in the town for re-classification. The Chaplain informed me the major had suggested I appear as a witness in his behalf. When the case came up before the Board, about the middle of November, he had requested the Chaplain to "sound me out" as to willingness to testify.

This request was nerve with a capital "N," coming from an officer whom I had emphatically informed, while on the front, that I had no confidence in his ability to command a battalion, and had also told him that any further orders from him would not be obeyed by me until the Commanding Officer of the 114th Infantry had been acquainted with my action.

Having no desire to crucify this officer by testifying against him, yet I most certainly could not testify in his behalf and tell the truth. To appear before the reviewing board would mean one of two things, for or against the major. If I testified in his behalf I would be lying. In order to be honest with myself and the men who had been under my command I decided the best thing to do was to get out of *Blois* before the trial came up. This may seem like running away under fire, but I was sick and tired of this everlasting condition, officers getting themselves into trouble and then trying to get their brother officers to appear as witnesses in their behalf, in an effort to evade punishment. Of all the hospitals in France it was my luck to be sent to *Blois,* where I was again brought up against more arguments. Not for me. I had had enough of it. So decided to leave the hospital, with or without permission, at the first opportunity.

With the help of one of the doctors whom I discovered had some relatives in my home city, and emphasizing how healthy I was and that there was no sense in my being in a hospital when I could be of service up front with my regiment, he finally agreed to help me try to get away. But not before much argument, and apparently against his own opinion. On Sunday, November 10th, I managed to get an order permitting me to leave the hospital.

I worked the order all right, but how many times in the intervening years have I paid for being in such a rush to get back to the 29th Division.

\*　　\*　　\*　　\*　　\*　　\*　　\*

ALL OVER! It was difficult to realize the war was over. On November 11th I was in *Tours,* changing trains on the way back to the 114th Infantry. While waiting I went through the city and heard considerable talk of an armistice being signed but was unable to obtain any official information. The natives were very much excited. They seemed unable to realize that the end of more than four years of war was only a matter of minutes.

During the afternoon it became generally known that the fighting had stopped; then the women and children flocked to the city hall, or as the French call it, "Hotel de Ville," in an effort to obtain information about their men folks who were still at the front when hostilities ceased. Altogether the scene was one of happiness, yet this feeling of uncertainty about the men who had survived put a damper on their enthusiasm for several hours. However, this feeling of gloom gradually disappeared and then burst out into a celebration that lasted for several days.

November 12th in *Le Mans* and the next day in *Paris*, where I stayed until the night of the 14th. The scenes in all the towns and villages passed through were the same. In *Paris* the natives, as well as the soldiers and sailors of the Allied nations, were celebrating in every conceivable manner. It seemed to me that every avenue and boulevard had several impromptu parades, moving in opposite directions at the same time. Then every few minutes the National anthem of each of the Allies would be heard, when the soldiers and sailors in the vicinity would render the prescribed salute. Along the sidewalks, in the cafes and public buildings, there was a scene of wild abandon that I am unable to describe. The French girls were even more jubilant than the men, throwing their arms around the foreign soldiers and begging for souvenirs. Who could blame them, after that terrible long period of suffering? We were all the same—wild with joy to think that the war had ended and in our favor.

It is hard to imagine which place I would rather have been in when the order to "cease firing" was given, on the front lines or in *Paris;* neither place will ever be forgotten. All in the A.E.F. were mighty proud of the fact that we had played a small part in helping to bring the war to an end, but especially proud of being soldiers or sailors of the United States.

Leaving *Paris* late on the 14th I finally caught up with the regiment on the evening of the 16th, at *Vavincourt.* Arriving in the regimental area was almost as good as being at home; by this time a feeling of satisfaction and contentment came over us when we returned to the organization after any absence. Both officers and men had been through so many hardships and suffering together that a feeling of comradeship and respect for each other had grown up, leveling all differences in rank except in a strictly military sense.

Arriving at *Vavincourt,* the first duty was to report my return to the headquarters of the 114th Infantry, then to pay my respects to Lieutenant Colonel Minnigerode, who you will remember had been the commander of the regiment when I was ordered to the hospital. Knocking on the door of his billet I was directed to enter. On so doing I found the Colonel bending over an open fire trying to coax a spark of life into it. As I entered the Colonel, without rising, turned to see who it was. He just stared at me until I felt that something was wrong. After a couple of minutes he stood up and coming towards me exclaimed, "Captain Reddan, you are the last man I wanted to see come back to this regiment; you have received a rotten deal."

For a moment I was stunned at Colonel Minnigerode's remark. Since leaving the hospital, the anticipation of rejoining the regiment was uppermost in my mind. I had not given a thought to what might have occurred in the regiment, or to possible changes in the officer personnel, nor to the political complex that had worked such havoc in the regiment during active operations. The Colonel did not keep me long in suspense. After shaking hands and inquiring if I had completely recovered from the gas and wound, he explained that he was no longer in command, but that Colonel George Williams, a regular army cavalry officer, had been assigned to command, several days previously. He also explained that as I had been wounded and sent to the hospital the recommendation for my promotion had been cancelled. Colonel Minnigerode explained that a new order had been issued stopping further promotions in the A.E.F., and this would prevent future recommendations for me; later on we will see that this order was continually broken. Colonel Minnigerode expressed his regret at the misfortune, as he termed it, that seemed to be following me.

During the conversation the Colonel told of the conditions on the front, how, after I had been evacuated, he was compelled to lead the regiment into its position on October 24th when the battalion commanders apparently became lost in attempting to occupy the positions assigned to their organizations. He also spoke of it being necessary for him to relieve one battalion commander and to censure another while on the front lines, because these officers stayed in dug-outs while the men under their command were being shot to pieces. He

related several other incidents which occurred during the last
tour of duty.

Rather a sad commentary on the battalion leadership in
the regiment. As explained on several previous occasions the
regiment had excellent company officers and enlisted men, they
were unsurpassed, but unfortunately the commanders of the
battalions were not up to snuff. The officer who was sent to
the rear by the Colonel should never have been given the
command of a combat battalion; he was the outgrowth of a
'click' that for years had used the former National Guard as
a social organization, and who never gave a serious thought to
the possibility of getting into a war. The reason this officer
was relieved at *Molleville Farm* was exactly the same
as had been demonstrated at *Bois de Ormont*—consigning
troops to battle and then taking cover in dug-outs, with no
consideration for the lives of the men under their command.
It is hard to write of these conditions, but how much harder
it was to see the men alongside of me wither and die under a
murderous fire, because of this inefficiency. It was unfortunate that the commanding officer had failed to recognize this
weak spot three months earlier.

Leaving Colonel Minnigerode, I went to the 1st Battalion
P.C. and reported my return to duty to the battalion adjutant,
the battalion commander being out for the evening; then I
went to find Company B. On the way to the company I met
one of the lieutenants of the battalion whom I had known for
a number of years. This officer had been at school during the
active operations of the regiment around *Verdun* and so
missed the hard service. He was the type who was continually
in trouble and avoided court-martial only through the leniency
of his brother officers, one of those given to making life for
himself as easy as possible by exciting sympathy. When the
lieutenant saw me he immediately commenced to explain how
bad conditions were in the battalion and wound up by saying:
"Bill! You are the senior captain and entitled to command the
battalion. You are not going to let him get away with it, are
you?" To which I replied that this was my affair, one that I

would attend to, and for him to take care of his own 'knit-ting.' Knowing this officer it was easy to understand his rea-soning. If he could induce me to put in a claim of seniority and in that way become the battalion commander, the lieu-tenant had it all figured out that life for him would be much easier. Such men were wonderful strategists where their own well-being was affected. It was peculiar, but several months later, while in temporary command of the battalion, it was necessary for me to severely censure this officer after a series of derelictions that were very annoying, to say the least, and which under another battalion commander would have re-sulted in trial by court-martial.

Upon my return to the 1st Battalion I found Captain John S. Cooke in command of the battalion. He was the regimental adjutant during our front-line duty and had been given com-mand of the battalion after I was sent to the hospital; up to the time of my return his promotion had not come through. As the senior captain of the regiment, several years senior to Cooke, according to army regulations I was privileged to de-cline service under a junior officer. Had I followed this course and refused to serve under him it would simply have meant that I would have been transferred away from Company B, if not out of the regiment. There had been one example of this in the regiment already. Towards the end of hostilities, while on the front line, one of the best captains of our regiment declined to serve in battle under a junior captain who had been given temporary command of the battalion. The result? The senior captain was promptly relieved of command of the com-pany he had entered the service with, trained and then success-fully commanded in nearly four months of front-line duty. This captain was sent to the rear for re-classification under the same stigma as an officer who was relieved for cowardice. No, thank you, none of this for me.

With a new colonel in command of the regiment, and realizing what would happen if any objection was made, I simply put pride in my pocket and went back to duty with Company B, confident in my ability to avoid trouble. The war was over and I didn't care a 'damn' who was in command of the battalion; it was all the same to me if a Chinaman was given the command. Like everyone else, all I wanted was to get out of "this man's army." Service in the 29th Division had cured me of any further desire to 'play soldier.'

Several weeks later Captain Cooke's promotion came through and officially he was our battalion commander until the regiment was mustered out. During the period that Major Cooke was in command there never was any trouble between us, in fact he gave me every liberty that I could reasonably expect and never interfered in the administration of the company. At various times he was absent from the battalion and I was in temporary command. Upon his return he always appeared to be satisfied with the condition of the battalion.

Despite the many unpleasant things it had been my misfortune to witness since the organization of the regiment, I was glad to be back with the outfit. The welcome I received from the members of Company B, who had survived the fighting, the manner in which each man came up to the salute and then broke out into a smile of welcome was something unexpected. I appreciated their expression of goodwill and came to understand that in spite of the necessity for strict discipline, these men seemed to consider me as a comrade.

Taking over the command of the company from Lieutenant Heinzmann seemed like being assigned to an entirely different outfit. Heinzmann was the only one of my old lieutenants still on duty with the company. Lieutenant Henry Bateman, one of the company officers who had been on special duty with the battalion scouts during the fighting, had been promoted to captain and was now the regimental adjutant. The new officers with the company were Lieutenants Chester Clasby and Luby Royall, both of whom had been with the 114th Infantry at *Bois de Ormont;* also Lieutenants Philip T. Boone and Earl Colby, newly assigned to the division. The company ranks had been filled with replacements from the 38th Division, men from the Middle Western States. It was at this time that Lieutenant Heinzmann told of the conditions the company had been facing in the vicinity of *Molleville Farm*. The report of the Lieutenant has already been given in a previous chapter; he was very bitter and biting in his criticism of the manner in which his men had been unnecessarily exposed and sacrificed without any assistance. This verbal report of the Lieutenant, in addition to what others in the regiment told me, gave a vivid picture of the rottenness existing.

Sunday morning, November 17th, I had my first glimpse of Company B. They were in good physical condition and ready for whatever might be in store for them. A number of men believed we would keep moving, right down to the coast and then home; some asserted we would be in the United States before Christmas. This view was discouraged as much as possible. I explained to the men that with so many divisions in France it would be impossible to have all troops leave at once; probably the organizations longest overseas would be the first to go home. I also suggested the possibility of our being ordered into Germany. This seemed to satisfy most of the men. Of course we had some die-hards who were willing to back up their opinions by making all sorts of bets; if I attempted to collect all the boxes of cigars, cartons of cigarettes, candy, etc., that these men wanted to wager, when I suggested that we would be lucky to be home for Easter, I would still be smoking their cigars and cigarettes.

## Chapter XVII

## CHATILLON-*sur*-SAONE

### "WINTER IN SUNNY FRANCE"

On November 18th at 8.30 A.M. the company left *Vavincourt* and arrived at *Silmont*, 11.30 A.M., remaining at this place until the 20th. At 4 P.M. we moved to *Tronville* and then by train to *Passavant,* arriving there at 1 P.M., November 21st. From this point we 'hiked' to *Chatillon-sur-Saone* arriving at 3.30 P.M. the same day.

*Chatillon-sur-Saone.* The winter of 1918-1919, with its long, weary months in a small village. The rain, snow, cold, dreary and draughty billets; other than routine duty, no way in which to pass the days of waiting. It is to the credit of the men that they controlled their loneliness and inactivity as well as they did. In the months we were stationed here I never received a complaint of any serious nature and never had to punish a soldier for wanton destruction of property or in any manner interfering with or disturbing the French natives. Once in a while some soldier would break loose and indulge a little too freely in 'greased lightning,' Vin Blanc. Usually he was taken care of by a 'buddy' who got him into his billet before any harm was done and before it became necessary for an officer to interfere. On the whole, maintaining discipline was not a very difficult task.

Upon arrival in this region, officially designated as the 11th Training Area, 29th Division Headquarters at *Bourbonles-Bains,* the division received a schedule of training that was ideal for a 'batch' of recruits being prepared to enter a war, rather than for troops who had been in the Federal service for nearly two years and who had been in battle for several months. Of course there was a reason for this intensive training, the necessity of keeping troops busy and out of trouble—the old army principle of "a grumbling soldier is happy." It is my experience that soldiers who are worked hard, treated fairly, properly fed and comfortably billeted will growl at being worked too hard, but rarely get into trouble. The American soldier appears to consider it as his privilege to protest and grumble. I believe the average soldier would 'kick' if he was being fed five times a day, with chicken served for breakfast in bed, no drills or fatigues on the schedule and each day a pay-day.

In describing our existence at this station, no attempt will be made to enter into details, merely a touching on the major events. A general survey will be sufficient to give a fair idea of the life around us and of which we were a part. For instance a chapter might be written about road building and road repairs, or as the men called it "manicuring the face of France." No matter how many times we had to perform this task, the work was always the same, digging out the worn spots, filling them in again with broken stone and then raking over the road surface. This work was very necessary, although the men could never appreciate the necessity for it. The country roads were being subjected to an amount of traffic, horse drawn and motorized, for which they had never been built; it was vital to our own comfort and sustenance, not considering the natives at all, that these roads be kept passable.

Stationed in the village was the Commanding Officer and Staff of the 114th Infantry, Commanding Officer and Staff of the 1st Battalion, Companies A, B, C and Headquarters Company. Company D of our battalion was stationed in another village a short distance away. In a small village this additional number of men, more than a thousand, gave us a crowded condition. Every available inch of space was occupied by us for billeting the troops; every barn, cowshed, woodshed, etc., was used. Company B was fortunate in this place. It had been assigned to a grain mill at the junction of the Saone and

Apance rivers, on the main road at the entrance to the village. This made things better for the men and easier for the officers to keep check on them; also eliminating complaints from a number of property owners.

Accustomed, as we were in the United States, to tents or barracks in large areas these billeting conditions were always unsatisfactory. The sanitary conditions were of the most primitive type, accommodations for personal cleanliness were very meager, each man having to wash his clothing in the river and wash his face and hands at the town pump. Bathing the entire body in the river was usually accomplished at night, or if in daylight hours a soldier would be on the lookout for the town ladies crossing the river. At an alarm the bathers in their birthday suits would dive into the river. Cleanliness was insisted upon at all times, no matter what the weather conditions might be, rain, snow, mud, etc. All were required to keep clothing, equipment and person scrupulously clean; each man required to shave daily. Many times the men had to break a hole in the ice to shave and wash. Every man had his bedsack filled with straw for sleeping on; sleeping of course on the floor of the billet. In spite of daily inspection by the officers and non-commissioned officers of the company the cleanest of us would, at times, discover that our 'Old Pal' the 'Cootie' was still with us, he had no respect for rank or position. As a matter of opinion I believe the 'Cooties' rather enjoyed 'picking on' an officer. He could be made to feel much more uncomfortable than an enlisted man, especially if the officer was standing at attention in front of his organization and a 'Coot' was enjoying a meal between the officer's shoulder blades. Sometimes, in memory, I still feel those pests.

Inspections of quarters and personnel of the organization were made by the regimental and battalion surgeons at regular intervals so that cleanliness and the general health of the command was kept very good. At intervals each company was required to have all clothing, blankets, bedsacks, etc., put through the "delousing" machine, an instrument of torture supposed to eliminate 'cooties' by placing the material in a machine and subjecting it to intense steam pressure. Theoretically the cooties would be dead when the clothing was removed from the machine, actually they were very much alive. The effect of the steam pressure appeared to be mostly on the uniforms. When given back to the soldier they were a mass of wrinkles that took weeks to remove; the clothing was shrunk so that a blouse which had gone into the machine a good size would go back to its owner many sizes too small. At one period, uniforms had been issued of rather a poor quality, with buttons of a composition material instead of the usual metal buttons. When that bunch of uniforms came out of the delouser they were a mess; sleeves up above the wrists, bottoms of the breeches up to the knees and the composition buttons unrecognizable.

In spite of the many hardships and handicaps the health of the company was very good and at no time was it necessary to punish the organization for carelessness of person or in the living quarters. No confinement to quarters such as had been the case when I assumed command of the company in January, 1918, at Camp McClellan.

The food was good and plentiful, but as might be expected limited in variety, usually the same general issue every day, making it necessary for the kitchen crew to think up new 'kinks' in disguising prunes to taste like grapefruit or perhaps serving beans that tasted like bananas, etc. I have eaten prunes in every conceivable form: stewed, fried, baked, roasted, raw, and on several occasions we had them made into pies. So with all the food, it was rather monotonous, and in a small village such as we were in it was impossible to buy any additional food supplies to help vary the menu.

While on the subject of food I would like to say a word of commendation for a small group of men in Company B who most certainly did their duty in both the active operations and after the cessation of hostilities. Not by actual participation in the battles, but by the simple process of obeying orders, doing their part in the company kitchen and under all conditions keeping food prepared so that we were always sure of something to eat if we were able to get near our kitchen, or as they often did, sending hot food up to the men on the front lines, although many times it did not reach our men. Theirs was a job under fire all the time; no hope of decorations or promotions, merely the satisfaction of duty exceptionally well done. To Mess Sergeant Chris. Galanos; Cooks Edward Stevens, Edward Fairchild, Charles Biehler, Joseph Leonard and the two assistant cooks, William Landers and Henry Hoffmann, I would say that the officers and men of your company appreciated your service and wish it were possible to show a more substantial form of commendation.

The periods around the holidays, Thanksgiving and Christmas, were rather trying times on all of us. The numerous changes that had taken place during the year and especially since arriving in France, from deaths, wounds, etc., had made an entirely different company. The many new faces in ranks caused us to miss the 'Old Gang' who had "Gone West" or to 'Blighty.' As a result a feeling of depression seemed to overshadow the few men who still remained with the company. Efforts were made to keep up the spirits of these men. Special menus were prepared for each holiday and various games were arranged for the afternoon, so that everybody was busy and as far as possible kept from thinking too deeply of their own troubles. It was only natural for the soldiers to celebrate in their own way by having a few drinks. Several times on Christmas Day, and again at New Year's, I had to side-step military rules long enough to join a few of the men in their celebrations. It was pleasant to know that these men, who had followed me through "Hell at *Verdun*," had enough respect for me to ask that I join them in their little festivities. After all we were soldiers, who had seen many hardships together. While regulations are necessary to maintain discipline in the service, and those who served under my command will hardly say that I was in the habit of overlooking regulations, an officer who has earned the respect of his subordinates, by service in battle with them, has no need to depend on shoulder bars to get the respect due his rank or to have his authority recognized. So passed 1918 and into the New Year of 1919.

The New Year brought no let-up in the training; this continued during the winter and spring months, a great deal of time being spent on the rifle range, practicing with the service rifle, automatic rifle, pistol firing, grenade throwing and practice with all weapons that an infantry company is armed with. In addition we had field maneuvers of all kinds, from the battalion up to and including the entire division. If we had not known that the war was officially over we might have believed we were preparing to enter more fighting; every small detail was just as closely supervised and minutely executed as in our early training days. There was no let up, men and officers were being sent to the service schools the same as in Camp McClellan. Then there were reviews of all sorts, usually by brigade, for the purpose of awarding decorations.

Each evening, weather permitting, the 114th Infantry Band rendered a short concert prior to retreat. One thing that always gave me a good laugh, during these band concerts, was to see the men of the outfits dancing with each other, using army field shoes with hob-nail soles for dancing shoes. It appeared to me that the dancers derived as much enjoyment out of these dances as if they had been dancing on the armory floor at home, as I had seen them doing so many times before the war.

You will understand that ours was a rather hum-drum, dreary sort of existence, during these winter months, with the long nights, the only light being from a few flickering candles and the only way to keep warm, in the cold, draughty billets, was to get in between the blankets. In my own case, living in much more comfortable quarters than the men, I felt the cold. For the billets in which stoves or fireplaces were available it was almost impossible to beg, borrow or steal any firewood.

"Sunny France." I'll wager that whenever a veteran of the A.E.F., who spent the winters of 1917-1918 and 1919 over there, hears that expression he will automatically button up his coat collar, no matter how hot the day may be at home. It seems to me that from the beginning of November to Easter it was raining, snowing or bitter cold all the time, with often a combination of all within the day.

In spite of the many discomforts, it was surprising, and in many instances amusing, how readily the troops adapted themselves to existing conditions and provided amusement more interesting and enjoyable than the supervised games, etc., on the schedule. About early February we had a heavy fall of snow which remained on the ground for some time; with all the wagon traffic and troops marching over it, the snow became packed quite hard; before long some of the soldiers had a slide in full swing, others had improvised a couple of bobsleds and were having the time of their young lives taking the 'village belles' for a real sleigh-ride, the real fun of the occasion, of course, being to overturn the party.

Then at times the men would become very playful and 'kittenish.' Such things as 'swiping' a little wood from some Frenchman's woodpile or chopping down a tree to help keep warm, might be considered as a boy's trick in the States, but 'Over There,' due to a general shortage of wood, it was a serious matter. Many times I had my hands full trying to appease a wild-eyed 'Frog,' who insisted that all Americans were gangsters, thieves, pickpockets, burglars and some other kind of criminal that he could not remember; in addition we were all crazy. It was odd how easily they could be pacified by handing them a few francs. More than likely those Frenchmen still have in storage the same francs that we gave them in 1918.

Another favorite pastime was fishing; those soldiers really caught fish and with far less effort than the fishermen at home. No traveling long distances with a load of fishing tackle and then waiting hours for a bite; not for those scheming soldiers. They had enough 'hiking' during drill hours, anyway they had a much simpler and more effective method, that gave them fish in a very few minutes. Usually in the wee, small hours of the morning, when all good soldiers were supposed to be in bed, a muffled explosion would be heard down by the river. Just as sure as I arrived at the orderly room next morning there would be another villager complaining that "les soldat Americain" had been fishing again, by the simple expedient of exploding a hand grenade in the river. The result of said explosion was a fine mess of fish, the offenders sneaking out into the woods during the day and enjoying a feed of fried fish.

Oh! to be an officer in the army, especially a company commander; it was such an easy, simple life; nothing to worry about—just one 'damn' complaint after another.

Another of the many laughable incidents was the village crier. In other chapters the duties of this functionary have been explained, how he would take a position in the village center and after giving several rolls on his drum would proceed to read out the news of general importance, usually orders of the French government. During the fighting he gave the official bulletins as to how the war was progressing; then news of the armistice.

During our stay in *Chatillon* the news had changed from the serious to matters of less importance, which news lost interest to our troops. As a result some of the men, who had learned to speak a little A.E.F. French, had a fine time poking fun at the crier. There was a sergeant in Company C, billeted on the main street of the village, about where the old crier would halt to beat his drum. As soon as the drummer started in to attract attention, this sergeant would stick his head out of the window or door and at the top of his voice roar out in the celebrated A.E.F. French: "Finis Cognac pour les soldats, Americain," meaning generally, no more cognac for the American soldiers, or some other remark equally facetious, which set everybody laughing, including the natives, thereby lowering the crier's dignity, of which a Frenchman is very touchy. If he occupies an official position, no matter how small, he is very dignified and takes himself very seriously; for a time this old 'codger' was quite insulted, but after a time he saw that it was all in fun and joined in the laughter at his own expense.

Lest you feel that French customs are continually being ridiculed let me hasten to say that such is not my intention, merely an endeavor to show how we lived and passed the time during the long wait for orders to return to "God's country," our own United States. Naturally French living conditions were very much different from what we were used to in the States. It was very hard to become a part of them and as a result of unfamiliarity with their customs we were continually blundering into something that at home would be quite all right but in France was all wrong. Undoubtedly those natives are now telling their children what a bunch of wild men the American soldiers were during the war.

In spite of all our difficulties and blunderings a bond of friendship existed between us and these simple peasants, that did more for the future good-will and understanding between the United States and France than all the national agreements ever drawn up at any peace table or between the political statesmen of either nation. Our men are not forgetting the cold billets, in which many contracted colds that developed into pneumonia, nor how those old French mothers, with possibly sons of their own in their army, took those sick boys of ours into their homes and treated them for the cold by putting their feet into hot mustard baths, then a plaster on the chest and dosing them with hot wine, then into a good warm bed, until the cold was sweated out of the patient. As one 'wag' remarked after this treatment, "The plaster on my chest was so strong I thought it would draw my shoes up through the bed and blankets as well as draw the cold out of my chest." To these women of France the A.E.F. probably appeared rough, careless, even wild, but it was only on the surface. Down in our hearts we did then and still continue to remember and appreciate their kindness to us.

In addition to the routine duties of a company or battalion commander, I had been detailed as a member of the Claims Board, to adjust claims of the natives for damages, real or fancied, against our troops in the vicinity. These claims were usually for small amounts to cover property damage in the billets, such as broken windows, etc.; whenever possible, if due to carelessness, the soldier responsible would have the amount deducted from his pay. Should the damage be the result of ordinary military usage, the claim would be reported as a proper claim against the United States.

At one time a claim came in for 1500 francs, made by an old lady who stated that her house had been wrecked by the American soldiers and the wood stolen. On the face of it the claim appeared to be exorbitant, even before making any investigation. In the village center, near the church, in the area occupied by Headquarters Company and Company A, was an old stone building, on which the claim had been made. It had no roof, no front wall, merely a skeleton, with the sidewalls held up by the adjoining buildings and its own floor beams. If *Chatillon* had been in the forward area during the fighting, I would have said that a bomb from an enemy aeroplane had dropped on it. A casual survey showed that the building was falling apart from old age and lack of repairs. More than likely our men had helped to 'keep the home fires burning' by swiping a little of the wood from the building, and by the same token, it was not at all unlikely that the natives had purloined a few bits of the wood for their own use; to me it appeared a neat trick to have Uncle Samuel pay out good coin, supposedly for repairs, and after we left the village, more than likely the building would be torn down. The claim was quickly adjusted by the simple method of having the village mayor report to me at the building and, with the aid of our company interpreter, tell 'His Honor' that while the Americans at times might appear to be slightly crazy, they were not altogether fools and the claim would be disapproved and no payment allowed. It appeared for a few minutes as though he was about to have a 'conniption fit,' hemorrhage or something, but as it seemed to have no effect on me the mayor then tried sympathy. With tears in his eyes he explained how much the old lady needed the money. Listening to his explanations and expressing the sympathy of the American army I still failed to see where this was a claim against us and informed the mayor that the claim was disapproved. Nothing more was heard of that claim.

On another occasion, going out to drill with the battalion one morning there were splotches on the snow that looked like dried blood. Asking the adjutant if there had been any report of men being hurt during the night, he replied there had been no such report. These spots continued down the road, at intervals of about three feet, about the length of a man's step, zigzagging from the edge to the center of the road and then back to the edge again. This red track continued until we came to the side road leading to the drill grounds, where the trail was lost. The thing had me puzzled until we returned from drill at noon; there was a memorandum on my desk stating that soldiers had broken into a native's cellar and taken a keg of wine; accompanying the memo was a claim for one hundred francs for the wine and damage to the cellar door. Going back to the house at the cross-roads I met the villager who lived there. He showed me the cellar door where the entrance had been made and in a very excited manner explained how the keg of wine had been stolen. I thought to myself, you are lucky they took only one keg, there are men in the village who would never have been satisfied with one. Returning to the road the trail was easily picked up. Following the red spots which led right into the village center and stopped alongside one of the billets, I entered and found three soldiers enjoying their wine. At first they denied any knowledge of wine being stolen, claiming the wine they were drinking had been purchased from an adjoining town; imagine trying that on an old soldier! A little pressure on them combined with an explanation of the seriousness of a conviction for burglary, with its long term in a French prison, soon made them willing to own up to a little spree the night before, claiming that on the way home they found this farmer's cellar door open, so went in and took the keg of wine back with them. The red splotches seen on the road were of wine leaking from the bung as they rolled the keg up the road. I directed the men to take the wine back to the farmer, who was willing to accept fifteen francs and forget the affair. And so ended another episode in the life of an army officer. We had to be all

things to all men, at all times, from a mule driver to a diplo-
mat, to successfully carry on with our varied duties.

Another duty was as a member of the Division General
Court-Martial Board for the trial of persons charged with military offenses. Most of the charges coming up were against
men who had been missing from their units during the battles,
or having entered the fighting had disappeared from the line
without proper authority. Most of these men were able to give
a complete account of their activities and whereabouts and
were exonerated. There were a few men whom it was necessary to punish, usually by assigning them to Labor Battalions
that were scheduled to remain in France until all other units
had gone home. On this tour of duty I cannot recall a single
case that was proved to be real cowardice; a few looked
suspicious but the benefit of the doubt was given to the accused.
The officers and non-commissioned officers, who had been in
the fighting, could be depended upon to show little consideration to any man who had failed in his duty 'up there.'

The above recalls an incident that occurred at one of the
maneuvers, shortly after the armistice. While passing through
one of the Machine Gun companies I met a sergeant whom I
knew. After the usual courtesies, we talked of friends who
had been killed or wounded and inquired for others whom
we had missed. While we were talking a number of soldiers
were standing about. One soldier in particular was very interested in the conversation and several times attempted to 'butt
in.' Finally the soldier remarked: "Well I fooled them." The
sergeant asked, "What do you mean, you fooled who?" and
the reply from the soldier was: "I mean the draft board.
They tried to get me for a year but I kept out of it until last
July." This soldier was one of the replacements who had
joined the Division after we left the front, so had not been in
any fighting. The sergeant just kept looking at the soldier,
as though sizing him up, then remarked, "You rat, if you
ever make a remark like that again I'll beat you to a pulp. To
think real men had to die up there so that the likes of you
could live. Take that with my compliments." He let go with

his fist straight to that soldier's chin and he went down like a log. If you were in my place what would you do? Place the sergeant under arrest for hitting a subordinate or do as I did, wink at the sergeant and walk away? After all he was merely doing what I would have liked to have done, the difference in rank helped the sergeant get away with it. I was satisfied that soldier would never again brag about dodging the draft board, at least not while my friend was around.

In reciting the incidents that were part of our existence, the telling of one tale generally leads to another. This seems to be a habit when old campaigners get together, one man tells of some serious or comical incident and as soon as he is finished some one else chimes in with, "do you remember!" And so on without end.

Speaking of maneuvers calls to mind a rather laughable incident that happened during one of our combat exercises in December 1918. Orders for a Division Combat problem were issued, in which all troops of the 29th were to participate. Details were arranged in strict accordance with so called military efficiency. The infantry was to attack an imaginary enemy position, we were to be supported by theoretical artillery and machine gun fire, which was to place a theoretical creeping barrage in front of the advancing infantry. The plan, arranged in all seriousness by the various staffs of the division, required all officers to issue the necessary orders just as though an actual battle with a real fighting enemy was in progress. The problem was to be held under the eagle eye of our Corps Commander, Major General C. P. Summerall; there is no disrespect calling the General 'Eagle-Eye,' he never missed a trick. Our instructions very definitely directed close attention to the manner in which the infantry was to make the advance according to the time schedule and at the required rate of speed. The details were explained to the men and every kind of dire threat promised if there was any slip-up.

At last the zero hour arrived and off we started. The rate of advance was about 100 meters in three minutes, rifles with bayonets fixed carried at the 'high port,' ready to be thrown to the front in the attacking position if any theoretical enemy appeared. The real war being over, ball cartridges were not carried on this maneuver. The First Battalion, of which my company was a unit, was advancing through a dense woods, the men in perfect formation, the only sound being the noise made as we crashed through the underbrush, everybody wishing the 'higher ups' would call the war off and let us go home. Staff Officers were all over the place, watching every move. They were even way up front with the infantry. There were more of them up front in this sham battle than ever came near any position we held in the fighting around *Verdun*. The maneuver was becoming tiresome, when suddenly there was a loud grunt, then a crash, as a good-sized hog and several young ones dashed out of the brush. They were heading for home at express speed. Our little war was over then and there; down went the bayonets and with a yell off went a group of soldiers after those pigs. It looked like old times on the western front, another charge into the enemy lines. The officers and N.C.O.'s could yell their heads off for the men to get back into formation, it had no effect; apparently those men had developed a sudden case of deafness. With the prospects of roast pig in front of them, who could blame those soldiers for breaking formation?

Oh me! Oh my! Did we get raked over the coals when the problem ended? General Summerall was really peeved; he had seen the incident but luckily did not know the outfit that was to blame. The General's language was the choicest of a really good soldier, upholding the best army traditions. He is a past master in giving expression to his opinion when he is displeased.

So passed the time. The incidents referred to are but a few in an otherwise monotonous existence. Many more could be told but space will not permit. They served to liven things up a little and were the cause of many a 'chuckle,' in spite of all the 'bawlings out' that the officers gave to the men. With all the fun that cropped up at unexpected moments, there was no let up in the discipline. Neatness in appearance, smartness in performing military duties were insisted on at all times. In fact it seemed to me that the staff officers, in many cases, developed a mania on this subject, unable to see anything except some luckless 'doughboy' who failed to render them the proper salute at a half-mile distance. I have often thought of the difference in the men at this period, and one year before. With the easy-going type of discipline that had existed at Pompton in the early days we could never have held the men under the conditions they were living in 1919. These men had become real soldiers and showed it in their every move. Very little grumbling, obeying orders promptly, and patiently, very patiently, waiting for the ship to take them home.

From the beginning of 1919 we were continually being inspected by officers from the Brigade, the Division, the Corps and occasionally by officers from G.H.Q. Many of the inspecting officers, especially from the Brigade or Division, while strict on the essentials seemed to understand and gave us credit for doing our best under very trying conditions. Occasionally, however, an inspector from a higher unit would pay us a visit and then we discovered that we were not soldiers, never had been and never would be soldiers, and from the attitude of these inspectors I assumed we were just so much dirt cluttering up the earth. The type of officer referred too, usually was some 'doll', always dressed up as though going to a social tea. In my humble opinion the hardest battle these officers had ever fought was "The Battle of Paris" and the only attack they had ever led was through a 'barrage of champagne corks.' It was a tough war on them; being required to mingle with the common herd of soldiers was an offense to their dignity. Incidentally they had managed, in some manner without going into the battles, to obtain fairly high rank, usually as lieutenant colonels, colonels, even as high as brigadier generals.

Inspections were not always held by order, at a prescribed time or place. On one occasion I found myself answering a lot of questions 'thrown at me' by a brigadier general, whose attitude was anything but that of an officer and a gentleman.

On this particular afternoon, shortly after noon mess, a verbal order was received from the battalion commander directing that, due to bad weather conditions, the scheduled drills and athletics for the afternoon were canceled, the time was to be devoted to school in such subjects as each company commander desired. In compliance with the order I directed the lieutenants to assemble their platoons and each to hold a class in such subjects as military courtesy, the proper method for a soldier to report, a subject that the inspectors seemed to have developed a mania on about this time, and other details that appeared to bother inspectors; then to have the men, under the supervision of the 'non-coms', disassemble their rifles and pistols for a thorough cleaning.

A couple of weeks prior to the above-mentioned day I had issued instructions on how to empty the company billet in case of fire. This was necessary with more than two hundred men sleeping in one building. Shortly after the classes were assembled on the afternoon referred to without warning I directed the company bugler, Musician A. Ross, to sound the 'fire call.' I went outside the building to watch the men get out by the prescribed exits; while standing there an automobile, with a silver star on the windshield, crossed the bridge, going in the direction of the 114th Infantry P.C. in the village. The car was only of passing interest; Brigadier Generals usually had no business with me so I continued the exercises. I was mistaken. That Brigadier General evidently did have business with me, for in a very short time a runner from Regimental Headquarters ran up and said, "Colonel Minnigerode directs the Battalion Commander report to the P.C. immediately." I told the runner to go and find Major Cooke, he was the Battalion Commander. The runner explained that he was sent for me and I was to report at once. This was one of the few times I was not the acting commander of the battalion, as Major Cooke was on duty with the organization. Without understanding the order, but suspecting the auto that had crossed the bridge was in some way connected, I ran up to the P.C. and reported to Colonel Minnigerode, explaining about the supposed error. The Colonel hurriedly told me that he was unable to locate Cooke and for me to report, as acting Battalion Commander, to the Brigadier General, an inspector from G.H.Q. This was one job there was no desire for, but the old army game was "obey orders." I did and "a pleasant time was enjoyed by those present" for the next fifteen or twenty minutes, with me playing the part of the goat.

The General asked all kind of questions about the troops. What schedule of instruction was being used, how the troops were billeted, etc. One question was, "What are the troops doing now?" My answer, "Holding company school." Immediately he berated me for not having the men out in the field for drill. I tried to explain that due to the prolonged period of wet weather, with all clothing soaking wet and the two pairs of shoes of each man water soaked, permission had been granted to have the men remain in for the afternoon. The General then told me that one company was not holding school, but evidently playing a game, as he saw them when he crossed the bridge. I explained that that was my own company holding fire drill and he then wanted to know "who ever heard of fire drills in the A.E.F." I explained there was a general order directing that fire drills be held in all billets where a platoon or larger unit was quartered. Even this did not suit "His Majesty," he still continued to find fault because the men were not drilling. I inquired if the General desired to inspect the men or the billets? "Certainly not, he had seen enough." Incidently he was not going to get any mud on his boots. Mud was only for common soldiers. This was the type of officer who antagonized every junior he came in contact with by his supercilious, sneering attitude. He with his highly polished boots and spurs, not a speck of mud on him, "crabbing" because our mud-soaked men were not out drilling and getting wetter. This brand of officer was one of the reasons why staff officers, generally, were so thoroughly disliked and criticized by the line officers.

Various forms of entertainment were inaugurated to help

pass the time. In December, 1918, leave details were granted so that each man, in turn, was allowed seven days official leave, plus traveling time, to such resorts as *Aix-le-Bains, Grenoble, Lamalou-les-Bains, Menton, Nice, Monte Carlo* and various other points. A limited number even visited England and Ireland. All expenses of the enlisted men for transportion, etc., were paid by the U. S. Government, so that the men had a very enjoyable time at these prominent tourist resorts.

In Company B the men who had been up on the lines were the first to go on leave, then down through the company according to the length of time that a man had been in France.

The Y.M.C.A. at intervals provided some entertainment at the recreation hut in the village. The 29th Division gathered together a group of amateur actors who traveled through the Division area, giving productions of a musical comedy known as "Snap it Up"—a very good show. The 114th Infantry had an amateur cast, producing a similar show called "Hello Buddy!" A number of men from Company B were in the regimental troupe, Cooks Charles Biehler and Joseph Leonard playing two of the leading parts. Many organizations of the division produced these amateur shows that traveled in each billeting area. Some of the shows were very good and some were not so good, but the worst of them was enjoyed, even when the only thing to laugh at was the actors.

On Monday, March 24th, 1919, occurred one of the highlights in the existence of the 29th Division. The Commander-in-Chief of the A.E.F., General John J. Pershing, reviewed our division and awarded decorations. General Pershing inspected the division, not as did the inspector mentioned in a previous paragraph, but by actually walking around the infantry, in the mud, and inspecting each company, talking with many of the men especially those who had wound chevrons on their sleeves; asking questions as to how the man was wounded, what he was doing at the time and in what battle he was wounded.

Naturally all of us were anxious to get a close-up view of

our celebrated commander, the man who, for many months, literally had our lives in his hands. The various stories heard about the General had led us to consider him a hard-boiled martinet of the old regular army, who never came into contact with the rank and file of the Service. On this occasion, as the acting commander of our battalion it was my duty to report to the Commander-in-Chief and accompany him during his inspection of the 1st Battalion. The short time with the General was a good opportunity to observe the man and the soldier. A tall, slim, clean-cut soldier, one glance at a man and he saw every inch of him. The General's questions to both officers and men were short and to the point and the Lord help any officer who hesitated in replying. Reporting to the General was a ticklish task, but as the inspection progressed the feeling passed and I came to understand that his questions were not superficial but rather showed a keen desire to know conditions among the personnel. Altogether it was apparent the A.E.F. had a real soldier as its commander and the unpleasant things we encountered were caused, not by the Commander-in-Chief, but by his subordinates.

The subject of our respected Commander recalls a story that was quite prevalent among the combat forces about the end of the war. A body of troops about to take part in the contemplated attack on Metz were resting along a road. Two of the 'doughboys' were discussing the impending battle and one remarked to his 'buddy,' "General Pershing says he will take Metz if it costs a hundred thousand lives." The other soldier thought for a moment and then remarked, "Generous son-of-a-gun, ain't he, especially with other peoples lives."

\*          \*          \*          \*          \*          \*          \*

Through the recital of these experiences it is hoped a picture has been created of the actual conditions existing both on the stage of military life and those taking place behind the scenes. On the stage it was an open play for all to see and understand, operated according to military rules, regulations, and orders. This is the picture, usually in the minds of the people at home, as gathered from newspaper accounts, published at the time. It will be understood that war correspondents with the armies in the field were not allowed to publish anything indicating another side of the picture, although these correspondents knew such conditions existed. Several books, published since the war prove this fact. It is my belief that conditions in the 29th Division especially among the New Jersey troops, were worse than elsewhere, or Major General Morton exaggerated conditions and unduly punished the 114th Infantry. Judge for yourself. You are familiar with conditions existing in our training days and later in active operations. Now look at the back stage during the winter of 1918-19. The mad scramble for decorations, promotions, assignments to staff positions—anything that might be of use after discharge from the service in the post-war adjustment at home.

Just as soon as it become certain the war was over and there would be no more fighting, with its dangers and discomforts, there was an influx of officers (men who had been on duty in the rear area during the battle days) into organizations that had been in the fighting. You will appreciate that returning to the home town and explaining how the war had been won would be much easier if one could say "My regiment captured this or that village," or "My company fought against the Prussian Guard at *Verdun*," or "My battalion was in the fighting at *Bois de Ormont*," etc. Friends at home pictured every soldier in France as a real fighting man and it would be extremely embarrasing for these officers to explain that they had spent their sojourn overseas counting beans or buttons, or 'riding' some luckless combat doughboy for getting drunk after spending weeks in that "Hell Hole Up Front."

Transfers and assignments to combat units were made easier as the result of an order, issued immediately after the Armistice was signed, directing there be no more promotions in the A.E.F., until all surplus officers in the replacement depots were assigned to active duty with organizations. Where all these surplus officers had been during the fighting still remains a mystery. Certainly they could have been used at the lines. Remembering that our organizations, at the cessation of hostilities, were merely skeleton units, with only a few enlisted men and officers surviving in each company, lieutenants and sergeants commanding companies, captains in command of battalions, etc., having proven their ability in battle, was it unreasonable for these officers and non-commissioned officers to expect that their leadership and service would be recognized by promotion to the next higher grade? Some promotions did get through. How? Why? There would be no cause for complaint if this order had been rigidly enforced, but it was not carried out when some favored one, at the various headquarters, was anxious to get back home with higher rank.

This condition was particularly aggravating to those junior officers, the combat leaders, who found themselves after the Armistice in their original unit, under the command of men with no experience as organization commanders in battle. In some cases these new commanders had been junior in rank to the men they were now commanding. As previously stated, the 1st Battalion, 114th Infantry, was under the command of a new major who had never commanded men in battle and who had been a junior as a captain. His promotion came through some time after this order was issued. Of the company commanders in the 114th Infantry, who remained with their companies from the beginning to the end of the fighting, only one had been promoted. A few lieutenants were promoted to captains, but the senior captains were still 'doing business at the old stand.' What more these men could have done to prove their ability of fitness for higher rank it is impossible to imagine. Most of them received commendations, citations and decorations for their work. You have read of the 'clicks' working in spite of Major General Morton's effort to break them up. Then add to this the orders barring future promotions and you will understand that the man without influence, attending strictly to business and not a part of the 'official family,' was simply out in the cold.

In the 29th Division, among the New Jersey Troops, officers

were being promoted as high as lieutenant colonels, who less than two years before had been lieutenants or captains. In one case a man entered the service from civil life, appointed a captain in 1917 and came back from France in 1919, a lieutenant colonel. Another case a man, without previous military service, enlisted in the summer of 1917 as a private; through a series of fortunate circumstances this soldier became a captain in the fall of 1918. The majority of these advancements went to men who had not been in action. On what basis were these promotions made? It would seem as though the best brains of the 'Jersey' units were in organizations other than the fighting infantry; possibly the infantryman lacked enough intelligence to appreciate his danger, and was too 'dumb' for a promotion. Are you able to figure it out?

Perhaps you think too much stress is being given to an officer's battle experience. Years of peace-time training, service in the regular army, etc., are all very fine, and to a certain extent prepare a man to take his place as a leader on the front line when needed, but taking part in one battle teaches a man more than a lifetime of peace-time soldiering and maneuvers. Another thing, no one can tell what any man will do when he goes under fire. Men who have spent their lives in soldiering, in the Regular Army and the National Guard, broke down and had to be relieved when they reached the front. Training cannot put into a man's system what his Maker left out.

Here is an example of one promotion made early in 1919. A vacancy for major occurred in the 114th Infantry. Knowing the manner in which these promotions were obtained, and with a colonel in command of the regiment who had been with another division during active operations and was not acquainted with what the individual officers of our regiment had done, it was possible for any captain to be advanced, without regard for seniority or ability. This promotion was finally given to a staff captain of the 114th on the grounds that "Having served in the regular army, the promotion would be more valuable to him upon returning to the regular service. The civilian officers would return to business after discharge; therefore, the promotion would be of no value to them."

Do you recall a staff captain becoming sick as he was due to take command of a patrol going up to *Etraye Ridge* on October 22, 1918? Do you remember also that two lieutenants became sick at the same time? The patrol finally went up with one captain and a sergeant. Well, the above-mentioned promotion was given to the sick staff captain. What was the use of trying to honestly perform duty? A smirking affability was more valuable.

The same conditions prevailed in the awarding of decorations. Men and officers who by their work on the lines should have been decorated with the Distinguished Service Cross did not receive it. Others were being decorated and it would take a long stretch of the imagination to picture such men performing the deed for which they were being cited. The enlisted men knew more about how each officer behaved in battle than they were given credit for, and whenever possible let the world know that they did not agree with the citations.

On one occasion, during a review at which several Distinguished Service Crosses were being awarded, Company B, as a part of the regiment, was standing at attention. Hearing some mumbling in the ranks I ordered it stopped. Recognizing the voice, upon our return to *Chatillon* I had the soldier on the carpet for his breach of discipline; this man, one of the sergeants, when asked for an explanation of his conduct replied, "Captain, one of those officers," mentioning the officer by name, "was given a D.S.C. for bringing in wounded men, after himself being wounded. I was at the first-aid station when he was brought in, and instead of he bringing in wounded, he was being helped in by three men from his own company." At the time it would not have been good discipline to side with the sergeant and I informed him that it was none of his business what the citation read; someone had made the recommendation, it had been approved and that was all that was necessary. This is but one instance and others could be told.

On another occasion, checking up on a recommendation for a D.S.C. that was of interest, and on which apparently no action had been taken, it was disclosed that the recommendation had been approved at the 114th Infantry P.C. and forwarded. Further inquiry led to the discovery it had been approved by the Commanding General of the 57th Brigade and forwarded to G.H.Q. through military channels. As it had been approved sometime previously and we had not heard of its being approved or disapproved higher up, further inquiry brought this remark from a Division Staff Officer: "G.H.Q. is receiving so many of these recommendations for the D.S.C. that I believe they are not even reading them, they are probably throwing them into the waste paper basket."

There you have an example of how things could happen if a man was given a recommendation for promotion or decoration. It could easily disappear if some member of a board, or if an officer had a 'grudge.' A check-up on recommendations made has ended in mystery, it was impossible to find any trace of them. As the French said "C'est la Guerre." The war behind the lines was worse than the war up front. At least we could see our enemies 'up there', behind our backs we could not see them. Don't forget that jealousy was a factor in the army.

When the honors had all been awarded, the next thing was to get out of France and home, to display 'manly' breasts covered with decorations, and incidentally to obtain the 'jump' on political preference before the common herd came home. So in the early spring of 1919 a number of our 'comrades' were seeking discharge and leaving us. When we arrived in the United States, in May, we found them safely billeted in 'soft jobs.'

Remember, please, that reference is made only to those individuals who had been using army service for their own selfish interests, and in seeking an early return to the States did so in order to profit on their service at the expense of their comrades still overseas. Some men had a legitimate reason for seeking discharge as early as possible; these men had given nearly two years in the service and their business needed them. Of these men and the sick and wounded who had been invalided home, of course, there can be no criticism. They had done their duty. There were many officers, however, who either lacked the brains to ask to be discharged, or else took their duty too seriously and made no effort to get out, but preferred to "stick it out" with the few survivors and go home with them.

Through the months of February and March, preparations were being made for the journey home and discharge. Every effort was made to get the organizations into shape so that when orders arrived there would be no unnecessary delay, and able to pass the various inspections made of all homebound troops. Records of each man were completed and prepared for his muster out of the service.

"Going Home." At last, April 6th, orders were issued relieving the 29th Division from duty with the 8th Corps and the 1st Field Army. Needless to say, from then on things began to move fast. There was no need to watch the men to see if orders were being obeyed; they were executed before they had been issued. "Going Home." All of us had waited so long and as patiently as possible for that glad word. When the orders were received I was again in command of the 1st Battalion, Major Cooke being away at school. After a conference with the company commanders of the Battalion and directing the preparations we were ready to move in a few days. Orders were issued for the 1st Battalion, 114th Infantry, to leave *Chatillon-sur-Saone,* on Saturday, April 12th, at 8 o'clock, and to march, with full pack to *Passavant,* a distance of about fifteen miles.

Shortly before leaving the village, with the battalion already formed on the road, an order was received to hold the battalion at that place, as trucks were being sent to transport us to the railroad. Luck was with us at last, or perhaps General Morton was sorry for having been so unkind to us in the past, and was "trying to make up with us." Whatever the reason we were satisfied and asked no questions.

While waiting for the trucks the natives of the village had turned out to bid us "Bon Voyage." As the men climbed into the trucks and we started to pull out many of the villagers were crying. These may have been tears of joy at getting rid of us, a 'bunch of wild Yanks,' but I believe the natives were really sorry we were leaving them. We had made many friends while stationed there, many of the men had been almost adopted by those good people, who had cared for our sick and had tried to make us comfortable under the circumstances. They seemed to be grateful for our little assistance in driving the Austrian and German armies out of their "La Belle France." At last all is ready and we move out. While waiting for the last truck to leave a little girl about twelve years old came rushing up to me all excited and in tears to bid, as she said, "Moi Capitaine," good-by. She was the little daughter of the inn-keeper, where the officers of Company B had taken their meals. This little girl had been a great favorite with our officers during the stay in the village. In leaving, all of us felt a little sad at parting with these friends, but we had the prospect of a greater pleasure, of joining the greatest soldiers of all, those who had waited for us at home in suspense.

The trip to *Passavant* was uneventful. Upon arrival there we immec ately boarded our old friends, the "40 and 8" troop trains, and left about 17 o'clock (5 P.M.), for the *Le Mans* area where preparations for the sea voyage would be completed. Detraining at *Beaumont* on the afternoon of the 14th, the battalion marched about 12 miles to our billeting area. Companies A and B at *Montbizot,* C and D at *St. James-sur-Sarthe.*

The stay in this area was short but every minute was used in preparing records and passenger lists. The company commanders and their clerks were especially busy. Due to their untiring efforts we were able to move to the coast in short order. The men and junior officers made a complete overhauling of the equipment and clothing, and turned in all surplus, in preparation for the field inspection to be held on

the 20th.   Passing this inspection would be our passport to
the boat and home.   April 21st we again marched to *Beaumont*.  It was surprising how easy we could make these marches
now, so much different than when we had been in this place
a year ago.

At *Beaumont* we again entrained for *St. Nazaire* arriving
at that port about 5 o'clock the next morning, the 22nd.   Then
we marched out to Camp No. 1, only a short distance from
the place we had been camped on our arrival in France the
previous year.   During the morning the final medical examination was held.   Now that all inspections had been successfully
passed all we needed was a boat.   Some of us were so anxious
to get home we might even have considered swimming home
if the Port Officers had asked in a nice way.

From the information gained upon our arrival the usual
procedure for home-bound troops was to remain at this camp
for about two weeks, awaiting their turn as the transports
arrived.   This looked like a long wait, with nothing to do
but more drilling.   A little mixing with the officers and clerks
on duty in the embarkation offices disclosed a few points that
were very interesting.   First, the organization scheduled to sail
before us was not quite ready; second, this organization was
anxious to sail direct to Philadelphia but the boat, then ready
for them, was to sail for Newport News; third, that one of
the higher officers in charge of embarkation had served with
us as an instructor on the Mexican border.   This information
was passed to the Commanding Officer of the 114th Infantry,
with the suggestion that possibly the embarkation officer might
still be interested in us.   Whatever the reason, shortly before
noon on the 23rd my battalion was ordered to move out of
camp for embarkation at one o'clock P.M.   Needless to say we
were ready and went aboard the "S. S. *Madawaska*," an
old German liner taken over by the United States at the beginning of the war.   We remained on the transport and sailed
about noon the following day, the 24th of April.

At last we were going home.

As the shores of France faded from view the thoughts of

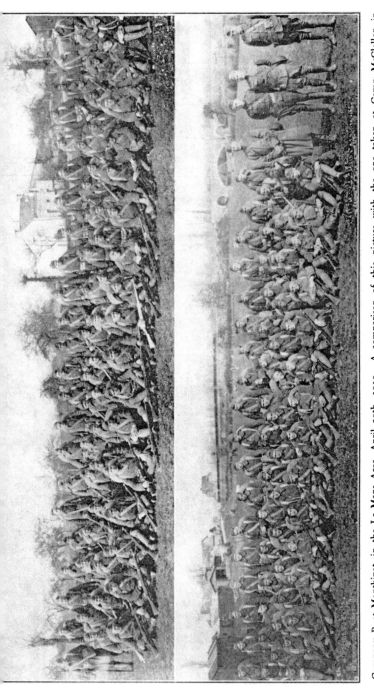

Company B at Montbizot, in the *Le Mans* Area, April 20th, 1919. A comparison of this picture with the one taken at Camp McClellan in March, 1918, emphasizes the severe change in personnel in a year's time.

Cast of the 114th Infantry play, "Hello Buddy." Several of the "ladies" in the cast, in addition to two comedians and a few "sweet-voiced" tenors, were from Company B.

"Home Again." S.S. *Madawaska* docking at Newport News, Va., May 6th, 1919, with regimental headquarters and the 1st Battalion, 114th Infantry, returning from France.

each of us must have varied. We were all happy to be going home, but there was no particular hilarity. It is hard to express my own feelings. The company now going back would never be recognized as the same Company B that had landed in France less than a year ago; very few of the old familiar faces were in the ranks. As we moved farther away from shore, standing alone on deck in the rear of the boat, my thoughts turned to the East up around *Verdun*. Reverently standing at attention I saluted, not France, but "Forty-Four Enlisted Men and One Officer" whom it had been my privilege to command and to accompany into battle, but who were now "SLEEPING IN A SOLDIER'S GRAVE."

As long as life shall last the memory of those heroes will be my most cherished memory. I still see them. "ADOIS, MY BUDDIES, until we all shall meet in Heaven, where there is no hardship, no suffering, no long night marches, no more war."

\*　　　\*　　　\*　　　\*　　　\*　　　\*　　　\*

As previously stated, when the orders to prepare for home reached us at *Chatillon* I was in temporary command of the First Battalion, and had been for several weeks prior to that time. Accordingly the entire preparation and movement was in my hands; in the train movement also attached to my command were several additional companies of the 114th until we reached St. Nazaire. Although Colonel George Williams and his staff accompanied us in the journey, the colonel did not assume command, as only a part of the regiment was moving at that time. It looked as though I was to be privileged to lead the "OLD BATTLE-SCARRED" 1st Battalion, 114th Infantry back home. This would have been an honor to be proud of. Although I had often "cussed them out," rode them, I also had been in training with them and soldiered alongside of them in battle. They knew me and I knew them, and my thought was that they respected me, not because of the bars on my shoulders or as their commanding officer, but rather as a comrade who had been in the same dangers and hardships with them. Is too much emphasis being given to the prowess of these men? My reply is that the A.E.F. had no better men than those of the 114th Infantry. With anything like intelligent command on the part of the battalion a much more pleasant story could be told; in fact there would have been no reason for this recital. To have led these men home would, to me, have been some recompense for the "Lost" promotions. However, "Lady Luck" was still playing against me. Shortly before going aboard the transport Major John S. Cooke, the actual commander of the 1st Battalion, reported back to the regiment for duty, he having heard while at school that the regiment was on its way home. His return automatically returned me to duty with Company B; my return also relieved Lieutenant Heinzmann as the company commander. The return of the major also blocked any possible chance of a last minute promotion for me and at the same time prevented Heinzmann from receiving the advancement that rightfully belonged to him. So we marched on board the *Madawaska* in exactly the same position as we landed in France. Again "C'est la Guerre."

Before continuing our homeward journey let me express one thought that has often occurred to me. Recalling what I have previously written of Major General Morton's opinion of the New Jersey Troops, it has always been a mystery to me why the 114th Infantry was selected as the first regiment to leave the Division. Was 'The Old Man' glad to get rid of us? Or were we so efficient that we were ready before other units? My own opinion is that it was combination of both reasons. With us out of the way, he was getting rid of the organization that had been a source of trouble to him in the early days of the division's existence. There must have been some efficiency in the 114th when we were ready to move from *Chatillon* in six days, and then travel down to the coast to pass successfully the various rigid inspections and be sailing in eighteen days after we first received our orders. Judge for yourself. If you are able to answer this and other questions asked, then you are a better man than I am.

The sea voyage was uneventful, nothing but a little guard duty and general policing to be done. It was each man's individual problem to make himself comfortable and enjoy the trip. There were band concerts each day by either the ship's band or our own 114th Infantry Band. During these band concerts we again saw the men dancing with each other or a sailor dancing with a soldier for a partner. The regimental show troupe gave a production of 'Hello Buddy' for the benefit of the ship's crew and the casuals on board, As usual the show was well rendered and enjoyed by all of us. Lieutenant J. J. Flaherty and the troupe deserve a great deal of credit for their efforts. Among the soldiers we again heard our friends the 'Galloping Ivories'. Many a sly game being played below decks, or in some dark corner, with both soldiers and sailors participating. In passing through the officer's quarters it was not unusual to hear strange language like "I'll raise four bits," "Come again," or "I'll call" and similar expressions. Perhaps you will know what they mean; I never saw them in any drill manual. The weather was good and fairly calm, except for the first few days at sea, when it rained, and with a choppy sea caused some seasickness. Altogether it was a very pleasant voyage, radically different from the east-bound trip. No one to forbid smoking at night, no continual wearing of life-belts, no 'stand to' in the early morning or evening. When we went to bed here we were reasonably sure there would be no alarms during the night, and no possibility of submarine attack. More like a personally conducted Cook's Tour.

Being informed that we were approaching the shores of the United States everybody was up and on deck before daylight, May 6th; in the distance we could see lights. When the day broke there was the 'old Virginia shore' ahead of us. What a feeling! Back in God's country at last! All were so excited it was quite a task to get them down to breakfast. After mess all hands crowded on deck again, the 114th Infantry Band playing as they never played before; amid the cheering and din from the naval vessels in the harbor we gradually approached the dock. During the band playing I saw the only demonstration of a mass remembrance of the men we had left in France; all of us were overjoyed at returning, singing the old favorites of the A.E.F. As the band finished playing one piece some of the men would call for another. Just before we pulled into the dock someone called for the band to play "Hail! Hail! The gang's all here." The request was killed as quickly as it had been made. This was one song that was not appropriate. "The Gang was Not all here." Only a small minority of the old 114th Infantry were now on board as we returned to the port we had left less than a year before. Eventually we were tied into the same dock that we had sailed from on the outbound trip and about ten o'clock the debarkation was completed.

Coming down the gang-plank, the first person met was Lieutenant Colonel T. Murphy of the U. S. Regular Army, whose home had been in Orange, N. J. Colonel Murphy had been the Captain of Company I, 2nd N. J. Volunteers during the Spanish-American War, and after that service had entered the regulars. The sons of many of these older volunteers were members of the returning regiment. The colonel was on duty at the Debarkation Center. We were also met by The Honorable D. F. Minnahan, Mayor of Orange, Mayor Chas. P. Gillen of Newark, and Rev. W. P. Donnelly of East Orange, N. J., whose brother was a sergeant in the Machine Gun Company of the regiment. It was good to meet these friends from home, our only regret being that we did not land at New York so that our families and friends could have been at the dock to greet us as we landed.

When the troops were all ashore we took up the march to camp, being halted in the streets several times to give the newspaper photographers an opportunity to take some pictures of the outfits for the 'home town papers.' As a soldier, I could never get used to living on a boat. To have my feet once more on dry land made me feel much more comfortable. As the companies were formed the regimental band struck up our old marching tunes and out we swung into the streets. Coming through the gates at the docks we were greeted by a roar from the bystanders. What a serenade! A victorious combat regiment returning from the wars. History repeating itself, even as the ancient Romans returned from their wars in France. We too were returning with decorated colors, bands playing and the sweetest music of all to an infantryman's ears, the rhythmic 'clank' of hob-nailed shoes on the pavement. It was 'a grand and glorious feeling.' We were back again in our own country. Forgotten, for the moment, were our hardships and privations.

Not for long were we allowed to forget. Within an hour after reaching our billets in Camp Stuart. While making an inspection of the men's quarters, in passing from one building to another, I came across a former officer of the 114th Infantry, who had beaten us home, accompanying the Governor of New Jersey. The first requirement was for me to salute my superior officer, a major. Then I turned to enter the billet. We were not in the country three hours before the political element was on the spot, even as they had been in Camp McClellan before we went overseas. As I started to enter the building the Governor remarked: "I believe I know that officer." To which the major replied: "That is Captain Reddan from Orange." Then the major called me. Going over to them I saluted and remained at attention until the major asked: "Captain, do you know the Governor?" to which I replied: "I have met His Excellency." The Governor complimented the regiment on its work in France and remarked: "It was hard going, captain. The enemy put up a strong resistance." Taking a long chance, I could not resist the opportunity to express my opinion, I replied: "The enemy in front of us put up a good fight and we knew it, but they were not nearly as dangerous as the enemy in rear of us, in our own organization." His Excellency making no reply, I felt that I was excused and saluting again continued with my duty.

Talking in this manner to the Governor may have appeared disrespectful. It was not intended as such. It was my opinion, and if other officers of the regiment had been interviewed the same opinion would have been expressed. Right then and there our home-coming was spoiled. The crowd who had been responsible for much of our misfortune overseas must have considered us as just ordinary idiots, lacking the smallest degree of intelligence. They probably thought that a few soft words would be deeply appreciated by us. If they had only shown a little consideration and allowed us to return to our homes without any display of simulated appreciation or coming around telling us how proud they were of us, in the excitement of returning, we might have been able at least for the time being to forget what was behind us. No, they still had to "have their names and faces in public places," also to have the photographers take pictures of them with the returning 'heroes'; then a newspaper article telling how the state officials had made a special trip to "meet the boys from home" as they landed. All of this was good publicity and made interesting reading to the 'folks back home.' To us it meant nothing; we were not looking for credit from that direction, we had seen too much of the underhand work that had taken place.

Even yet we were not through with the 'greetings.' On the 9th we were all herded into a building and for more than an hour compelled to listen to more 'ballyhoo' from New Jersey officials. None of us wanted to listen, but were required by order to attend; even instructed just how the men were to behave and holding the officers of the regiment strictly responsible for the conduct of the men. Was it possible someone had an idea that embarrassing questions might be asked, or remarks made, that were not on the program? If so, they were mistaken. Members of the 114th would, at least, respect the office. That was one of the lessons we had learned in the army.

Many times since the demobilization I have had a laugh upon reading old newspaper clippings describing the excitement at our return; letters being written to the War Department urging that the returning 29th and 78th Divisions be permitted to parade in Camden, Trenton, Newark, 'Squedunk and all points west'. As usual the hard-boiled War Department was non-committal, making no promises other than to get the men out of the service as quickly as possible. Various trips were made to Washington for the same purpose. Why this sudden interest in us? Of all the clippings and newspaper accounts read, I failed to note where the officials were making trips to the Capital to find out why the 114th Infantry suffered such heavy casualties, although many newspapers carried articles in November and December, 1918, calling attention to our exceptionally heavy losses. As one newspaper stated "Something went wrong at *Ormont Farm.*" Those of us who knew something of the workings in France can appreciate that no official notice of our misfortune was taken for the simple reason that any impartial investigation would have brought out one of the worst political 'messes' known, and would have ruined the political ambitions of some men.

The only reason any interest was shown upon our return was that it was the popular thing at the moment, giving office seekers a wonderful opportunity to shine in the reflected glory of a victorious fighting organization that had made a name for itself in spite of all the intrigue within its ranks. All of us realize the citizens of New Jersey were proud of their soldiers and sailors and anxious to show appreciation for the task just finished. What the veterans, and the civilians, resented was the attempt of self-seeking politicians to use the honorable record of our returning soldiers and our comrades who had made the Supreme Sacrifice for their own personal benefit.

At Camp Stuart preparations were immediately begun to transfer the men to the camp nearest their homes for discharge. This was to be the last station at which Company B would be together as a unit of the military service. It was hard to think of this fine body of men being scattered all over the United States, and within a few days some of them would pass out of each others lives, never to meet again and nothing to carry through the ensuing years but a memory of service together.

As each detachment of the company was assembled to leave

us a final inspection was made. I wished them good luck and a safe journey home. As I shook hands with each man at leaving some comical remarks were heard and there were some queer looks. Many a man, whom it had been necessary to censure at some time, and that applied to nearly all of them, would give me a quizzical look and smile, as much as to say: "Gee! The 'skipper' is getting sentimental. What will he do now that he won't have me to pick on." I believe that with all the past memories each man left with a feeling that he had served with and been a soldier in the best company in the A.E.F., and was proud of Company B, 114th U. S. Infantry, as I was.

The stay at Camp Stuart was short. On May 12th, we again started entraining for Camp Dix, N. J., having only those men and officers with us whose homes were in or near New Jersey. Reaching Camden, N. J., the next morning we paraded to the armory of the old Third Regiment, N. J. N. G., which was approximately our 2nd Battalion. At the armory we had dinner and then to the trains again for Camp Dix, where we arrived about 4 o'clock the same afternoon.

When our train moved into the Camp Dix depot we saw a great crowd waiting for us. As those on the platform recognized individual friends and relatives on the train a roar went up. It was a wonderful sight. Then as we stepped off the train, what a rush. I was in the middle of a milling mob before my feet touched the ground. After considerable effort we managed to get the crowd back and form the companies for the march into camp. Meeting our families and friends here was a great joy, all our hardships were well paid for by this reunion.

Marching the organizations into camp our services as commanders ended. The enlisted men were automatically transferred to Casual Companies, and the officers transferred to Casual Officer Detachments, all to await discharge. Official Records of the company were transferred to the Records Office. About Retreat, May 13th 1919, Company B. 114th Infantry, 29th Division, United States Army, officially passed into history.

For more than two years, Company H and Company K, 5th Regiment Infantry, New Jersey National Guard, later designated as Company B, 114th Infantry, had been on active duty in the service of the United States. Prior to that time, many of these men had spent about five months on duty along the Mexican border. They had certainly done their duty to the limit, from the hot sands of Arizona to the cold winter in the *Vosges Mountains* of France. They had served fearlessly; facing the endless, monotonous training, long marches, raids and battles; they had seen their comrades sicken and die, others wounded and killed in action alongside of them. Now they were about to return to civil life. 'Uncle Sam' owed them much. In what manner would it be repaid?

As this story of Company B comes to a close I take this opportunity to say a final word to the men who had the hard task of aiding me to make the company the efficient organization it was. With their unfailing loyalty and brave leadership success was assured. To my lieutenants, sergeants and corporals l extend my sincere thanks and appreciation. Without your assistance and co-operation the task would have been impossible.

To all who served, in Company B, 114th U. S. Infantry, the 'Skipper' salutes you.

"Au revoir, mes braves."

# APPENDIX

## The Westward Way.

Our eyes are turned to the westward,
We look to the way called home,
We long for a sight of the homeward sea
And to gaze at the churning foam.

There's an itch in our feet to be moving,
We wait for our orders to come.
There's a brawny back, to carry each pack
As we gaze at the dying sun.

There's a home o'er the sea that awaits
And that's a Westward Ho!
There's a girl, a wife, or a mother there
Whom we're longing so to go.

We shall leave with hearts so happy
And with thoughts so bright and gay;
But there's a thought in our minds a lingering,
A thought that's come to stay.

It's a thought for the 'Buddies' who've fallen,
Who have gone to the long, long rest.
We sigh for them, we pray for them
That they too, might go home 'To the West.'

They lie in the hills and the valleys,
They rest in the fields o' France,
And up in the *BOIS de ORMONT*
Where they fell in their last advance.

The laurel wreath of victory
Is a Halo 'round their heads;
They went to glory, fighting,
Did all these honored dead.

Our eyes are turned to the westward,
We wait for the bugle's sound.
Their eyes, to the Heavens above them,
They too, are Homeward Bound.

By Corporal Malcolm C. Murray,
*Company B, 114th U. S. Infantry*
*Dec. 5th, 1918.*

Chatillon-*sur*-Saone,
Haute Vosges, France.

HEADQUARTERS 29th DIVISION
AMERICAN E. F.,
1 Nov. 18.

*General Orders,*
  No. 59.

Now that its part in the action north of Verdun is finished, the Division Commander wishes to take occasion to express his deep appreciation of the skill, endurance and courage shown by the officers and men of the division, including both staff and line, in a most difficult and prolonged fight.

Everything was opposed to our success. We had a most determined enemy in our front and one skilled by four years of warfare, whereas this was the first real fight of our division. On most days the weather was bad and the ground difficult, added to the fact that the fighting was largely in woods. On account of the woods, ravines and dampness, gassing of our troops was easily accomplished and full advantage of this fact was taken by the enemy to whom the use of gas was an old story.

Without exception the organizations of the division and their commanders responded heroically to every call upon them and at the end of the fight we had not only gained our objectives, but we held them and turned them over to our successors. We advanced some eight kilometers through the enemy's trenches, and captured over 2,100 prisoners, 7 cannon, about 200 machine guns and a large quantity of miscellaneous military property. We had the pleasure of seeing two hostile divisions withdrawn from our front, one of which was composed of some of the best troops of the German Army. On many occasions captured prisoners stated that our attack was so rapid and our fire so effective that they were overwhelmed and had nothing to do but to retire or surrender.

In this brief summing up the results of its first fight the Division Commander feels that every officer and man participating, whether in planning or in executing, should feel a just pride in what has been accomplished. This is but repeating the praise that has been bestowed upon the division by both American and French superior commanders.

By command of Major General Morton:

S. A. CLOMAN,
*Colonel of Infantry*
*Chief of Staff.*

*Official:*
  HARRY COOPE,
  *Adjutant General,*
    *Adjutant.*

## HEADQUARTERS FIRST ARMY

AMERICAN EXPEDITIONARY FORCES, FRANCE,

ADVANCE COPY:                                 9 April, 1919.
*General Orders,*
  No. 20.

1. Pursuant to the telegraphic instructions from G.H.Q., A.E.F., the 29th Division was relieved from duty with this Army April 6, 1919.

The 29th Division came under the command of the First Army September 15, 1918.

The Division Served in Army Reserve until October 3d when it was marched to the vicinity of VERDUN and advanced into action, commencing with an attack on the morning of October 8th, participating in the operations of the 17th Corps (French), east of the Meuse river, until October 30th when its relief from duty in the line was completed and it passed again to the reserve of the Army. During its service in the line the Division or units thereof, took part in the operations against *Bois de Chaume, Bois Plat Chene, Molleville Farm, Bois de la Reine, Bois d'Ormont* and *Grand Montagne.* These operations accomplished an advance of seven kilometers and resulted in the capture of *Molleville Farm, Grand Montagne* and the ridge of *d'Etrayes,* a feat of arms of which the Division Commander and his fine Division have cause to be very proud.

2. The Army Commander takes this opportunity to express his appreciation of the services of the 29th Division while a part of this Army and wishes it God-speed in the final phase of its services as a part of the American Expeditionary Forces.

By Command of Lieutenant General Liggett;

                                        H. A. DRUM,
                                        *Chief of Staff.*

*Official:*
  H. K. LOUGHRY,
  *Adjutant General.*

HEADQUARTERS 57th INFANTRY BRIGADE,
AMERICAN E. F.

France, 19 April 1919.

*Memorandum,*
No. 46.

1. In view of the early muster out of the service of the 57th Brigade, the Brigade Commander desires to express to all officers and men his appreciation of their soldierly qualities shown on the battlefield and also in the Training Area.

2. During the long wait for news of when you were to go home, in the mud and rain of "sunny France" since the Armistice, the morale of the Brigade has never been lowered.

3. The Brigade Commander wishes every member of the Brigade to know that he will take back into civil life with him his best wishes for a long, happy and successful life.

4. It has been a great pleasure to command as fine an organization as the 57th Brigade. You have served your country well.

5. This Memorandum will be read to each organization at the first formation after its receipt.

L. S. UPTON,
*Brigadier General, U. S. A.*

*Distribution:*
To include company commanders.

HEADQUARTERS 29th DIVISION,
AMERICAN E. F.,
20 April 1919.
*General Orders,*
No. 13.

1. The 29th Division, which began its official existence 25 August 1917, is now about to be dissolved. From a large number of National Guard organizations with superb material but with little training or discipline it has become a perfectly trained, organized and disciplined fighting machine, which can at any time be put into any military situation without anxiety as to the result.

The record of the division during the year and a half of its history has been superb. At Camp McClellan, Alabama, the organization of the division was perfected, its discipline brought up to high standard and its training made effective. Those who were not considered up to a proper professional or physical standard were eliminated. The division thus formed was embarked for France in June 1918 and with but little delay was placed in the trenches facing foes with four years war training behind them. During the two months spent in the trenches the division received its baptism of fire. Immediately upon leaving the trenches it was transferred to the First American Army and entered the great fight of the war, the Meuse-Argonne Offensive, where it stayed on the line almost as many days as any division in the army. Its behavior in this great fight brought commendation from the Commander-in-Chief of the American Army, from the Commander of the First Army, from the French Army Corps Commander under whom it served, and from all others under whose notice it came.

Withdrawn from action but a few days before the armistice was signed, the division was placed into winter billets where under adverse conditions of cold, rain, snow and mud it still maintained the same superb discipline for which it has been famous.

The fallen will have the honor of the great country which sent them forth to battle for human freedom and of their comrades in arms.

And now on the eve of returning home, the division commander desires to thank every officer and man for the magnificent work that has been done and to wish for each one long life, health and prosperity wherever he may go.

C. G. MORTON,
*Major General, U. S. Army,*
*Commanding.*

HEADQUARTERS 29th DIVISION,
Aμεrican E. F.,
20 April 1919.

FROM:      The Commanding General, 29th Division.

TO:        The Commanding Officer, 114th Infantry.

SUBJECT: Commendation.

1. On the eve of your departure for a base port enroute to the United States, the division commander wishes to commend and thank every officer and man of your regiment for the hard, conscientious work performed during the time of your existence.

2. During the great fight in which it was your privilege to take part you showed most gallant spirit under most adverse conditions. You were assigned to one of the most difficult tasks in the whole war, and at a time when the troops on your right and left failed to advance you went forward gallantly nevertheless and did your part in the winning of the Meuse-Argonne Offensive.

3. The Officers and Men of your regiment who have fallen will always be honored by their comrades and by the people of their state and country. To those who remain and are soon to be back in their homes, the division commander wishes every good fortune that may come to brave and gallant soldiers.

C. G. Morton,
*Major General, U. S. Army.*


1st. Ind.

Hqrs. 114th Infantry, U.S.S. Madawaska, 29th April 1919. To Battalion and Company Commanders.

1. To be read to organizations at first formation.

By order of Colonel Williams;

Henry E. Bateman,
*Captain, 114th Infantry,*
*Adjutant.*

## FINAL ROSTER of COMPANY B, 114th U. S. INFANTRY, 29th DIVISION.

\*      \*      \*      \*      \*      \*      \*

This list compiled from copies of rosters made at varying times during the service. Containing the names of Officers and Enlisted Men, attached or assigned to the company for any period of time, between the date of reorganization at Camp McClellan, October 11th 1917, when the organization came into official existence, and Muster Out of Company B at Camp Dix, N. J., May 13th 1919.

Because a name does not appear in this roster is not proof, positive, that a man did not serve with the company.

\*      \*      \*      \*      \*      \*      \*

COMMISSIONED OFFICERS

| Last Name | First Name | Rank | On Duty From | | To | | Remarks |
|---|---|---|---|---|---|---|---|
| Ashton, Norville | | 2nd Lieut. | 4 Dec. | 1917 | 21 Dec. | 1917 | Attached |
| Averill, Henry | | 2nd Lieut. | 26 Aug. | 1918 | 3 Sept. | 1918 | " |
| Bateman, Henry E. | | 1st Lieut. | 5 Sept. | 1918 | 24 Nov. | 1918 | Assigned |
| Boone, Philip T. | | 2nd Lieut. | 11 Nov. | 1918 | 20 March | 1919 | " |
| Brooks, Joseph J. | | Captain | 6 Jan. | 1918 | 25 Jan. | 1918 | Attached |
| Burns, John H. | | 2nd Lieut. | 15 Dec. | 1918 | 15 Jan. | 1919 | " |
| Bussey, George L. | | 2nd Lieut. | 20 May | 1918 | 23 Oct. | 1918 | Assigned |
| Clasby, Chester F. | | 1st Lieut. | 1 March | 1919 | Discharge | | " |
| Colby, Earl | | 2nd Lieut. | 10 Nov. | 1918 | " | | " |
| Cooley, Charles G. | | 2nd Lieut. | 29 May | 1918 | 2 Oct. | 1918 | " |
| Cooley, Edward L. | | 2nd Lieut. | 4 Nov. | 1918 | 8 Nov. | 1918 | Attached |
| Deahn, Larene C. | | 1st Lieut. | 4 Nov. | 1917 | 11 Dec. | 1917 | Resigned |
| Derrom, Andrew T. | | 1st Lieut. | 5 Nov. | 1917 | 8 Aug. | 1918 | Assigned |
| Elms, Chester H. | | 2nd Lieut. | 22 July | 1918 | 12 Oct. | 1918 | Wounded in action |
| Farrell, Vincent J. | | 1st Lieut. | 11 Oct. | 1917 | 6 Nov. | 1917 | Assigned |
| Heathcote, Luther | | 2nd Lieut. | 27 Jan. | 1918 | 3 May | 1918 | Attached |
| Heinzmann, Grover P. | | 1st Lieut. | 3 May | 1918 | Discharge | | Assigned |
| Johnson, Roscoe R. | | Captain | 11 Oct. | 1917 | 22 Jan. | 1918 | Discharged S.C.D. |
| Kennedy, Robert A. | | Captain | 7 Dec. | 1917 | 1 Feb. | 1918 | Attached |
| Livingstone, Robt. E. | | 2nd Lieut. | 11 Oct. | 1917 | 15 Jan. | 1918 | Discharged S.C.D. |
| McNally, Robert C. | | 1st Lieut. | 11 Oct. | 1917 | 3 May | 1918 | Assigned |
| Mitchell, Robert L. | | 2nd Lieut. | 6 Oct. | 1918 | KILLED in Action, Oct. 12, 1918 | | |
| Myers, David G. | | 2nd Lieut. | 13 Feb. | 1919 | 5 March | 1919 | Attached |
| Palmer, Charles D. | | 2nd Lieut. | 5 Jan. | 1919 | On S.D. with Supply Co. | | |
| Pickardt, William E. | | 2nd Lieut. | 11 Oct. | 1917 | 17 Oct. | 1917 | Assigned |
| Reddan, William J. | | Captain | 23 Jan. | 1918 | Discharge | | " |
| Royall, Luby F. | | 2nd Lieut. | 23 Oct. | 1918 | Discharge | | " |
| Sabol, Stephan A. | | 1st Lieut. | 25 May | 1918 | 30 May | 1918 | " |
| Schultz, Fred'k W. | | 1st Lieut. | 30 May | 1918 | 7 Dec. | 1918 | " |
| Stanton, Guy H. | | Captain | 14 Nov. | 1917 | 15 Jan. | 1918 | Attached |
| Walker, Lewis D. | | 1st Lieut. | 11 Oct. | 1917 | 2 Feb. | 1918 | Assigned |

ADDENDUM

Funger, Robert F., Jr., 2nd Lieut. Co. H, 5th N. J. Inf., transferred 11 Oct. 1917.
Gray, Roger D.,          2nd Lieut. Co. K, 5th N. J. Inf., transferred 11 Oct. 1917.

## ENLISTED MEN.

| Last Name | First Name Initial | Rank |
|---|---|---|
| Adamitz, | Joseph | Private |
| Albro, | Frank | Corporal |
| Allen, | Frank F. | Priv. 1st class |
| Allin, | George H. | Private |
| Anderson, | William | Private |
| Andrews, | Henry A. | Private |
| Archambeau, | Charles M. | Priv. 1st class |
| Arrestiba, | Edward | Private |
| Arthur, | Glenn M. | Mechanic |
| | | |
| Bacesky, | Stanley | Private |
| Baker, | Frank J. | Private |
| Baldwin, | Harry W. | Corporal |
| Ball, | William H. | Private |
| Barge, | George W. | Private |
| Barnes, | Benjamin W. D., Jr. | Private |
| Barth, | Joseph P. | Priv. 1st class |
| Bauer, | William E. | Corporal |
| Beccaccine, | Frank | Private |
| Bell, | Harry A. | Private |
| Benjamin, | William | Private |
| Berger, | Charles A. | Corporal |
| Berninger, | Harold O. | Corporal |
| Betak, | Joseph | Private |
| Bez, | Giovanni B. | Priv. 1st class |
| Bickler, | Harry | Corporal |
| Biehler, | Charles W. | Cook |
| Bisonio, | Arthur | Corporal |
| Block, | Raymond A. | Private |
| Bloomer, | Edgar N. | Sergeant |
| Blumstein, | Soloman | Priv. 1st. class |
| Boetsch, | George D. | Private |
| Bohannon, | Harry L. | Sergeant |
| Boswell, | Miles | Private |
| Bowman, | Elmer E., Jr. | Priv. 1st class |
| Boyce, | Blaine | Corporal |
| Boyce, | Edward P. | Corporal |
| Braaz, | Herman | Priv. 1st class |
| Brady, | Frank L. | Corporal |
| Brady, | Frank T. | Private |
| Brady, | Leonard J. | Private |
| Brennan, | Benjamin J. | Priv. 1st class |
| Brooks, | Henry P. | Private |

| Last Name | First Name Initial | Rank |
|---|---|---|
| Brown, Allan | | Corporal |
| Brown, Frank M. | | Private |
| Browne, Harrison E. | | Priv. 1st class |
| Browne, William H. | | Private |
| Buehler, Jacob E., Jr. | | Corporal |
| Buffo, Peter | | Private |
| Burchaum, Orlondo E. | | Private |
| Burns, John J. | | Corporal |
| | | |
| Cable, Russell H. | | Private |
| Campanell, Christopher J. | | Corporal |
| Campbell, Harvey E. | | Private |
| Campbell, Pierce | | Priv. 1st class |
| Caragliano, Gaetano | | Priv. 1st class |
| Carey, William J. | | Priv. 1st class |
| Chance, Clyde | | Private |
| Chapman, Omer M. | | Corporal |
| Chiofolo, Joseph | | Priv. 1st class |
| Christino, William | | Private |
| Clarke, James A. | | Priv. 1st class |
| Clarke, James T. | | Priv. 1st class |
| Clifford, Edward C. | | Private |
| Climie, John S. | | Private |
| Cobb, Ralph | | Corporal |
| Cochran, Earl | | Priv. 1st class |
| Coeyman, Allison J. | | Private |
| Cogswell, Harold I. | | Priv. 1st class |
| Colabelli, Anthony | | Private |
| Conroy, Edwin F. | | Private |
| Cooley, Horace J. | | Corporal |
| Corbat, Joseph | | Private |
| Corliss, Elo A. | | Priv. 1st class |
| Corrigan, John P. | | Priv. 1st class |
| Coucher, Herman E. | | Corporal |
| Coufield, Harold F. | | Private |
| Coull, William L. | | Private |
| Covello, Joseph | | Private |
| Cowan, Jack F. | | Private |
| Cowan, William W. | | Private |
| Crecca, William F. | | Private |
| Cribari, Joseph | | Private |
| Crismore, Floyd C. | | Private |
| Cucinelli, Henry | | Private |
| Cummingham, Joseph K. | | Corporal |
| Cummings, Walter J. | | Private |

| Last Name | First Name Initial | Rank |
|---|---|---|
| Daggett, George E. | | Sergeant |
| Dambel, John | | Private |
| Dangler, Douglas W. | | Private |
| Dangler, John E. | | Private |
| Dann, Bernard W. | | 1st Sergeant |
| Dean, Albert J. | | Private |
| Dean, William | | Private |
| DeBella, Vincent | | Private |
| DeBruler, Gifford | | Sergeant |
| Deckenbach, John H. | | Corporal |
| Decker, Ralph A. | | Cook |
| Delaney, John J. | | Private |
| DelFavaro, Peter | | Priv. 1st class |
| Dempsey, Cornelius | | Private |
| Dennis, Elmer | | Private |
| Denny, Derry U. | | Corporal |
| Denton, Paul | | Private |
| DiAugustine, Albert | | Private |
| Dondreo, Angelo | | Private |
| Donohue, James W. | | Private |
| Doody, William J. | | Priv. 1st class |
| Dooling, William F. | | Private |
| Dove, John B. | | Private |
| Downard, Hugh G. | | Private |
| Doyle, Frank L. | | Corporal |
| Doyle, James L. | | Private |
| Dresch, Alfred | | Priv. 1st class |
| Drews, Joseph | | Corporal |
| Dries, John W. | | Supply Sergeant |
| Drummond, Oliver | | Corporal |
| Drury, Peter J. | | Sergeant |
| Dury, Francis J. | | Private |
| Duncan, Leslie O. | | Corporal |
| Dunn, William T. | | Private |
| | | |
| Earnest, Burl E. | | Private |
| Easterling, Ellison C. | | Private |
| Edling, Walter E. | | Sergeant |
| Edwards, Quinton | | Sergeant |
| Elam, Grover C. | | Priv. 1st class |
| Ellison, James J. | | Priv. 1st class |
| Elworthy, Reginald J. | | Private |
| Ely, Meredith A. | | Private |
| Enderlin, Herbert T. | | Corporal |
| Endres, Roy R. | | Corporal |

| Last Name | First Name Initial | Rank |
|---|---|---|
| Epstein, Abraham | | Corporal |
| Erickson, Edward A. | | Priv. 1st class |
| Estes, Thomas | | Private |
| Everett, Edward S. | | Private |
| | | |
| Fachet, Joseph C. | | 1st Sergeant |
| Fairchild, Edmund | | Cook |
| Falcetto, Joe F. | | Priv. 1st class |
| Farah, Wydah | | Private |
| Faraher, James F. | | Corporal |
| Farrar, Willie G. | | Private |
| Farrell, Arthur C. | | Private |
| Fayle, Earl E. | | Priv. 1st class |
| Ferguson, Frank F. | | Priv. 1st class |
| Finan, Charles F., Jr. | | Supply Sergeant |
| Finnegan, Edward A. | | Private |
| Finneran, James | | Sergeant |
| Fitzgerald, Joseph P. | | Private |
| Fitzpatrick, Edward J. | | Priv. 1st class |
| Fitzpatrick, Michael A. | | Sergeant |
| Flay, Edward H. | | Priv. 1st class |
| Flood, James J. | | Supply Sergeant |
| Flynn, Thomas J. | | Private |
| Folkes, Louis | | Private |
| Fortuna, Andrew | | Private |
| Frady, James | | Private |
| Frame, Harry | | Private |
| Franklin, John C. | | Sergeant |
| Franks, Morey J. | | Corporal |
| Friedmann, Julius | | Priv. 1st class |
| Fryer, Gilbert | | Corporal |
| | | |
| Galanos, Chris. | | Mess Sergeant |
| Gardner, John J. | | Private |
| Gaston, Charles M. | | Sergeant |
| Genthe, Raymond A. | | Private |
| Ghelberg, Abraham | | Private |
| Gillespie, Edward J. | | Corporal |
| Gilpatrick, George M. | | Private |
| Glass, Robert M. | | Private |
| Glennon, John T. | | Priv. 1st class |
| Goldstein, Hyman | | Private |
| Grady, John J. | | Private |
| Graham, John | | Private |
| Greene, Alfred J. | | Private |

| Last Name | First Name | Initial | Rank |
|---|---|---|---|
| Grenner, | Oliver | D. | Corporal |
| Griffin, | Walter | J. | Priv. 1st class |
| Grois, | Joseph | P. | Private |
| Gumport, | Leslie | I. | Private |
| | | | |
| Hackett, | William | | Private |
| Hall, | Frank | P. | Private |
| Hall, | Joseph | L. | Musician |
| Hamerson, | Peter | | Private |
| Hand, | John | | Private |
| Harris, | Gideon | A. | Private |
| Harvey, | Charles | D. | Private |
| Hattersley, | John | W. | Private |
| Heichel, | George | L. | Sergeant |
| Hendrickson, | Frank | | Private |
| Hendrickson, | George | | Private |
| Hengeveld, | Prentice | | Private |
| Henry, | Edward | M. | Private |
| Henry, | Joseph | F. | Sergeant |
| Herold, | George | H. | Private |
| Heusser, | Edward | F. | Priv. 1st class |
| Heyen, | Walter | | Sergeant |
| Higgins, | Peter | J. | Private |
| Higgins, | William | H. | Private |
| Hintzen, | Walter | | Priv. 1st class |
| Hockman, | Jacob | | Private |
| Hoffman, | Henry | | Priv. 1st class |
| Horrocks, | Sampson | M. | Sergeant |
| Hostetler, | Marvin | | Corporal |
| Howard, | Raymond | F. | Private |
| Hughes, | Harry | | Private |
| Hughes, | James | F. | Priv. 1st class |
| Hurd, | John | P. | Priv. 1st class |
| Hynes, | Thomas | J. | Sergeant |
| | | | |
| Inman, | Leeman | D. | Corporal |
| Irvine, | Walter | L. | Musician |
| Italiano, | Albert | | Private |
| | | | |
| Jacobs, | Harry | | Priv. 1st class |
| Jacobus, | George | | Private |
| Jacobus, | Wallace | L. | Corporal |
| Jacovini, | James | F. | Private |
| Jaggers, | James | F. | Priv. 1st class |
| Jansen, | Gustav | B. | Mechanic |

| LAST NAME | FIRST NAME INITIAL | RANK |
|---|---|---|
| Johns, | Charles H. | Priv. 1st class |
| Johnson, | Allen E. | Private |
| Johnson, | William H. | Mechanic |
| Jolke, | Fred. | Private |
| Jones, | Herbert E. | Musician |
| Jordan, | Fred G. | Private |
| Judy, | Anderson W. | Corporal |
| Jurgens, | Fred. W. | Corporal |
| | | |
| Kaiser, | Joseph R. | Priv. 1st class |
| Kashuba, | John K. | Corporal |
| Kearney, | Thomas J. | Private |
| Keenan, | Joseph A. | Priv. 1st class |
| Keifer, | Joseph R. | Private |
| Kelly, | John J. | Private |
| Kent, | Gerald E. | Private |
| Kesler, | Ruben S. | Corporal |
| Kettler, | Samuel | Cook |
| Kiely, | George J. | Private |
| King, | Clarence D. | Priv. 1st class |
| King, | Frank J. | Corporal |
| Kleimpf, | George P. | Private |
| Klein, | Otto W. | Private |
| Kleinknecht, | Kenry | Priv. 1st class |
| Kretzschmar, | Willie M. | Private |
| Kunz, | Francis W. | Corporal |
| Kurowski, | John | Priv. 1st class |
| | | |
| Lamb, | Thomas | Private |
| Landers, | William R. | Priv. 1st class |
| Landrum, | Robert C. | Private |
| Larkins, | George F. | Private |
| Laruffa, | Dominick | Private |
| Latham, | Charles F. | Priv. 1st class |
| Laugel, | John F. | Corporal |
| Laurent, | William | Private |
| LeGlise, | Thomas M. | Corporal |
| Leonard, | Howard | Cook |
| Levin, | William | Priv. 1st class |
| Littlefield, | Everett A. | Private |
| Lombardi, | Pasquale | Private |
| Loprete, | Joseph | Private |
| | | |
| McCarrick, | Raymond M. | Private |
| McCarthy, | William M. | Private |

| Last Name | First Name Initial | Rank |
|---|---|---|
| McChesney, Edward D. | | Private |
| McCoom, Grant M. | | Priv. 1st class |
| McCormick, Charles | | Private |
| McEnerney, Frank A. | | Private |
| McGuirk, George J. | | Corporal |
| McKlennan, Thomas | | Corporal |
| McMahon, James E. | | Corporal |
| McManus, Laurence E., Jr. | | Private |
| McMillan, James H. | | Private |
| McNally, John J. | | Private |
| McPherson, Harry G. | | Private |
| Madigan, Anthony | | Priv. 1st class |
| Maggiolo, Joseph | | Private |
| Majewski, Frank | | Private |
| Manning, Fred. J. | | Sergeant |
| Manthey, Emil | | Corporal |
| Marion, Abe | | Private |
| Markley, Herman | | Private |
| Markowitz, Max | | Private |
| Marriott, Vincent | | 1st Sergeant |
| Martin, William F. | | Corporal |
| Mathias, Harry | | Private |
| Maull, Ellis R. | | Private |
| May, George, Jr. | | Private |
| May, Roman | | Private |
| Mazzio, Sabato | | Priv. 1st class |
| Meath, Frank A. | | Private |
| Merriott, Walker L. | | Private |
| Mesker, Frank | | Priv. 1st class |
| Metzger, Chris. | | Priv. 1st class |
| Metzik, Max | | Private |
| Miller, Alston G. | | Priv. 1st class |
| Miller, George | | Private |
| Miller, Herbert W. | | Corporal |
| Miller, Oscar | | Priv. 1st class |
| Miller, Percy A., Jr. | | Corporal |
| Mingen, John A. | | Priv. 1st class |
| Mitchell, Frank | | Private |
| Mock, Raymond D. | | Private |
| Mondrella, Frank | | Private |
| Mongotich, Rudolph | | Private |
| Morabito, Alfred | | Private |
| Morgan, John | | Private |
| Morio, Frank | | Private |
| Moritz, Edward A. | | Private |

| Last Name | First Name | Initial | Rank |
|-----------|-----------|---------|------|
| Morrison, | Leo | L. | Corporal |
| Moskevich, | John | | Private |
| Mulholland, | John | H. | Private |
| Mullen, | Joseph | J. | Priv. 1st class |
| Murray, | James | J. | Priv. 1st class |
| Murray, | James | P. | Private |
| Murray, | Malcolm | C. | Sergeant |
| Muro, | Vincenzo | | Private |
| | | | |
| Naccaralla, | Antonio | | Priv. 1st class |
| Nance, | Thomas | F. | Corporal |
| Newcombe, | Joseph | | Private |
| Newton, | Thomas | | Private |
| Nighland, | Eugene | F. | Private |
| Norton, | William | J. | Private |
| Nucker, | William | A. | Corporal |
| | | | |
| Oakley, | Charles | A. | Private |
| Oates, | Joseph | | Sergeant |
| O'Brien, | Herbert | F. | Cook |
| O'Connell, | John | | Priv. 1st class |
| O'Connor, | John | J. | Priv. 1st class |
| O'Grady, | John | J. | Private |
| Oldfield, | John | | Private |
| Orgero, | Robert | E. | Private |
| O'Shea, | William | | Priv. 1st class |
| Oswald, | Oliver | O. | Private |
| | | | |
| Palin, | Felix | L. | Private |
| Panapolis, | Peter | J. | Corporal |
| Panettiere, | Antonio | | Private |
| Pendorf, | George | A. | Private |
| Perl, | William | | Private |
| Peters, | Anthony, Jr. | | Sergeant |
| Petrucelli, | James, Jr. | | Private |
| Pickett, | John | | Private |
| Pickles, | William | B. | Private |
| Pierson, | Charles | W. | Private |
| Piolella, | Michele | | Private |
| Postelanczyk, | John | F. | Private |
| Postin, | Ollie | C. | Private |
| Pottorf, | John | M. | Priv. 1st class |
| Powers, | William | F. | Priv. 1st class |
| Price, | Frank | T. | Sergeant |
| Purcell, | James | E. | Corporal |

| LAST NAME | FIRST NAME INITIAL | RANK |
|---|---|---|
| Quint, Elmer F. | | Private |
| | | |
| Raphael, Joseph | | Corporal |
| Reiman, Francis R. | | Private |
| Reist, Albert | | Private |
| Renbold, George | | Corporal |
| Rhodes, Robert A. | | Private |
| Rhule, Jesse J. | | Corporal |
| Richardson, Benjamin J. | | Priv. 1st class |
| Richter, Jacob | | Private |
| Ridings, Lester | | Private |
| Risberg, Carter O. | | Private |
| Rivkind, Abraham G. | | Private |
| Roberston, Alexander | | Corporal |
| Robinson, Anglish N. | | Private |
| Robinson, Peter | | Private |
| Robinson, William A. | | Private |
| Robutta, Frank | | Private |
| Rochford, Waldron J. | | Private |
| Roman, William J. | | Sergeant |
| Rosen, Israel | | Private |
| Rosensweig, Joseph | | Private |
| Roskey, Edward B. | | Private |
| Ross, Augustus | | Musician |
| Ross, John A. | | Private |
| Roth, William L. | | Mess Sergeant |
| Rowe, Fred. S. | | Sergeant |
| Rowland, Harley J. | | Private |
| Rowland, Harold D. | | Sergeant |
| Rozetta, Joseph | | Sergeant |
| Rudolph, Shirley M. | | Sergeant |
| Rutherford, William | | Private |
| Ryan, James A. | | Mechanic |
| Ryan, John T. | | Corporal |
| | | |
| Sanchelli, Frank | | Corporal |
| Sanders, Nathan | | Private |
| Sanok, Leonard J. | | Sergeant |
| Sanok, Stephen J. | | Private |
| Santacroca, Antonio | | Priv. 1st class |
| Sayres, James E. | | Sergeant |
| Schmich, Emil | | Sergeant |
| Schwab, August H. | | Sergeant |
| Schwartz, Harry C. | | Corporal |
| Schwartz, John J. | | Priv. 1st class |

| LAST NAME | FIRST NAME INITIAL | RANK |
|---|---|---|
| Scomp, Vernon L. | | Supply Sergeant |
| Segel, George | | Private |
| Selig, Herbert M. | | Private |
| Semel, Alfred | | Private |
| Sheets, Alvin E. | | Private |
| Shellenberger, George H. | | Private |
| Shephard, Roy E. | | Corporal |
| Shields, Herbert T. | | Private |
| Shugert, William E. | | Private |
| Silverberg, David | | Private |
| Simpson, Frank J. | | Corporal |
| Sirgredias, John | | Private |
| Skonieski, Walter J. | | Mechanic |
| Slater, Walter S. | | Private |
| Slattery, James H. | | Priv. 1st class |
| Smack, Romeyn | | Sergeant |
| Smith, David M. | | Priv. 1st class |
| Smith, Jacob S. | | Priv. 1st class |
| Smith, Tilford | | Private |
| Snyder, Frank W. | | Private |
| Solberg, M. J. | | Private |
| Sonnenberg, Jacob | | Private |
| Spaulding, Joseph M. | | Private |
| Speer, Elmer A. | | Sergeant |
| Spence, Clarence C. | | Private |
| Squibb, William H. | | Private |
| Steciak, Stephen | | Private |
| Steinberg, Joseph | | Private |
| Stevens, Edward J. | | Cook |
| Stratton, Clarence A. | | Corporal |
| Strauss, Raymond | | Private |
| Sutker, Myer | | Priv. 1st class |
| Sutter, Gustave | | Private |
| Sweigart, William | | Private |
| Sylve, Herman | | Private |
| Tabachnick, Paul | | Private |
| Tackaberry, John | | Private |
| Taft, James H. | | Priv. 1st class |
| Tarantola, Harry | | Private |
| Thomas, William H. | | Priv. 1st class |
| Thompson, Dave T. | | Private |
| Thompson, Frank I. | | Private |
| Thompson, Raymond S. | | Private |
| Tichenor, Albert W. | | Private |

| Last Name | First Name Initial | Rank |
|---|---|---|
| Toelcke, Berthold H. | | Musician |
| Toomer, James C. | | Priv. 1st class |
| Torpey, David E. | | Musician |
| Totaro, Lucien M. | | 1st Sergeant |
| Townsend, Willie M. | | Priv. 1st class |
| Tracey, William J. | | Private |
| Troast, Abraham E. | | Sergeant |
| Trotter, John J. | | Private |
| Trotto, Mose | | Priv. 1st class |
| Tubo, Victor H. | | Supply Sergeant |
| Tuck, John W. | | Private |
| Tynan, Harold E. | | Corporal |
| | | |
| Umbriet, Lawrence | | Mechanic |
| Urbanski, Felix | | Priv. 1st class |
| Usher, Thomas H. | | Priv. 1st class |
| | | |
| Valese, Michael | | Priv. 1st class |
| Van Harken, David | | Private |
| Vernon, Clarence | | Private |
| Vnenchak, Jacob | | Private |
| Vreeland, Ralph W. | | Sergeant |
| | | |
| Wade, Charles T. | | Private |
| Walker, Floyd | | Priv. 1st class |
| Walker, Peter J. | | Priv. 1st class |
| Wall, Richard S. | | Private |
| Ward, Frank T. | | Sergeant |
| Ward, William H. | | Private |
| Watkins, John T. | | Private |
| Weakley, Emmett J. | | Private |
| Weakley, Gaston H. | | Private |
| Weaver, John E. | | Priv. 1st class |
| Wells, Dan L. | | Private |
| Weston, George | | Private |
| Wheeler, Halbert S. | | Sergeant |
| White, Claude | | Priv. 1st class |
| White, John | | Priv. 1st class |
| White, Julian | | Private |
| Whitehurst, Ed | | Private |
| Wilcox, Charley F. | | Private |
| Wiled, Henry | | Mechanic |
| Wilhelm, Edgar | | Private |
| Wilkinson, Ivy W. | | Private |
| Williams, Carl H. | | Priv. 1st class |

| LAST NAME | FIRST NAME INITIAL | RANK |
|---|---|---|
| Williams, | Edward | Private |
| Williamson, | Henry | Priv. 1st class |
| Wininger, | Jasper | Private |
| Wisniewski, | Stanley | Priv. 1st class |
| Wittenweiler, | Frank G. | Sergeant |
| Wood, | James L. | Priv. 1st class |
| Wood, | William | Priv. 1st class |
| Worcby, | Mike | Private |
| Wright, | Buren M. | Corporal |
| Wright, | Sidney | Private |
| Wylie, | William | Private |
| Wynimko, | Albert | Corporal |
| | | |
| Yackel, | Peter C. | Priv. 1st class |
| Yech, | Anthony J. | Priv. 1st class |
| | | |
| Ziegler, | George V. | Sergeant |
| Ziegler, | Herman | 1st Sergeant |
| Ziemba, | Andrew | Private |
| Zilka, | Otto | Private |
| Zitzman, | Robert | Private |
| Zukowski, | Peter | Private |

CPSIA information can be obtained
at www.ICGtesting.com
Printed in the USA
LVOW07s0423271017
553937LV00001B/31/P